CIMA

Paper E1

Enterprise Operations

Study Text

WORKING TOGETHER FOR YOU

CIMA Publishing is an imprint of Elsevier
The Boulevard, Langford Lane, Kidlington, Oxford, OX5 1GB, UK
225 Wyman Street, Waltham, MA 02451, USA
Kaplan Publishing UK, Unit 2 The Business Centre, Molly Millars Lane, Wokingham, Berkshire RG41 2QZ

Notice
No responsibility is assumed by the publisher for any injury and/or damage to persons or property as a matter of products liability, negligence or otherwise, or from any use or operation of any methods, products, instructions or ideas contained in the material herein.

British Library Cataloguing in Publication Data
A catalogue record for this book is available from the British Library

ISBN: 978-0-85732-455-9

Printed and bound in Great Britain

11 12 11 10 9 8 7 6 5 4 3 2 1

Contents

Paper Introduction

How to Use the Materials

These Official CIMA learning materials brought to you by Elsevier/CIMA Publishing and Kaplan Publishing have been carefully designed to make your learning experience as easy as possible and to give you the best chances of success in your *'Enterprise Operations'* exam.

The product range contains a number of features to help you in the study process. They include:

*   a detailed explanation of all syllabus areas;

*   extensive 'practical' materials;

*   generous question practice, together with full solutions;

This Study Text has been designed with the needs of home-study and distance-learning candidates in mind. Such students require very full coverage of the syllabus topics, and also the facility to undertake extensive question practice. However, the Study Text is also ideal for fully taught courses.

This main body of the text is divided into a number of chapters, each of which is organised on the following pattern:

*   *Detailed learning outcomes* expected after your studies of the chapter are complete. You should assimilate these before beginning detailed work on the chapter, so that you can appreciate where your studies are leading.

*   *Step-by-step topic coverage*. This is the heart of each chapter, containing detailed explanatory text supported where appropriate by worked examples and exercises. You should work carefully through this section, ensuring that you understand the material being explained and can tackle the examples and exercises successfully. Remember that in many cases knowledge is cumulative: if you fail to digest earlier material thoroughly, you may struggle to understand later chapters.

*   *Activities*. Some chapters are illustrated by more practical elements, such as comments and questions designed to stimulate discussion.

- *Question practice.* The test of how well you have learned the material is your ability to tackle exam-standard questions. Make a serious attempt at producing your own answers, but at this stage do not be too concerned about attempting the questions in exam conditions. In particular, it is more important to absorb the material thoroughly by completing a full solution than to observe the time limits that would apply in the actual exam.

- *Solutions.* Avoid the temptation merely to 'audit' the solutions provided. It is an illusion to think that this provides the same benefits as you would gain from a serious attempt of your own. However, if you are struggling to get started on a question you should read the introductory guidance provided at the beginning of the solution, where provided, and then make your own attempt before referring back to the full solution.

You should plan to attempt the mock tests just before the date of the real exam. By this stage your revision should be complete and you should be able to attempt the mock exam within the time constraints of the real exam.

If you work conscientiously through the official CIMA Study Text according to the guidelines above you will be giving yourself an excellent chance of success in your erxam. Good luck with your studies!

Icon Explanations

Definition - these sections explain important areas of knowledge which must be understood and reproduced in an exam environment.

Key Point - identifies topics which are key to success and are often examined.

Supplementary reading- indentifies a more detailed explanation of key terms, these sections will help to provide a deeper understanding of core areas. Reference to this text is vital when self studying.

Test Your Understanding - following key points and definitions are exercises which give the opportunity to assess the understanding of these core areas.

Illustration - to help develop an understanding of particular topics. The illustrative exercises are useful in preparing for the Test your understanding exercises.

Exclamation Mark - this symbol signifies a topic which can be more difficult to understand, when reviewing these areas care should be taken.

Study technique

Passing exams is partly a matter of intellectual ability, but however accomplished you are in that respect you can improve your chances significantly by the use of appropriate study and revision techniques. In this section we briefly outline some tips for effective study during the earlier stages of your approach to the exam. Later in the text we mention some techniques that you will find useful at the revision stage.

Planning

To begin with, formal planning is essential to get the best return from the time you spend studying. Estimate how much time in total you are going to need for each subject you are studying for the Managerial Level. Remember that you need to allow time for revision as well as for initial study of the material. You may find it helpful to read "Pass First Time!" second edition by David R. Harris ISBN 978-1-85617-798-6. This book will provide you with proven study techniques. Chapter by chapter it covers the building blocks of successful learning and examination techniques. This is the ultimate guide to passing your CIMA exams, written by a past CIMA examiner and shows you how to earn all the marks you deserve, and explains how to avoid the most common pitfalls. You may also find "The E Word: Kaplan's Guide to Passing Exams" by Stuart Pedley-Smith ISBN: 978-0-85732-205-0 helpful. Stuart Pedley-Smith is a senior lecturer at Kaplan Financial and a qualified accountant specialising in financial management. His natural curiosity and wider interests have led him to look beyond the technical content of financial management to the processes and journey that we call education. He has become fascinated by the whole process of learning and the exam skills and techniques that contribute towards success in the classroom. This book is for anyone who has to sit an exam and wants to give themselves a better chance of passing. It is easy to read, written in a common sense style and full of anecdotes, facts, and practical tips. It also contains synopses of interviews with people involved in the learning and examining process.

With your study material before you, decide which chapters you are going to study in each week, and which weeks you will devote to revision and final question practice.

Prepare a written schedule summarising the above and stick to it!

It is essential to know your syllabus. As your studies progress you will become more familiar with how long it takes to cover topics in sufficient depth. Your timetable may need to be adapted to allocate enough time for the whole syllabus.

Students are advised to refer to the notice of examinable legislation published regularly in CIMA's magazine (Financial Management), the students e-newsletter (Velocity) and on the CIMA website, to ensure they are up-to-date.

The amount of space allocated to a topic in the Study Text is not a very good guide as to how long it will take you. For example, the material relating to Section B 'Information Systems' and Section D 'Marketing' each account for 20% of the syllabus, but the latter has more pages because there are more models and illustrations, which take up more space. The syllabus weighting is the better guide as to how long you should spend on a syllabus topic.

Tips for effective studying

(1) Aim to find a quiet and undisturbed location for your study, and plan as far as possible to use the same period of time each day. Getting into a routine helps to avoid wasting time. Make sure that you have all the materials you need before you begin so as to minimise interruptions.

(2) Store all your materials in one place, so that you do not waste time searching for items around your accommodation. If you have to pack everything away after each study period, keep them in a box, or even a suitcase, which will not be disturbed until the next time.

(3) Limit distractions. To make the most effective use of your study periods you should be able to apply total concentration, so turn off all entertainment equipment, set your phones to message mode, and put up your 'do not disturb' sign.

(4) Your timetable will tell you which topic to study. However, before diving in and becoming engrossed in the finer points, make sure you have an overall picture of all the areas that need to be covered by the end of that session. After an hour, allow yourself a short break and move away from your Study Text. With experience, you will learn to assess the pace you need to work at.

(5) Work carefully through a chapter, making notes as you go. When you have covered a suitable amount of material, vary the pattern by attempting a practice question. When you have finished your attempt, make notes of any mistakes you made, or any areas that you failed to cover or covered more briefly.

(6) Make notes as you study, and discover the techniques that work best for you. Your notes may be in the form of lists, bullet points, diagrams, summaries, 'mind maps', or the written word, but remember that you will need to refer back to them at a later date, so they must be intelligible. If you are on a taught course, make sure you highlight any issues you would like to follow up with your lecturer.

(7) Organise your notes. Make sure that all your notes, calculations etc can be effectively filed and easily retrieved later.

Structure of subjects and learning outcomes

Each subject within the syllabus is divided into a number of broad syllabus topics. The topics contain one or more lead learning outcomes, related component learning outcomes and indicative knowledge content.

A learning outcome has two main purposes:

(a) To define the skill or ability that a well prepared candidate should be able to exhibit in the examination

(b) To demonstrate the approach likely to be taken in examination questions

The learning outcomes are part of a hierarchy of learning objectives. The verbs used at the beginning of each learning outcome relate to a specific learning objective e.g.

Explain process design.

The verb **'explain'** indicates a level two learning objective.

PAPER E1
ENTERPRISE OPERATIONS

Syllabus overview

This paper addresses several functional areas of business, as well as introducing candidates to the economic, social and political context of international business. For each of the sections dealing with information systems, operations, marketing and managing human capital, the learning requirements alert students to major developments in the field as well as tools and techniques important to each functional area.

Syllabus structure

The syllabus comprises the following topics and study weightings:

A	The Global Business Environment	20%
B	Information Systems	20%
C	Operations Management	20%
D	Marketing	20%
E	Managing Human Capital	20%

Assessment strategy

There will be a written examination paper of three hours, plus 20 minutes of pre-examination question paper reading time. The examination paper will have the following sections:

Section A – 20 marks
A variety of compulsory objective test questions, each worth between two and four marks. Mini scenarios may be given, to which a group of questions relate.

Section B – 30 marks
Six compulsory short answer questions, each worth five marks. A short scenario may be given, to which some or all questions relate.

Section C – 50 marks
One or two compulsory questions. Short scenarios may be given, to which questions relate.

E1 – A. THE GLOBAL BUSINESS ENVIRONMENT (20%)

Learning outcomes
On completion of their studies students should be able to:

Lead	Component	Indicative syllabus content
1. explain the social, political and economic context of business.	(a) explain the emergence of major economies in Asia and Latin America; (b) explain the emergence and importance of outsourcing and offshoring; (c) explain the impact of international macroeconomic developments (e.g. long-term shifts in trade balances), on the organisation's competitive environment.	• Cross-cultural management and different forms of business organisation. • Emerging market multinationals. • Liberalisation and economic nationalism. • Outsourcing and offshoring. • Major economic systems including US, European and transition economies. • National account balances (especially from international trade), monetary policy, and their impact on markets.
2. analyse the relationship between the internal governance of the firm and external sources of governance and regulation.	(a) explain the principles and purpose of corporate social responsibility and the principles of good corporate governance in an international context; (b) analyse relationships among business, society and government in national and regional contexts; (c) apply tools of country and political risk analysis; (d) discuss the nature of regulation and its impact on the firm.	• Corporate governance, including stakeholders and the role of government. • Principles of corporate social responsibility and the scope for international variation, e.g. between developed and developing economies. • Business-government relations in developed and developing economies. • Regulation in the national and international context and its impact on the firm. • Role of institutions and governance in economic growth. • Corporate political activity in developed and developing markets. • Country and political risk.

E1 – B. INFORMATION SYSTEMS (20%)

Learning outcomes
On completion of their studies students should be able to:

Lead	Component	Indicative syllabus content
1. discuss the wider business context within which information systems operate.	(a) identify the value of information and information systems organisations; (b) discuss the reasons for organisations' increased dependence on information systems; (c) discuss the transformation of organisations through technology.	• The role of information systems in organisations. • Emerging information system trends in organisations (e.g. Enterprise-wide systems; knowledge management systems; customer relationship management systems, e.g. E-business, Web 2.0 tools). • Information technology enabled transformation; the emergence of new forms of organisation. • Geographically dispersed (virtual) teams; role of information systems in virtual teams and challenges for virtual collaboration.
2. analyse how information systems can be implemented in support of the organisation's strategy.	(a) discuss ways for overcoming problems in information system implementation; (b) discuss ways of organising and managing information system activities in the context of the wider organisation.	• Assessing the costs and benefits of information systems; criteria for evaluating information systems. • Privacy and security. • System changeover methods (i.e. direct, parallel, pilot and phased). • Information system implementation as a change management process; avoiding problems of non-usage and resistance. • Information system outsourcing (different types of sourcing strategies; client-vendor relationships). • Aligning information systems with business strategy (e.g. strategic importance of information systems; information systems for competitive advantage; information systems for competitive necessity).

E1 – C. OPERATIONS MANAGEMENT (20%)

Learning outcomes
On completion of their studies students should be able to:

Lead	Component	Indicative syllabus content
1. explain the relationship of operations management to other aspects of the organisation's operations.	(a) explain the shift from price-based to relational procurement and operations; (b) explain the relationship of operations and supply management to the competitiveness of the firm; (c) explain the particular issues surrounding operations management in services; (d) explain the importance of sustainability in operations management.	• Supply chain management as a strategic process. • An overview of operations strategy and its importance to the firm. • Supply chains in competition with each other; role of supply networks; demand networks as an evolution of supply chains. • Design of products/services and processes and how this relates to operations and supply. • The concept of sustainability in operations management.
2. apply tools and techniques of operations management.	(a) apply contemporary thinking in quality management; (b) explain process design; (c) apply tools and concepts of lean management; (d) illustrate a plan for the implementation of a quality programme; (e) describe ways to manage relationships with suppliers.	• Different methods of quality measurement (e.g. Servqual). • Approaches to quality management, including Total Quality Management (TQM), various British and European Union systems as well as statistical control processes. • External quality standards. • Systems used in operations management: Manufacturing Resource Planning II (MRPII); Optimized Production Techniques (OPT) and Enterprise Resource Planning (ERP). • Use of process maps to present the flow of information and product across supply chains and networks. • Methods for managing inventory, including continuous inventory systems (e.g. Economic Order Quantity, EOQ), periodic inventory systems and the ABC system (Note: ABC is not an acronym; A refers to high value, B to medium and C to low value inventory). • Methods of managing operational capacity in product and service delivery (e.g. use of queuing theory, forecasting, flexible manufacturing systems). • Application of lean techniques to services. • Practices of continuous improvement (e.g. Quality circles, Kaizen, 5S, 6 Sigma). • The characteristics of lean production. • Criticisms and limitations of lean production. • Developing relationships with suppliers, including the use of supply portfolios.

E1 – D. MARKETING (20%)

Learning outcomes
On completion of their studies students should be able to:

Lead	Component	Indicative syllabus content
1. explain developments in marketing.	(a) explain the marketing concept, and the alternatives to it; (b) describe the marketing environment of a range of organisations; (c) explain marketing in a not-for-profit context; (d) explain the social context of marketing behaviour; (e) describe theories of consumer behaviour.	• The marketing concept as a business philosophy. • The marketing environment, including societal, economic, technological, political and legal factors affecting marketing. • Marketing in not-for-profit organisations (i.e. charities, non-governmental organisations; the public sector). • Theories of consumer behaviour (e.g. social interaction theory), as well as factors affecting buying decisions, types of buying behaviour and stages in the buying process. • Social marketing and corporate social responsibility.
2. apply tools and techniques used in support of the organisation's marketing.	(a) explain the relationships between market research, market segmentation, targeting and positioning; (b) apply tools within each area of the marketing mix; (c) describe the business contexts within which marketing principles can be applied; (d) describe the market planning process; (e) explain the role of branding and brand equity.	• Market research, including data gathering techniques and methods of analysis. • Segmentation and targeting of markets, and positioning of products within markets. • How business to business (B2B) marketing differs from business to consumer (B2C) marketing in its different forms (i.e. consumer marketing, services marketing, direct marketing, interactive marketing, e-marketing, internal marketing). • Promotional tools and the promotion mix. • The 'service extension' to the marketing mix. • Devising and implementing a pricing strategy. • Experiential marketing. • Marketing communications, including viral, guerrilla and other indirect forms of marketing. • Distribution channels and methods for marketing campaigns. • The role of marketing in the business plan of the organisation. • Brand image and brand value. • Product development and product/service life-cycles. • Internal marketing as the process of training and motivating employees so as to support the organisation's external marketing activities. • The differences and similarities in the marketing of products, services and experiences. • Product portfolios and the product mix.

E1 – E. MANAGING HUMAN CAPITAL (20%)

Learning outcomes
On completion of their studies students should be able to:

Lead	Component	Indicative syllabus content
1. explain the relationship of Human Resources (HR) to the organisation's operations.	(a) explain how HR theories and activities can contribute to the success of the organisation; (b) explain the importance of ethical behaviour in business generally and for the line manager and their activities.	• Theories of Human Resource Management relating to ability, motivation and opportunity. • The psychological contract and its importance to retention. • The relationship of the employee to other elements of the business. • Personal business ethics and the fundamental principles (Part A) of the CIMA Code of Ethics for Professional Accountants.
2. discuss the activities associated with the management of human capital.	(a) explain the HR activities associated with developing the ability of employees; (b) discuss the HR activities associated with the motivation of employees; (c) describe the HR activities associated with improving the opportunities for employees to contribute to the firm; (d) discuss the importance of the line manager in the implementation of HR practices; (e) prepare an HR plan appropriate to a team.	• Practices associated with recruiting and developing appropriate abilities including recruitment and selection of staff using different recruitment channels (i.e. interviews, assessment centres, intelligence tests, aptitude tests, psychometric tests). • Issues relating to fair and legal employment practices (e.g. recruitment, dismissal, redundancy, and ways of managing these). • The distinction between development and training and the tools available to develop and train staff. • The design and implementation of induction programmes. • Practices related to motivation including issues in the design of reward systems (e.g. the role of incentives, the utility of performance-related pay, arrangements for knowledge workers, flexible work arrangements). • The importance of appraisals, their conduct and their relationship to the reward system. • Practices related to the creation of opportunities for employees to contribute to the organisation including job design, communications, involvement procedures and appropriate elements of negotiating and bargaining. • Problems in implementing an HR plan appropriate to a team and ways to manage this. • HR in different organisational forms (e.g. project based, virtual or networked firms) and different organisational contexts. • Preparation of an HR plan (e.g. Forecasting personnel requirements; retention, absence and leave, wastage).

Understanding the CIMA Verb Hierarchy for E1

Chapter learning objectives

CIMA VERB HIERARCHY

CIMA place great importance on the choice of verbs in exam question requirements. It is thus critical that you answer the question according to the definition of the verb used.

The E1 syllabus contains 38 learning outcomes using the following verbs that you need to understand:

Level 2 verbs

- "Explain" - occurs 17 times
- "Describe" - occurs 6 times
- "Illustrate" - occurs once
- "Identify" - occurs once

Level 3 verbs

- "Apply" - occurs 4 times
- "Prepare" - occurs once

Level 4 verbs

- "Discuss" - occurs 7 times
- "Analyse" - occurs once

The verbs given in the syllabus limit the scope of the question requirements that the examiners can ask.

For example, syllabus learning outcome C2(b) is "**explain** process design". "Explain" is a level 2 verb, so the examiner would not be allowed to ask you a level 3 or 4 verb here, such as to "**discuss**" a firm's process design approach.

This chapter looks at the verbs and the differences between them.

1 Operational Level Verbs

It is vital that you identify which verb is used in an exam question requirement and answer accordingly. The examiner has repeatedly said that students in the real exam are generally good at the knowledge aspects of questions but poor when discussion and/or application to a scenario is required.

Level 1: KNOWLEDGE

What you are expected to know

VERBS USED	DEFINITION
List	Make a list of
State	Express, fully or clearly, the details of / facts of
Define	Give the exact meaning of

Level 2: COMPREHENSION

What you are expected to understand

VERBS USED	DEFINITION
Describe	Communicate the key features of.
Distinguish	Highlight the differences between.
Explain	Make clear or intelligible/state the meaning or purpose of.
Identify	Recognise, establish or select after consideration.
Illustrate	Use an example to describe or explain something.

Level 3 - APPLICATION

How you are expected to apply your knowledge

VERBS USED	DEFINITION
Apply	Put to practical use.
Calculate	Ascertain or reckon mathematically.
Demonstrate	Prove with certainty or exhibit by practical means.
Prepare	Make or get ready for use.
Reconcile	Make or prove consistent/compatible.
Solve	Find an answer to.
Tabulate	Arrange in a table.

Level 4 - ANALYSIS

How you are expected to analyse the detail of what you have learned.

VERBS USED	DEFINITION
Analyse	Examine in detail the structure of.
Categorise	Place into a defined class or division.
Compare and contrast	Show the similarities and/or differences between.
Construct	Build up or compile.
Discuss	Examine in detail by argument.
Interpret	Translate into intelligible or familiar terms.
Prioritise	Place in order of priority or sequence for action.
Produce	Create or bring into existence.

2 Further guidance on operational level verbs that cause confusion

Verbs that cause students confusion at this level are as follows:

Level 2 verbs

- **The difference between "describe" and "explain".**

  An explanation is a set of statements constructed to describe a set of facts which clarifies the **causes**, **context**, and **consequences** of those facts.

  For example, if asked to **describe** the features of a marketing orientation you could talk, among other things, about understanding the customer's needs and adopting a strategy producing products with the benefits and features to fulfil these needs. This tells us what the marketing orientation looks like.

  However if asked to **explain** the marketing orientation, then you would have to talk about why firms may be dissatisfied with alternative approaches to selling their products and may consider switching to the marketing orientation, and the implications for firms (consequences) in terms of the benefits of adopting a marketing orientation.

  More simply, to describe something is to answer "what" type questions whereas to explain looks at "what" and "why" aspects.

- **The verb "to illustrate"**

  The key thing about illustrating something is that you may have to decide on a relevant example to use. This could involve drawing a diagram, performing supporting calculations or highlighting a feature or person in the scenario given. Most of the time the question will be structured so calculations performed in part (a) can be used to illustrate a concept in part (b).

  For example, you could be asked to explain and illustrate what is meant by an "quality programme".

Level 3 verbs

- **The verb "to apply"**

  Given that all level 3 verbs involve application, the verb "apply" is rare in the real exam. Instead one of the other more specific verbs is used instead.

- **The verb "to reconcile"**

This is a numerical requirement and usually involves starting with one of the figures, adjusting it and ending up with the other.

For example, in a bank reconciliation you start with the recorded cash at bank figure, adjust it for unpresented cheques, etc., and (hopefully!) end up with the stated balance in the cash "T account".

This verb will rarely be used in paper E1.

- **The verb "to demonstrate"**

The verb "to demonstrate" can be used in two main ways.

Firstly it could mean to prove that a given statement is true or consistent with circumstances given. For example, the Finance Director may have stated in the question that the company will not exceed its overdraft limit in the next six months. The requirement then asks you to demonstrate that the Director is wrong. You could do this by preparing a cash flow forecast for the next six months.

Secondly you could be asked to demonstrate **how** a stated model, framework, technique or theory could be used in the particular scenario. Ensure you do not merely describe the model but use it to generate some results.

Level 4 verbs

- **The verb "to analyse"**

To analyse something is to examine it in detail in order to discover its meaning or essential features. This will usually involve breaking the scenario down and looking at the fine detail, possibly with additional calculations, and then stepping back to see the bigger picture to identify any themes to support conclusions.

For example, if asked to analyse a set of financial statements, then the end result will be a set of statements about the performance of the business with supporting evidence. This could involve the following:

(1) You could break down your analysis into areas of profitability, liquidity, gearing and so on.

(2) Under each heading look at key figures in the financial statements, identifying trends (e.g. sales growth) and calculating supporting ratios (e.g. margins).

(3) Try to explain what the figures mean and why they have occurred (e.g. why has the operating margin fallen?)

(4) Start considering the bigger picture - are the ratios presenting a consistent message or do they contradict each other? Can you identify common causes?

(5) Finally you would then seek to pull all this information together and interpret it to make some higher level comments about overall performance.

The main error students make is that they fail to draw out any themes and conclusions and simply present the marker with a collection of uninterpreted, unexplained facts and figures.

- **The verb "to discuss"**

To discuss something is very similar to analysing it, except that discussion usually involves two or more different viewpoints or arguments as the context, rather than a set of figures, say. To discuss viewpoints will involve looking at their underlying arguments, examining them critically, trying to assess whether one argument is more persuasive than the other and then seeking to reach a conclusion.

For example, if asked to discuss whether a particular technique could be used by a company, you would examine the arguments for and against, making reference to the specific circumstances in the question, and seek to conclude.

- **The verb "to prioritise"**

To prioritise is to place objects in an order. The key issue here is to decide upon the criteria to use to perform the ordering. For example, prioritising the external threats facing a firm could be done by considering the scale of financial consequences, immediacy, implications for the underlying business model and so on.

The main mistake students make is that they fail to justify their prioritisation - why is this the most important issue?

2

Introduction to the Global Business Environment

Chapter learning objectives

Lead	Component
A1. Explain the social, political and economic context of business.	(a) Explain the emergence of major economies in Asia and Latin America.
	(b) Explain the emergence and importance of outsourcing and offshoring.
	(c) Explain the impact of international macroeconomic developments (e.g. long-term shifts in trade balances), on the organisation's competitive environment.
A2. Analyse the relationship between the internal governance of a firm and external sources of governance and regulation.	(c) Apply tools of country and political risk analysis

1 Introduction

Today's global business environment is changing at a fast pace. This presents a number of challenges for global managers who must be able to deal with a wide range of labour, environmental, social, cultural, ethical and governmental issues.

Some of these will give rise to opportunities for the firm, for example:

- New markets in developing nations
- The possibility of reducing production costs by outsourcing and off-shoring
- The achievement of economies of scale through becoming a multi-national company (MNC)

However, there may be problems and threats to deal with as well, such as:

- Domestic markets may become open to competition from foreign firms
- Some countries may be difficult to penetrate due to them joining a regional trade bloc.
- World Trade Organisation (WTO) intervention may change the balance of power in some markets

Today's global managers are expected to possess entrepreneurial qualities beyond those of judgement, perseverance and knowledge of business. Above all, global managers must have an understanding of the complexities of the modern world and how to deal with people from a wide range of backgrounds and cultures.

The real issue facing many of today's global leaders is what to say about corporate governance when the rules and expectations of society are changing so quickly. What do you teach managers about the global competitive landscape, when countries like China and India are fundamentally changing the rules of the game?

Chapters 2 and 3 explore some of these issues in more detail and also review the role of government in the global business environment.

2 Free trade and protectionism

2.1 Liberalisation and nationalism

In this section we consider the issue of free trade, the arguments for and against it, different methods of protectionsim and the institutions that influence these factors. All of these are key issues for a business that operates in more than one country.

 Liberalisation is a broad term that usually refers to fewer government regulations and restrictions in the economy. As a result, international trade, i.e. free trade, will be encouraged.

> ### Illustration 1 - Fewer regulations in the economy
>
> The deregulation of the bus industry in the UK in the 1980s opened it up to private sector operators. The elimination of this government monopoly aimed to increase efficiency, reduce prices and increase quality.

Economic nationalism, on the other hand, refers to a set of policies that favour the home nation, e.g. the restriction of free trade or of foreign investment. As a result, international trade will be discouraged (protectionism).

2.2 Free trade

"Free trade" means that there are no barriers to the free flow of goods and services between countries.

In theory, free trade between nations is desirable, but often in practice various forms of protection are used.

Benefits of free trade

The main arguments in favour of free trade are as follows:

- World trade allows **specialisation** enabling different nations with differing skills and resources to gain the rewards from the division of labour. In theory, nations specialise in the production of goods for which they have a natural advantage.

  For instance, Saudi Arabia extracts oil, Argentina rears beef and Britain provides financial services.

  Specialisation usually enables an industry to benefit from large-scale production and make the maximum use of resources.

- This should improve the **economies of scale** which can be obtained are determined by the size of the market.

  As international trade opens up new markets, it facilitates economies of scale. Such efficiency has benefits for the trading economies because it should produce lower prices and better products, leading to improvements in general living standards.

- **Surpluses and deficits removed**, thus improving economic prosperity and the standard of living.

  A country with a surplus, e.g. of oil, can export its resource and a country with a deficit can import the resource.

- **Competition** should be fostered by world trade, particularly free trade.

  A domestic market which is controlled by a monopolist might be subject to a foreign competitor. Alternatively, the market of a few complacent home suppliers might be revitalised by the entry of foreign firms (e.g. Japanese and American companies in British consumer goods industries).

- **Lower prices and greater choice** should be available to consumers.

  The increased choice which results from international competition is particularly evident in the British car industry. However, it must be noted that these benefits perhaps need to be set against the loss of employment in domestic industries.

- For **political reasons.**

  For example, the USA actively supported the free trade in flowers with Colombia so that farmers would grow carnations rather than cocaine.

Arguments for restricting free trade

The main arguments given for limiting free trade are as follows:

- **Protection for infant industries** - likely in developing countries where new industries are too small to have gained economies of scale, workers will be inexperienced and there is inadequate finance for expansion.

- **Self-sufficiency** - the country may wish to maintain a degree of self-sufficiency in case trade is cut off in times of war.

- **Prevents dumping** - a country may produce an excess of a good, e.g. wine or beef, and in order to get rid of the excess they may export it at a low price. The countries receiving the dumped goods would therefore be facing unfair competition from abroad.

- **Prevents the establishment of a foreign based monopoly** - competition from abroad could drive domestic producers out of business. The foreign company, now having a monopoly, could charge high prices for sub-standard products.

- **To reduce the influence of trade on national culture** - for example, the developing countries may object to the influence of Western consumerist values expounded by companies such as Starbucks and McDonalds. France has resisted the import of American culture through cinema and radio for a number of years and has media legislation in place restricting the amount of broadcasts in languages other than French.

- **To prevent the import of harmful goods** - the import of goods, such as drugs or live animals, may be barred.

- Free trade reduces **national security** by reducing border controls.

- International free trade is inefficient, as consumer expectations are increased. Many people in the developed world are no longer satisfied with seasonal produce and the cost of shipping out of season fruit and vegetables around the world, usually by air, is high to the consumer and **damaging to the environment**.

- The **influence of multinationals** is often so strong in the country in which they operate that it can be used to corrupt the political system.

Free trade agreements

In many parts of the world, governments have created trade agreements and common markets to encourage free trade. However, the World Trade Organisation (WTO) is opposed to these trading blocs and customs unions (e.g. the European Union) because they encourage trade between members but often have high trade barriers for non-members.

From a business perspective such agreements give major opportunities to firms within the area specified but create barriers to entry for those outside. This is the reason why Japanese car manufacturers have built factories within the EU, so they can avoid quotas.

The different types of agreement are as follows:

Bi-lateral and multi-lateral trade agreements

These are agreements between two or more countries to eliminate quotas and tariffs on the trade of most (if not all) goods between them. Examples include:

- The Closer Economic Relations (CER) agreement between Australia and New Zealand.

Free trade areas

If the members of a multi-lateral free trade agreement are all in the same geographical area then it is sometimes described as a free trade area. Examples include

- The North American Free Trade Agreement (NAFTA) between Canada, the United States, and Mexico.

- The ASEAN Free Trade Area (AFTA) is an agreement by the Association of Southeast Asian Nations (Brunei, Indonesia, Malaysia, Philippines, Singapore, Thailand, Vietnam, Laos, Myanmar and Cambodia).

- South Korea is currently negotiating a free trade agreement with the EU. Trade between South Korea and the EU totalled $92.2 billion in 2010.

Customs unions

A customs union is a free trade area with a common external tariff. The participant countries set up common external trade policy, but in some cases they use different import quotas. Examples include:

- Mercosur is a customs union between Brazil, Argentina, Uruguay, Paraguay and Venezuela in South America.

Countries may chose to move from a FTA to a customs union to eliminate some of the trade distortions of FTAs where different member countries have different export rules to the same target country. To avoid local regulations producers may sell to a partner in another member country with less stringent regulations who then sells to the target customer. This results in the need for rules to determine the origin of goods.

Single markets (economic communities)

A single market is a customs union with common policies on product regulation, and freedom of movement of all the four factors of production (goods, services, capital and labour). Advocates argue that this gives a more "level playing field" for producers in different countries as they all have to meet the same standards.

Examples include:

- The Economic Community of West African States (ECOWAS).

Economic unions

An economic and monetary union is a single market with a common currency.

The largest economic and monetary union at present is the Eurozone. The Eurozone consists of the European Union member states that have adopted the Euro.

Arguments abound regarding the effects of regional trading blocs.

- Their supporters say that they encourage *trade creation by harmonizing economic policies* and standards within member countries and reducing prices as trade restrictions are removed.

- Opponents state that they lead to *trade diversion*. Member countries buy within the regional trading bloc when cheaper sources are available outside.

- Common external tariffs can encourage a regional fortress mentality which can lead to conflicts between different regional trading blocs. For example, NAFTA has complained over the EU's agricultural imports while the EU has complained over NAFTA's restrictions on steel imports.

- The fear is that regional trading blocs could lead to the development of protectionism worldwide at a time when the WTO is seeking to create free trade.

2.3 Balanced trade

There are a number of alternatives to free trade policies.

- In some instances two countries will attempt a policy of 'balanced trade', whereby they will try to maintain a fairly even relationship between their respective imports and exports so that neither country runs a large trade deficit.

- Another approach is to actually try to protect the local market by restricting imports. This is known as economic nationalism or, more commonly, protectionism.

2.4 Protectionism

Trade involves costs as well as benefits. Therefore, countries may erect barriers to trade. These include:

- **Tariffs** – customs duties on imports.

Illustration 2 - Tariffs

In 2002 the US steel industry was making heavy losses. As a result, George W. Bush (the US President at the time) announced that the industry was to receive protection from imported steel. Tariffs of between 8% (on steel wire) and 30% (on steel plates) were imposed. The decision was met with dismay from throughout the world. The Americans were accused of putting domestic politics ahead of the country's international legal agreements.

- **Quotas** - restrictions on the amount of certain goods that can be imported.
- **Embargoes** - ban on certain imports or exports.

Illustration 3 - Embargoes

In 2006, a European Commission ban on British beef exports officially ended, 10 years after it was imposed to prevent the spread of BSE or "mad cow disease" throughout Europe.

- **Subsidies** - on domestic products to give them a price advantage over imports.
- **Administrative regulations** - designed to deter imports, e.g. excessive paperwork.
- **Government action** - for example, the government may favour domestic producers when purchasing defence equipment.

If we are the domestic producer in a country that practises protectionism, then we will benefit from the reduced competition and lower risk, both of which should result in higher profitability. However, the methods described above may present a firm with powerful barriers to entry into new markets. One way of trying to get round such barriers is to consider some form of alliance or joint venture with a domestic firm in that market.

Test your understanding 1

Explain the problems associated with restricting free trade.

Institutions influencing free trade

Most companies will face markets where free trade dominates and others where there is more protectionsim. However, these situations are rarely set in stone so here we consider some of the major institutions that influence free trade.

The World Trade Organisation (WTO) and the General Agreements on Tariffs and Trade (GATT)

As trade began to recover after the Second World War attempts were made to reduce barriers to free trade around the world. The General Agreements on Tariffs and Trade (GATT) came into being in 1948. Regular rounds of talks were held to agree trading patterns around the world and to negotiate removal of trade barriers.

These negotiations have become more prolonged and complex as time has gone on.

In 1995 the World Trade Organisation based in Geneva replaced GATT. It has a number of roles:

- to ensure compliance of member countries with previous GATT agreements

- to negotiate future trade liberalisation agreements

- to resolve trading disputes between nations.

The WTO has much greater authority than GATT as it has the power to police and 'enforce' trade agreements. It faces an increasingly difficult role as the facilitator for global free trade talks.

The WTO is opposed to the development of trading blocs and customs unions such as the EU and NAFTA. Although they promote free trade between members of the union, there are normally high trade barriers for non-members, e.g. the difficulties faced by non-EU food producers when they attempt to export to the EU.

Example

There is growing tension between the developed and the developing world. The developing world regards heavy subsidy of EU and American farmers as a huge barrier to trade for their domestic farmers. At the same time, the developed world complains about export of low cost manufactured goods from the developing world that are not subject to the same health, safety and environmental regulations that they face.

The European Union (EU)

The EU is an example of a single market and, within the Euro zone, an economic union (see above). It has its origins in the Treaty of Rome (1957).

The aims of the treaty were as follows:

- the elimination of customs duties and quotas on imports and exports between member states

- the establishment of a common customs tariff and a common commercial policy towards non-member states

- the abolition of obstacles to the free movement of persons, services and capital between member states

- the establishment of common policies on transport and agriculture

- the prohibition of business practices that restrict or distort competition

- the association of overseas countries in order to increase trade and development.

The Group of Eight (G8)

The Group of Eight (G8) consists of Canada, France, Germany, Italy, Japan, Russia, the United Kingdom, and the United States. Together, these countries represent about 65% of the world economy.

The agenda of G8 meetings is usually about controversial global issues such as global warming, poverty in Africa, fair trade policies and AIDS but has implications for global trade.

The 31st G8 summit in 2005 resulted in a stated commitment to reduce subsidies and tariffs that inhibit trade.

The G8 summit has consistently dealt with:

- Macroeconomic management
- International trade
- Energy issues and climate change
- Development issues and relationships with developing countries
- Issues of international concern such as terrorism and organised crime.

The G8 does not have any formal resources or powers as is the case with other inter-national organisations such as the WTO. However, it provides a forum for the most powerful nations to discuss complex international issues and to develop the personal relations that help them respond in effective collective fashion to sudden crises or shocks. The summit also gives direction to the international community by setting priorities, defining new issues and providing guidance to established international organisations.

3 Emerging markets

3.1 Globalisation

 Globalisation is the economic and social process whereby local markets and cultures are increasingly dominated by global markets and cultures.

Illustration 4 - Globalisation

Most people are affected by globalisation in a number of ways and are aware of global brands either through personal experience or via the media. Thinking about what you are doing at the moment, it is quite possible that:

- You are reading a book written in the UK
- Using software developed in North America
- Which was typeset in India
- Printed locally wherever you live
- Bought using a credit card issued by an international bank
- You are drinking a coffee made from Columbian beans
- Wearing trainers made in Vietnam
- Clothes made in China
- Or possibly from Egyptian cotton
- You may be listening to music recorded locally
- But playing on equipment made in Japan
- You may even be studying in a foreign country where you have gone to work

Illustration 5 - Globalisation and supermarkets

The expansion of European and American grocer retailers into global markets has been underway for a number of years. Limited growth opportunities at home resulted in the major players expanding their overseas operations with mixed success. Tesco entered the Thai market in 1998 and now has over 500 stores. The advantage for these international retailers was expertise in systems, distribution and the range of products. However, the businesses have had to learn to adapt to local conditions, e.g. Walmart sells whole roasted pigs and live frogs in its Chinese stores.

Test your understanding 2

Identify the main drivers of globalisation.

The impact of globalisation on firms

Firms are affected by globalisation in many ways, including:

Industrial relocation

As mentioned above, many firms have relocated their manufacturing base to countries with lower labour costs ("off-shoring").

However, this can give the impression that the only form of expansion is from "First World" to "Third World". This is not always the case as illustrated by Nissan (a Japanese company) building a car factory in Sunderland in the United Kingdom to avoid EU import quotas and tariffs.

Also, the motivation is not always cost. As mentioned before some non-Western countries are developing regional areas of excellence. For example, Bangalore in India is recognised globally for its expertise in telecommunications.

Managing (often complex) global supply chains has only been made possible by the advances in ICT mentioned above.

Emergence of growth markets

As mentioned above, many previously closed markets, such as China, are opening up to Western firms.

In addition, if tastes are becoming more homogeneous, then this presents new opportunities for firms to sell their products in countries previously discounted.

Access to markets and enhanced competition

The combination of firms' global expansion plans and the relaxation of trade barriers have resulted in increased competition in many markets. This can be seen in:

- greater pressure on firms' cost bases with factories being relocated to even cheaper areas

- greater calls for protectionism.

Developments in ICT have also facilitated greater access to markets, for example by selling via the internet.

Cross-national business alliances and mergers

To exploit the opportunities global markets offer many firms have sought to obtain expertise and greater economies of scale through cross-national mergers and acquisitions. For example:

- In 2004 American brewer Anheuser-Busch Limited purchased the Chinese company Harbin Brewery Company Ltd.

- The merger of Hoechst (a German company) and Rhone Poulenc (French) to create Aventis in 1999 created the second largest drugs manufacturer in the world at the time.

Widening economic divisions between countries

Many opponents of globalisation argue that it is creating new gaps between the rich and the poor. For example:

Rich countries have much greater access to the internet and communications services. In the current information age wealth is created by the development of information goods and services, ranging from media, to education and software. Not all poor countries are taking part in this information revolution and are falling further behind the "digital divide".

The relentless drive to liberalise trade, i.e. to remove trade barriers, promote privatisation, and reduce regulation (including legal protection for workers), has had a negative impact on the lives of millions of people around the world.

Many poor countries have been pressured to orientate their economies towards producing exports and to reduce already inadequate spending on public services such as health and education so that they can repay their foreign debt. This has forced even more people into a life of poverty and uncertainty.

3.2 Globalisation and developing countries

- In the past, many companies located much of their manufacturing in the developing countries of Asia and Latin America.

- Now they are increasingly locating service and knowledge-based jobs there too, e.g. telesales, research and development.

- This is because many countries in Asia and Latin America now produce a massive number of well educated and well trained individuals.

- These workers are cheap to employ compared to those in the US and Europe, resulting in lower costs and increased profits for companies.

- The developing countries have also benefited with economic growth and wage rises as a result of globalisation.

3.3 Transition economies

A **transition** economy is an economy which is changing from a planned economy to a mixed (or even a free market) economy.

- A planned economy - the government owns all the resources and makes decisions about their use on behalf of the population, e.g. The Soviet Union and China after the Second World War.

- A free market economy - Individuals decide how resources should be used acting as producers and consumers of goods and services.

- In a mixed economy some products are supplied by market forces like in a free economy but there is government intervention in other areas. The USA and the UK are examples of mixed economies - both come relatively close to the definition of a free market economy but there is a limited degree of government intervention in the provision of healthcare, education and welfare services.

> ### Advantages of planned economies
>
> - **Reduces inequalities in wealth** – the government controls the distribution of incomes. This reduces inequalities in wealth.
>
> - **Lower unemployment** – if individuals are free to pursue private profits, there will tend to be higher unemployment since firms making losses will lay staff off. This should not be an issue in a planned economy.
>
> - **Fairer treatment of consumers** – in a planned economy there will be no private monopolies. Monopolies can exploit the consumer, charging high prices for poor quality products and services. (Note: government monopolies may still exist.)
>
> - **Affordable goods** – government control of prices reduces the problem of inflation and can be used to ensure affordable basic goods for poorer members of society.

Advantages of a free market economic system

- **Consumer sovereignty** – consumers determine what is produced by producers, i.e. suppliers will only produce goods and services that consumers will buy.

- **Greater competition** – competition between firms should lead to improved efficiency and quality and lower priced goods and services.

- **Incentive to work hard** – individuals are free to make profit for themselves (and not the government). This increases the incentive to work hard.

The former Soviet Union and China would be placed as transition economies.

Transition economies have been triggered into growth by a number of factors. For example:

- Foreign direct investment (FDI) – overseas companies want to share in the growth of these countries and may invest by acquiring a local company or by creating new facilities in the host country to take advantage of local conditions.

- Offshoring (see earlier discussion).

How transition economies change

As countries seek to become more competitive, they will attract investment from overseas firms, eager to share in the growth of the country. The investment that those companies make is known as foreign direct investment (FDI).

The firms that make these investments are known as multinational enterprises (MNEs), and retain control of the entity in which they have invested. This is often met with mixed feelings by the population, who are grateful for the creation of wealth and jobs but resentful of the country being "bought by foreigners". Similarly there can be resentment in countries whose firms invest abroad, particularly when there is domestic unemployment.

The current trend to offshore call centres and computing services has been a hotly debated issue since it began, but it is a phenomenon that has been occurring for many years. Originally the preserve of OECD countries is now a truly global feature of the world economy.

There are two main types of FDI:

(1) Acquisitions, where the MNE acquires the shares of the local company, and control of the assets and markets of the acquired firm are transferred to the new parent. The local firm becomes a division of the new parent. Sometimes the acquiring firm will "collect" companies in adjacent countries and a cross border merger results in the production of a whole geographical region being coordinated. Unless the acquired company was in danger of imminent collapse, and was rescued by the new parent, there is no long-term benefit to the local economy, as all future profits are likely to be exported to the parent group.

(2) Greenfield investment occurs where a company creates new facilities in the host country to take advantage of local conditions. These are better for the host country, since they are likely to create jobs, productive capacity, knowledge transfer and access to the global economy. Although the profits that the parent makes are still exported to head office, the domestic economy should benefit from the wages earned by the workforce and the income earned by any local firms that supply the new facilities.

Many countries are seeing their economy boosted by the arrival of foreign firms, as is the case of Russia, where growth in the domestic economy is being fuelled by the arrival of multinational retailers who have established bases in the country. In 2005 Russia attracted $16.7 billion of FDI, with Coca Cola acquiring a fruit juice maker, Heineken acquiring local brewers and both Toyota and Volkswagen establishing automobile factories. Other companies establishing factories include Carlsberg, Nestle and Whirlpool (the domestic appliance manufacturer) in partnership with the Turkish company, Vestel Group.

FDI is often the "trigger" to an economy, and can lead to rapid growth in wealth and skills. Countries that are beginning to benefit from FDI are known as "transition" economies, and they sometimes develop significant domestic economic infrastructure as a result. Other transition economies are triggered into growth by offshoring, and the economic gain can lead to the development of a local pool of highly skilled labour. Some local organisations grow, until they too are ready to enter the world stage.

3.4 BRIC economies

A recent trend has been a rise in multinational companies from the emerging "BRIC" economies.

- BRIC are the world's largest emerging economies.

- Fast growth, strong economic foundations and large populations have made BRIC into the world's most promising economies.

- By 2050, the combined BRIC economies are expected to outstrip the G6 economies (Germany, France, Italy, Japan, UK and the USA).

- At this point, China is predicted to become the world's largest economy.

- In June 2009, the first summit of heads of state of the BRIC countries was held. The forming of an alliance will help to increase their economic and political power.

- Organisations in BRIC economies are moving from being recipients of foreign direct investment to actually investing in and even becoming owners of major Western businesses.

The future of the BRIC economies

The global financial meltdown in 2008 has resulted in a slowdown in the rate of growth of the BRIC economies. However, BRIC countries have a number of strengths which should allow them to continue to grow including:

- **Strong consumer demand** – high levels of consumer expenditure in the BRIC countries should help drive growth.

- **High levels of foreign exchange reserves** – these reserves will allow the government to boost public spending in the economy, e.g. on transport and infrastructure. This will enhance the environment and lead to further economic growth.

Threats for BRIC economies

The global slowdown of 2008 has resulted in a number of threats for the BRIC economies. For example:

- Foreign investment in BRIC economies from developed countries has slowed.

- Consumer demand in the developed world has slowed. This will impact the BRIC economies, e.g. two thirds of China's exports are to the developed world, with exports accounting for over one third of their wealth.

- India's economy depends on developed countries outsourcing services to them. A recession in the developed world will reduce the level of outsourcing.

The role of major institutions in fostering international

The principal institutions encouraging world trade have been discussed earlier in this chapter. Here we consider institutions more involved with international development and financing.

The World Bank

The International Bank for Reconstruction and Development (IBRD), also known as the World Bank, was created at the Bretton Woods meeting in 1944. The original purpose of the IBRD was to help finance the reconstruction of economies damaged by the war. However, it soon shifted the focus of its lending to countries of the developing world.

The bank now comprises three principal constituent elements:

1. The IBRD proper whose function is to lend long-term funds for capital projects in developing economies at a commercial rate of interest. The main source of these funds is borrowing by the IBRD itself.
2. The International Development Association (IDA) which was established in 1960 to provide 'soft' loans to the poorest of the developing countries. The IDA:
   (a) is mainly financed by 20 donor countries providing funds every 3 years. Funding therefore depends on the generosity or otherwise of these countries.
   (b) provides loans on concessionary terms, normally interest free loans repayable over 50 years.
3. The International Finance Corporation, which promotes the private sector in developing countries by lending or by taking equity.

The World Bank is clearly an important source of capital funds for the developing countries. However, it has been criticised in recent years over the nature of its lending conditions.

The International Monetary Fund (IMF)

The IMF was also founded in 1944 at Bretton Woods in the USA but did not really begin to fully function until the 1950s. The so called Bretton Woods System that the IMF was to supervise was to have two main characteristics: stable exchange rates and a multilateral system of international payments and credit.

In particular the IMF became responsible for:

- promoting international financial co-operation and establishing a system of stable exchange rates and freely convertible currencies

- providing a source of credit for members with balance of payments deficits while corrective policies were adopted

- managing the growth of international liquidity.

European Bank for Reconstruction and Development

The European Bank for Reconstruction and Development was established in 1991 when communism was crumbling in central and Eastern Europe and ex-soviet countries needed support to nurture a new private sector in a democratic environment.

Today the EBRD uses the tools of investment to help build market economies and democracies in 27 countries from central Europe to central Asia.

4 Multinational Companies (MNCs)

4.1 Introduction to multinationals

A **multinational** business owns or controls foreign subsidiaries in more than one country, i.e. it has production or service facilities in more than one country.

Size – most of the world's largest firms, e.g. Wal Mart and Shell, are multinationals but there are also thousands of very small multinationals

Owernership – Overseas subsidiairies may be wholly owned or joint ventures may be established

Nature of Business – cover all areas from manu-facturing to service provision and finance

Diversity among multinationals

Productive locations – may be located in a small or large number of countries

Overseas business relative to total business –only one fifth of Wal Mart's sales come from overseas subsidiaries compared to four fifths of BP's sales

Benefits of going multinational

Two major advantages of being a multinational

Lower costs – can locate each part of production in a country where the resource costs are lower

New market entry – can expand overseas once markets in the domestic economy have become saturated

Benefits of going multinational

Ownership advantages

- Ownership of superior technology – this will enhance productivity and result in superior-quality products.
- Research and development (R&D) capacity – multinationals can invest heavily in R&D since they can spread the cost over a large output.
- Product differentiation – can combine innovation with successful product differentiation.
- Managerial skills – managers of multinationals are more innovative in the way that they do things.

Locational advantages

Multinationals will take advantage of the most appropriate location to make their products or services. Can locate:

- where the required resources can be found.
- where labour is relatively cheap.
- where the quality of the resources is better.
- in a foreign country to avoid transport costs and tariffs.
- in a foreign country to take advantage of government incentives.

Internalisation

The cost of setting up an overseas subsidiary is often less than the cost of arranging a contract with an external party, e.g. an overseas importer.

5 Outsourcing and Offshoring

5.1 Outsourcing

Outsourcing means contracting-out aspects of the work of the organisation, previously done in-house, to specialist providers.

Outsourcing has become increasingly common in organisations. The advantages and disadvantages are as follows.

Advantages

The main reason for outsourcing is that it is cheaper. Cost advantages can come from a number of sources:

- A large supplier may benefit from economies of scale in production
- The firm concerned will benefit from reduced capital expenditure on machinery to make the items now outsourced
- Reduced headcount in terms of workers no longer needed to make the items.
- Research and development expenditure on the components, say, concerned will also be saved.

There can also be quality advantages:

- The supplier may have skills and expertise that allow them to make better products
- Outsourcing may solve the problem of the customer having a skills shortage in certain areas.

Other advantages include the following:

- The supplier have greater, leading to faster and more flexible supply of components. This could enable a just-in-time system, for example.
- The management of the customer are no longer distracted by fringe areas and so can focus on core business activities.
- The organisation can exercise buyor power over suppliers ensuring favourable terms and conditions.
- The organisation has greater flexibility to switch suppliers based on changing cost/quality considerations.

Disadvantages

The main reasons why firms do not outsource include the following:

Cost issues

- Presumably the supplier has to make a profit margin, so we will be charged a price to cover both costs and profit. This suggests it should be cheaper to do it in house as we only have to pay the costs then.
- If dealing with a major supplier we may be vulnerable to future price rises

Quality issues

- Loss of competitive advantage (if function being outsourced is a key competency) - see below

- Loss of in-house expertise if skilled staff are made redundant

- Risk of loss of confidentiality as key ideas and proprietary knowledge must be shared with the supplier in order for them to make our components

Other potential problems

- Risk to continuity of supply if the supplier has problems - for example, if they are in another country that has political unrest

- Difficulties in agreeing and enforcing contract terms.

Note that at least some of the potential disadvantages can be controlled though the use of effective service level agreements.

Service level agreements

Service level agreements should include the following factors:

- A detailed explanation of exactly what service the supplier is offering to provide.

- The targets / benchmarks to be used and the consequences of failing to meet them.

- Expected response time to technical queries.

- The expected time to recover the operations in the event of a disaster such as a systems crash, terrorist attack, etc.

- The procedure for dealing with complaints.

- The information and reporting procedures to be adopted.

- The procedures for cancelling the contract.

5.2 Core competencies in more detail

Before making a decision to outsource, a company should consider what competencies exist within their business. There are two types of strategic competencies:

- **Threshold competencies** – actions or processes that you must be good at in order to compete or survive. Effectively you must possess these competencies in order to participate in the market concerned.

For example, in clothes retail it may be the case that most firms have outsourced to Chinese manufacturers in order to gain low costs. Outsourcing may be essential just to be a feasible player in the market.

- **Core competencies** – something that you are able to do that drives competitive advantage and is very difficult for your competitors to emulate. You must possess these if you want to compete effectively in the market concerned.

  For our clothing retailer the core competences may relate to design and brand management.

  It may be unwise to outsource aspects of the work in which you have a core competence as this could erode your competitive advantage.

5.3 Transaction cost theory

"Transaction costs" are the expenses incurred by allowing some activity to be undertaken outside the organisation, for example through outsourcing.

Transaction costs arise from the effort that must be put into specifying what is required and subsequently co-ordinating delivery and monitoring quality.

A number of kinds of transaction cost have come to be known by particular names:

- Search and information costs are costs such as those incurred in determining that the required good is available on the market, who has the lowest price, etc.
- Bargaining costs are the costs required to come to an acceptable agreement with the other party to the transaction, drawing up an appropriate contract, etc.
- Policing and enforcement costs are the costs of making sure the other party sticks to the terms of the contract, and taking appropriate action (often through the legal system) if this turns out not to be the case.

If the product or service is a standard design, then specification will be straightforward and the transaction costs will be low. But unfortunately, with sophisticated products and services there needs to be a great deal of negotiation between the organisation and its supplier.

In the context of outsourcing, high transaction costs would suggest an in-house solution whereas low transaction costs would support the argument to outsource.

Test your understanding 3

Could Accountancy Services be outsourced? Are there problems in so doing?

Quinn and Hilmer

According to Quinn and Hilmer (1994), a major strategic factor in sourcing decisions is core competence. There are three basic tests that can be employed to identify the core competences of an organization.

- First, a core competence should provide potential access to a wide variety of markets.

- Secondly, a core competence should also make a significant contribution to the perceived benefits as experienced by the customer of the product.

- Finally, a core competence should be difficult to imitate by competitors.

Based on these ideas, Quinn and Hilmer developed a decision matrix incorporating three factors:

(1) The potential for competitive edge derived from the activity,

(2) Any strategic vulnerability introduced by outsourcing and the need for flexibility, and

(3) The transaction costs incurred due to outsourcing.

The output from the decision matrix identifies the level of control the organization needs to exercise on the particular activity. For example,

- If the potential for competitive edge derived from a given activity and the degree of strategic vulnerability are both "high," then a "high" level of control is in order. Coupled with a "low" need for flexibility required (due to demand variability, say), this suggests full ownership of the activity in question by the organisation.

- On the other hand, when the flexibility requirement is "high," then the authors propose outsourcing of the activity based on a short-term contract.

Naturally, there are other possible actions between these two extremes, such as partial ownership and long-term contracts, depending on the level of control and flexibility needs.

5.3 Transaction cost theory

"Transaction costs" are the expenses incurred by allowing some activity to be undertaken outside the organisation, for example through outsourcing.

Transaction costs arise from the effort that must be put into specifying what is required and subsequently co-ordinating delivery and monitoring quality.

A number of kinds of transaction cost have come to be known by particular names:

- Search and information costs are costs such as those incurred in determining that the required good is available on the market, who has the lowest price, etc.

- Bargaining costs are the costs required to come to an acceptable agreement with the other party to the transaction, drawing up an appropriate contract, etc.

- Policing and enforcement costs are the costs of making sure the other party sticks to the terms of the contract, and taking appropriate action (often through the legal system) if this turns out not to be the case.

If the product or service is a standard design, then specification will be straightforward and the transaction costs will be low. But unfortunately, with sophisticated products and services there needs to be a great deal of negotiation between the organisation and its supplier.

In the context of outsourcing, high transaction costs would suggest an in-house solution whereas low transaction costs would support the argument to outsource.

Transaction cost theory

Transaction cost theory (Wiliamson)

Organisations choose between two methods of obtaining control over resources:

- the ownership of assets (hierarchy solutions – decisions over production, supply, and the purchases of inputs are made by managers and imposed through hierarchies) and

- buying-in the use of assets (the market solution – individuals and firms make independent decisions that are guided and co-ordinated by market prices).

The decision is based on a comparison of the transaction costs of the two approaches.

Transactions have three dimensions that determine the costs associated with them:

- uncertainty – the more uncertain the environment the harder it is to write effective long-term contracts and the more likely vertical integration is;

- the frequency with which the transactions recur; and

- asset specificity – the extent to which the transacting firms invest in assets whose value depends on the business relationships remaining intact. The greater the specificity of the assets involved, the greater the likelihood that a transaction will take place within the firm.

These factors translate into 'make-or-buy' decisions: whether it is better to provide a service from within the organisation, with hierarchical co-ordination, or from outside the organisation, with market co-ordination.

Williamson argues that it is the third dimension, the degree of asset specificity, which is the most important determinant of transaction. The more specific the assets are to a transaction then, all other things being equal, the greater will be the associated transaction costs and the more likely that the transaction will be internalised into a hierarchy. Conversely, when the productive assets are non-specific the process of market contracting is the more efficient because transaction costs will be low.

Asset specificity

An asset is said to be transaction-specific if its value to a given transaction is greater than its value in its best alternative use. The greater the gap between these two values, the greater the degree of specificity of the asset. Williamson has suggested six main types of asset specificity:

- Site specificity – suggests that once sited the assets may be very immobile.

  For example, a car components manufacturer locating a components factory near to a large customer's manufacturing plant.

- Physical asset specificity – when parties make investments in machinery or equipment that are specific to a certain task these will have lower values in alternative uses.

  For example, a supplier of wet cement to building sites may invest in wet cement delivery trucks (a 'hierarchy' solution) since these trucks are so specific to this task that they cannot be sourced via a network.

- Human asset specificity – occurs when workers may have to acquire relationship-specific skills, know-how and information that is more valuable inside a particular transaction than outside it.

  For example, a consultant may have to acquire detailed knowledge of a client's in-house developed systems but this knowledge may not be useful on other clients.

- Brand name capital specificity refers to becoming affiliated with a well-known 'brand name' and thus becoming less free to pursue other opportunities.

  For example, an actor may become 'typecast' in a particular role or show.

- Dedicated asset specificity entails investments in general-purpose plant that are made at the behest of a particular customer.

  For example, the car components manufacturer above invests in dedicated machinery to make bespoke components for just one manufacturer. Should the contract be lost, these components may have to be adapted for sale elsewhere.

- Temporal specificity – arises when the timing of performance is critical, such as with perishable agricultural commodities where a farmer may struggle to find alternative processors at short notice.

5.4 Offshoring

Offshoring is the relocating of corporate activities to a foreign country

The bulk of offshored activities include call centres, IT enabled services (e.g. software development) and business process operations (e.g. human resource management and payroll processing).

Illustration 6

Reuters, the world's biggest news agency, employs dozens of journalists in Bangalore, India. They work overnight so that they can report US financial news live as it happens on the New York Stock Exchange.

These Indian financial journalists can be employed by Reuters for a fraction of the cost of employing a journalist in the New York office.

This system became feasible as a result of IT developments:

- **Obtaining information** – most US companies now put out their press releases on the internet, just as the stock market opens. Therefore, the journalists in Bangalore can access the same basic information as their colleagues in the US.

- **Sending information** – the reduced cost of telecommunications links means that the news written in Bangalore can be sent around the world as quickly as the news written in New York.

Test your understanding 4

Over the last decade, India has emerged as an attractive destination for offshoring. Explain why many UK companies have taken the decision to offshore their services to India.

Benefits of offshoring for the recipient countries

The benefits of offshoring for the recipient countries, such as India, include:

- The creation of much needed jobs
- Improvement in skills
- Advances in infrastructure and technology

Disadvantages of offshoring for the home country

The disadvantages for the home country, for example the UK, include:

- **Differences** - cultural, language and time differences between the home country and the recipient country may make offshoring difficult.

Illustration 7

A team of retired teachers from the UK have set up a company in India where they conduct general knowledge classes for the Indian call centre workers to teach them how to handle calls from UK customers. The call centre agents not only learn about regional accents around the UK, but also the cultural variations and political make-up of the UK.

- **Stability of the offshore countries** – economic and political instability exists in many of the countries providing the services.

- **Cost savings** – the promises of cost savings and improved productivity are not always realised

- **Job losses** – it is argued that when jobs are lost people are freed up to do higher skilled and higher paid work. But in reality, whilst the economy as a whole may evolve in time to a higher level, the individuals who lose their jobs are not necessarily the ones gaining the new jobs.

- **Safety of information** – there is an increased risk that confidential information, e.g. customer's details, may be lost.

- **Exchange rate effects** - make offshoring risky

In addition to the disadvantages for the home country, concerns to do with decent working conditions, e.g. wages, working hours, and other aspects of good practice (such as technology transfer), exist in the recipient country.

> ### Illustration 8
>
> Employees in Indian call centres are exposed to a host of health problems because of the time difference between India and the US. Working from late evening until early dawn can result in digestive problems, hair loss, back pain and stress.
>
> These factors contribute to the high turnover in Indian call centres; approximately 30-40% of employees resign each year.

6 Country and political risk

6.1 Introduction

Globalisation can be a huge opportunity for a company to engage in business with many countries around the world. However, investing abroad may be accompanied by risk. This section will review two such risks:

- Political risk

- Country risk

6.2 Political risk

Political risk is the possibility of an unexpected politically motivated event in a country affecting the outcome of an investment.

- Political risk is greater in countries with developing economies.

- A change in government can sometimes result in dramatic changes for a business.

- Political risk could have a direct effect on a business. For example:

  - The risk of nationalisation of foreign owned assets.

  - The risk of a government decision to raise taxation.

  - The risk of a government decision to restrict payments to foreign shareholders.

  - The risk that politically motivated terrorists cause damage to property and/or employees.

  - The risk of changes in the law, such as employment law.

  - The risk that contracts are cancelled or revised.

  - The risk that lobby groups within a country put pressure on the government to support home based business rather than foreign business.

- Political risk can also be indirect, because of the effect of government policies on the economy, e.g. changes in interest rates and exchange rates.

Illustration 9

In 2001, British Prime Minister Tony Blair had to personally intervene to protect the investment in the Ukraine by the British oil company JKX Oil and Gas plc. The Ukraine's State Property Fund had attempted to expropriate JKX's investment but after intervention by the British Prime Minister the Ukrainian court ruled that the action was illegal.

Managing political risk

Test your understanding 5

Explain what steps may be taken to manage political risk:

(a) before the investment takes place.

(b) during the period of investment.

(c) after the risk has been realised.

6.3 Country risk

Country risk is the risk arising from operating or investing in a particular country, with risks relating to matters such as political interference, political stability, the social and economic infrastructure, the culture of the country, and its attitude to foreign business.

Country risk is a much more general term than political risk and relates to all of the risks of operating or investing in a particular country.

Illustration 10

Oil company BP has explained on its website how it approaches the task of identifying and assessing country risk.

BP carries out a country risk assessment whenever it faces a strategic decision about whether to invest in a new country. Country risk assessments are also made when the political or social environment changes, or if a significant change in the size of investment is under consideration.

'This process culminates in an intensive discussion with active participation from outside experts and BP personnel with experience of the region and relevant BP operations. Over two days many strands of thinking and research are brought together to form a view of the country in question, which then informs all major decisions, including investment decisions, relating to BP's involvement in the country. The results of these assessments remain, by their nature, confidential to the business.'

Country risk analysis

```
          Country risk can be analysed
                 in three ways
```

Political analysis
Considers:
- stability of govern-ment
- corruption by officials
- different religious beliefs
- ethinic tensions

Financial analysis
- Can country meet its debt obligations?
- Consider factors such as exchange rate stability, past loan defaults

Economic analysis
- Growth in GDP (gross domestic product)
- Per capita GDP
- Inflation rates

When all of these risks are taken together, an overall assessment of country risk can be made.

Risk mapping

When an initial review is carried out to identify and assess risks, the assessment of both probabilities and impact might be based on judgement and experience rather than on a detailed statistical and numerical analysis.

- In an initial analysis, it might be sufficient to categorise the probability of an adverse outcome as 'high', 'medium' or 'low', or even more simply as 'high' or 'low'.

- Similarly, it might be sufficient for the purpose of an initial analysis to assess the consequences or impact of an adverse outcome as 'severe' or 'not severe'.

Each risk can then be plotted on a risk map. A risk map is simply a 2 × 2 table or chart, showing the probabilities for each risk and their potential impact.

		Impact/ consequences	
		Low	High
Probability/ likelihood	**High**		
	Low		

7 Cross-cultural management

7.1 Introduction

 Culture is the 'sum total of the beliefs, knowledge, attitudes, norms and customs that prevail in an organisation or country'.

Managers are increasingly exposed to working with, or within, many different business cultures. This involves working in other countries, working in organisations that have operations in other cultural environments, or working with colleagues from a wide range of cultures.

David Foster argues that cross-cultural management is a shorthand term that summarises a number of different elements:

- First, it describes the range of organisational behaviour which exists within both countries and cultures.

- Second, it compares and contrasts organisational behaviour across countries and cultures.

- Third, it seeks to understand to understand and improve the interaction of co-workers, clients, suppliers and partners from different countries and cultures."

Cross-cultural education and training are thus needed to achieve the following purposes:

- To encourage people to study and evaluate the components of their own culture so that they become more aware of their own hidden cultural assumptions which interfere with effective intercultural action.

- To expand people's repertoire of culturally appropriate behaviours so that they can operate more effectively in cross-cultural encounters in the workplace.

- To evaluate the impact of cultural factors on job performance. It can be argued that cultural traits and differences are so ingrained that it is hard for individuals even to understand they are there or that they have an influence on behaviour. These traits influence individual action, how relationships are formed and maintained, how products are perceived and located in markets and the success of communication.

HSBC brands itself as 'the World's local bank'. The company understands that there are cultural differences between the countries in which they operate and celebrate that people have different points of view. They believe that these points of view are supported by their business values and promote these values in their advertising. This understanding of cultural differences has helped this 'local bank' to become one of the world's largest and most successful banks.

7.2 The Hofstede model

With his work with IBM Hofstede found that national culture can be a greater influence on behaviour and performance than corporate culture. This means that even firms with a very strong corporate culture need to understand the different national cultures in which they operate. The challenge for managers is thus knowing where and how national cultures vary.

Hofstede has identified five dimensions in which national culture seems to vary:

Power distance index – how much society accepts the unequal distribution of power, for instance the extent to which supervisors see themselves as being above their subordinates. In some cultures, particularly South American ones, disparities of power were tolerated more than in North European cultures.

Individualism versus collectivism – how much people prefer a tight-knit social framework based on 'loyalty' to an involvement based on individual cost and benefit. Some cultures are more cohesive than others, with Anglo Saxon cultures more individualistic than the collectivist cultures of South America.

Masculinity versus femininity – used as shorthand to indicate the degree to which 'masculine' values predominate: e.g. assertive, domineering, uncaring and competitive, as opposed to 'feminine' values such as sensitivity and concern for others. A masculine culture is one where gender roles are distinct, with the male focus on work, power and success. Such cultures include Japan, and Italy. Feminine cultures, such as Finland, have smaller differences in gender roles and success is likely to be regarded as a social, rather than personal activity.

Uncertainty avoidance index – how much society dislikes ambiguity and risk, and the extent to which people feel threatened by unusual situations, paralleled by how far persons and ideas deviate from the accepted norm. Some cultures, such as France and Japan, dislike uncertainty and use planning and bureaucracy to reduce it. Other cultures, such as Jamaica and Denmark, tend to be less uncomfortable with uncertainty and ambiguity. High uncertainty avoidance traits means risk taking is discouraged.

Long term orientation (based on Confucian dynamism) – values associated with Long Term Orientation (e.g. China) are thrift and perseverance; values associated with Short Term Orientation (e.g. Germany) are respect for tradition, fulfilling social obligations and protecting one's 'face'.

Hofstede's five dimensions of culture

Individualistic	Individualism/Collectivism	**Collectivist**
Australia		Colombia
United States		Pakistan
United Kingdom		Venezuela

Lower power distance	Power distance	**High power distance**
Austria		Mexico
Denmark		India
Israel		Philippines

Low uncertainty avoidance	Uncertainty avoidance	**High uncertainty avoidance**
Singapore		Japan
Hong Kong		Portugal
Denmark		Greece

Masculine	Masculinity/Femininity	**Feminine**
Japan		Sweden
Austria		Denmark
Venezuela		Norway

High	Long term orientation	**Low**
China		Russia
Japan		Canada
Netherlands		Indonesia

It is important to see that Hofstede was attempting to model aspects of culture that might influence business behaviour, rather than produce national stereotypes

Culture in the BRIC economies

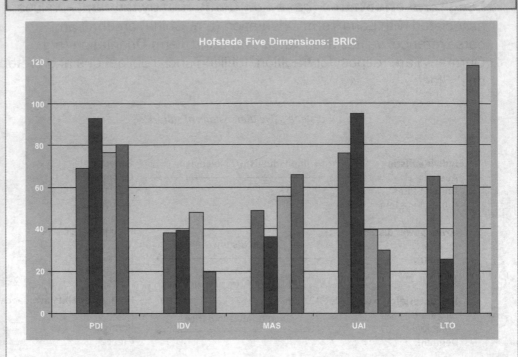

Key:

PDI = power distance

IDV = individualism

MAS = masculinity

UAI = uncertainty avoidance

LTO = long term orientation

For each dimension the chart shows the results in the order of Brazil: Russia: India: China.

Test your understanding 6

In the Hofstede model, a national culture which supports single status pay arrangements, informal styles of address in the workplace and self-managed team working would be classified as:

A individualist.

B masculine.

C low power distance.

D high uncertainty avoidance.

Test your understanding 7

Looking at the **Hofstede** traits, choose the classification that most closely fits Great Britain.

Individualistic or collective?

Large power distance or small?

Masculine or feminine roles?

The implications of Hofstede's categories for business

Dimension	Implication
High Power Distance	• Managers make autocratic decisions. • Structures tend to be tall (many levels of managers and supervisors). • Status differences between managers and subordinates.
High Individualism	• Self reliance. • Autonomy. • Individual achievement (not achievement of group) important.
High Masculinity	• Status through high earnings. • Advancement value. • Challenges sought.
High Uncertainty Avoidance	• Formalised organisational structures. • Depend heavily on rules and regulations. • Do not like anything that deviates from accepted norms.
High Long Term Orientation	• Strong work ethic; emphasis on perseverance. • High value placed on education and training. • Respect for tradition.

Hofstede also looked at cultural differences in work related attitudes. These include:

Leadership – in some countries, such as those in Latin America, leaders are expected to take a strong personal interest in employees and appear at private social functions, such as weddings, whereas in other countries such as Germany such social contact is discouraged. In other countries, notably in Asia and Africa, public criticism is intolerable as the loss of self-respect brings dishonour to the employee and his family.

Motivation – the incentives for effective performance must match the culture. It is pointless offering individual bonuses to workers where there are strong group and company loyalties, as in Japan, or where loyalty to an individual's superior is paramount as in Turkey and the Near East.

Structure – research showed that French firms are bureaucratic with orders and procedures set from above whereas German work organisation relies more on the professional expertise, which derives from the trained knowledge and skill of the more junior employees.

8 International economic developments

8.1 Macroeconomic policy objectives

Typically, governments will have four macroeconomic policy objectives:

- Economic growth – how can productive capacity be increased?
- Inflation – how can we ensure that general price levels do not increase?
- Unemployment – how can we ensure that everyone who wants a job has one?
- Balance of payments – how should we manage our relationship and trade with other countries?

These are discussed in more detail below.

More detail on policy objectives

Stagnation and economic growth

Most governments want economic growth. Growth should result in the following:

- more goods being demanded and produced
- people earn more and can afford more goods

- more people should have jobs. .

On the face of it, therefore, growth should result in an improved standard of living in a country and higher profitability for businesses.

However, growth is not without its problems.

- Is economic growth fast enough to keep up with population growth?
- Growth rates have to exceed inflation rates for benefits to arise (i.e. "real" growth has to occur).
- Growth may be in 'demerit' goods, such as illegal drugs.
- Growth may be at the expense of the environment or through exploitation of the poor.
- The gap between rich and poor may grow, as the benefits from growth are not evenly distributed.
- Rapid growth means rising incomes and this often 'sucks in' imports, worsening the balance of trade, rather than benefiting domestic producers.

Growth can be measured by looking at an the increase in two figures GDP and GNP:

- Gross Domestic Product (GDP) = the total value of income/ production from economic activity within a country.
- Gross National Product (GNP) = GDP + overseas income – income earned in the country by overseas residents.

Inflation

Most governments want stable prices and low inflation. The main reasons given include the following:

- Inflation causes uncertainty and stifles business investment.
- Not all incomes rise in line with inflation – the poor and those on fixed incomes suffer the most.
- In extreme cases of inflation, the function of money may break down, resulting in civil unrest.
- Inflation distorts the working of the price mechanism and is thus a market imperfection.

Note that high inflation can affect savings in different ways:

- inflation erodes the future purchasing power of funds so people may decide to save less but spend more now

- an alternative argument is that higher prices reduce individuals' real wealth and so they spend less. This could result in higher savings (the "real balance" effect).

Unemployment

Even in a healthy economy some unemployment will arise as people change jobs. However, mass unemployment is a problem due to the following:

- The government has to pay out benefits to the unemployed at a time when its tax receipts are low. This can result in the government having to raise taxes, borrow money and cut back on services.

- Unemployment has been linked to a rise in crime, poor health and a breakdown in family relationships.

- Unemployment is a waste of human resources and can restrict economic growth.

High unemployment could give firms higher bargaining power allowing them to pay lower wages to prospective employees.

Balance of payments

In the long-term government seeks to establish a broad balance between the value of imports into, and exports from, the country.

To run a persistent surplus or deficit can have negative macroeconomic effects.

- A long-term trade deficit has to be financed. The financing costs act as a major drain on the productive capacity of the economy.

- A long-term trade surplus can cause significant inflationary pressures, leading ultimately to a loss in international confidence in the economy and a lack of international competitiveness

The government will aim to balance a number of economic factors through the use of fiscal or monetary policies. The decisions made by a country's government will impact any company that trades with or within that country, e.g. companies will need to consider economic growth, inflation, unemployment and exchange rates.

8.2 Fiscal policy

Involves changes in:

- **Taxation** – the government raises revenue from individuals and businesses via taxes.

- **Government spending** – the way in which the government spends the money will impact the strength of the economy.

Taxation policy

Governments raise revenue from individuals and businesses via a variety of taxes. The way they spend that money can have a significant effect of the strength of the economy.

There are two ways we can look at taxation; we can consider taxation to be direct (in which case it deducted from earnings, either individual or corporate), or indirect, in which case it is levied on expenditure.

Direct tax

Direct tax is normally a percentage deducted from either earnings or profits. Invariably for businesses it is based on profits. Not all direct tax is levied on earned income and an individual may pay income tax on their salary but also a tax on dividends that they hold in a company unrelated to their work. This would be described as a tax on unearned income. Sometimes a special tax on individuals will be designated for a particular purpose, for instance a tax to provide for old age pensions.

Indirect taxes

Indirect taxes, sometimes called taxes on consumption, are levied on expenditure. This means that when we buy something the cost will have been inflated by a percentage which when the vendor receives it must be paid to the government. One of the advantages of this type of tax for the government is that they have to collect tax from fewer sources – there are fewer vendors in most economies than there are earners.

Types of indirect tax include;

- A **value added tax** – which can be levied on all goods, although a government may decide to apply different rates to different products to encourage (or discourage) patterns of consumption. For instance there is unlikely to be any VAT on this book – the government may want to encourage study – but if you have some chocolate whilst you are reading it that will carry VAT since it is a luxury.

- **Hydrocarbon tax** – a tax on the fuel that people use in their vehicles. Again there is a motivation for government over and above the mere raising of revenue; they may wish to discourage the use of cars and so tax fuel heavily. We shall discuss that again when we discuss the environment.

- **Tobacco tax** – aside from the revenue raised the higher the tax the more people are discouraged from smoking which will be good for the nation's health and, possibly, reduce the demands on the health provision in the country.

- **Import duties** – again governments will use this form of taxation to encourage or discourage particular patterns of consumption as we discussed earlier in the chapter.

For a government there are two further decisions to be made other than those implied in the decisions described above.

(1) Firstly they will need to decide whether the majority of the tax revenue should come from individuals or from companies.

Obviously businesses will consider the environment more favourable if there is a low level of corporate tax. If it isn't they may decide to relocate to a country with a more favourable tax regime.

Tax havens such as the Bahamas or Bermuda will have exceptionally low, or even no, income tax to attract foreign companies to set up branches there.

Governments may decide to have a threshold of income below which taxation is not paid by individuals, effectively helping the low waged to live. In the case of companies they may have a system of tax credits for particular industries to encourage investment in those areas.

The population would prefer the income tax levels to be low since they would prefer to keep the majority of their earnings to use as they see fit. Too high a level of taxation will not encourage people to work harder to raise their income levels.

(2) Secondly they will need to decide whether how much they wish to raise by taxing earnings compared to the amount the wish to raise via indirect taxation.

8.3 Monetary policy

Monetary policy refers to the management of money supply within the economy.

In particular, monetary policy may be concerned with:

- The **volume** of money in circulation – the stock of money in the economy (the 'money supply') is believed to have important effects on the volume of expenditure in the economy. This in turn may influence the level of output in the economy or the level of prices.

- The **price** of money – the price of money is the rate of interest. If governments wish to influence the amount of money held in the economy or the demand for credit, they may attempt to influence the level of interest rate. A rise in interest rates should result in:
  - a fall in spending
  - a fall in investment
  - a fall in asset values
  - foreign funds attracted to the country
  - a rise in exchange rates.

Test your understanding 8

Explain how changes in monetary policy can influence a business.

8.4 Balance of payments

The balance of payments records all of the transactions that have taken place between residents of a country and overseas residents during the period of a year. Just like any bookkeeping system, each transaction has a debit and a credit entry and overall the system should balance.

The balance of payments is split into three parts:

- current account (goods and services),
- capital account (e.g. buildings) and
- financial account (e.g. cash flows)

Exporting goods for cash would give rise to a debit in the financial account and a credit in the current account.(This is similar to sales being a credit in the income statement).

When discussing debits and credits we conventionally look at the current account, hence exports are a credit entry and imports a debit.

Balance of payments deficits

If a country is said to have a deficit on its balance of payments this means that there is a net outflow of funds from the country, for example through importing more than it exports. Clearly, this outflow cannot continue as a country cannot keep spending more than it earns in foreign currency – eventually it will run out of reserves and other countries will cease to be willing to loan it money.

Government can seek to reduce a balance of payments deficit in a number of ways. Traditionally the strategies that can be used are divided into:

- expenditure-reducing strategies
- expenditure-switching strategies.

Expenditure-reducing strategies

- This involves the government deliberately shrinking the domestic economy. By reducing overall demand in the domestic economy a government will be able to reduce demand for imports.

- Reducing demand in the home economy should also reduce inflationary pressures, reducing export prices and making them more competitive.

- Conversely, suppressing demand in the home economy could lead to an increase in unemployment.

- Examples of such strategies include contractionary monetary policy (see above) and contractionary fiscal policy.

Increasing interest rates

- Increasing interest rates will reduce demand for imports as domestic consumers and firms will have less money to spend.

- However, it will also discourage investment in the home economy as the cost of borrowing increases.

- It can cause a country's currency to strengthen (appreciate) due to demand for sterling from overseas investors. This can actually worsen the deficit as it increases the price of UK exports, whilst making imports cheaper.

Expenditure-switching strategies

> **Government takes steps to increase expenditure on domestically – produced rather than imported goods**

> **Restrict imports e.g.**
> - use tariffs or quotas
> - exchange controls limit the supply of sterling available to buy foreign currency to pay for imports

> **Increase exports e.g.**
> - subsidies provided to exporters will reduce prices

In this case the government seeks to change expenditure patterns of consumers by encouraging expenditure on domestically-produced rather than imported goods.

Import controls

Government could seek to restrict imports. This could be achieved by:

- direct imposition of tariffs or quotas

- or through exchange controls limiting the supply of sterling available to buy overseas currencies to pay for imports.

The imposition of trade barriers is highly controversial, however, and is likely to breach WTO regulations.

Boost exports

A government could seek to boost exports in a number of ways:

- Provide subsidies to exporters to allow them to reduce export prices.
- Extend export credit guarantees to more countries, reducing the risk for exporters of non-payment.

Lower the exchange rate

- In the case of a fixed exchange rate this is referred to as a devaluation. Where exchange rates are floating it is referred to as a depreciation. This strategy has the effect of making imports more expensive and exports cheaper (in their own currency) to an overseas buyer.
- This policy has a number of problems associated with it often making it a last choice of government. These problems include:
  - It may not work if it results in competitive depreciations or devaluations.
  - It may not work as the rise in import prices triggers domestic inflation.

Test your understanding 9

Which of the following policies for correcting a balance of payments deficit is an expenditure reducing policy?

A   Cutting the level of public expenditure.

B   Devaluation of the currency.

C   The imposition of a tariff on imports.

D   The use of import quotas.

Test your understanding 10

Which of the following might cause a country's exports to decrease?

A   A fall in the exchange rate for that country's currency.

B   A reduction in other countries' tariff barriers.

C   A decrease in the marginal propensity to import in other countries.

D   A rise in that country's imports.

9 Chapter summary

Outsourcing and offshoring
- Pros and cons of outsourcing
- What is offshoring?
- Pros and cons of offshoring

Liberalisation and economic nationalism
- Definition
- Pros and cons of free trade

International economic developments
- The balance of trade
- Reducing trade deficits
- Monetary policy

Introduction to the global business environment
Global business environment impacted by:
- social
- political and
- economic factors

Cross-cultural management
- What is culture?
- Hofstede's five dimensions

Emerging market multinationals
- Globalisation and developing countries
- What is a multi-national?
- The BRIC economies

Country and political risk
- Definitions
- Management of risk

10 Practice questions

Question 1

Risk relating to matters such as the political stability of a country, the social and economic infrastructure and the culture of the country is known as:

A   country risk.

B   financial risk.

C   accounting risk.

D   political risk.

(2 marks)

Question 2

In a free market economy, decisions and choices about resource allocation are determined by:

A   individuals.

B   the government.

C   a combination of individuals and the government.

D   the money markets.

(2 marks)

Question 3

Which of the following would NOT be a feature of a mixed economy?

A   private ownership of land

B   government control of interest rates

C   public ownership of all resources

D   the influence by the government on the private sector

(2 marks)

Question 4

The imposition of which one of the following would NOT act as a barrier to international trade?

A   quotas

B   tariffs

C   value added tax

D   embargoes

(2 marks)

Question 5

A country that has a culture where there are wide status differences between subordinates and managers would be said to have:

A   low masculinity.

B   high individualism.

C   high long term orientation.

D   high power distance.

(2 marks)

Question 6

Which of the following would NOT correct a Balance of Payments deficit?

A   re-valuing the currency

B   raising domestic interest rates

C   deflating the economy

D   imposing import controls

(2 marks)

Question 7

Explain FOUR reasons why a UK insurance company may be concerned about offshoring its customer call centre to India.

(4 marks)

Question 8

Briefly explain the similarities and differences between the economic systems of the UK and the US.

(4 marks)

Question 9

X Company is a manufacturer of non-alcoholic soft drinks and has a well-established position and brand recognition in country Z. The potential for future growth in country Z is, however, limited, with the market reaching saturation. One option for expansion is to move into new markets in other countries offering its existing product range.

The business development team is evaluating this option and is currently working on proposals to sell the company's range of drinks in country Y. One possible strategy to achieve market entry that the team is investigating is through a joint venture with a company that is already established in country Y, and is in the drinks distribution business.

The Board of X Company has given the business development team the task of undertaking a feasibility study to explore the viability of the proposed strategy. The feasibility study needs to assess the cultural compatibility of the ways of doing business in country Y compared to how X Company currently operates in country Z.

Required:

Explain how Hofstede's research could be used to assess the compatibility of X Company's strategy with the culture of country Y.

(15 marks)

Question 10

POOL Publishing is a publisher of books with a listing on the stock exchange of the country in which it is based. POOL has a large number of customers. Almost five years ago, it outsourced its accounting to an external service provider, ITW. The accounting system is fully computerised, and is a bespoke system developed several years ago for POOL, and updated occasionally since that time.

The service from ITW has operated fairly well until recently, but ITW now appears to have difficulty in dealing with the rapidly-growing accounting requirements of POOL, as its business has expanded.

A decision has therefore been taken that the contract with ITW will not be renewed when it expires in six months' time. The accounting work will be given to a different outsourcing firm.

As management accountant and internal auditor for POOL, you have been asked to plan the changeover from ITW to the new outsourcing firm. In addition, in accordance with the contractual agreement with ITW, you will be required to carry out an audit of the accounts system before the changeover occurs.

Required:

Describe the potential risks that need to be considered in the changeover from ITW to the new outsourcing firm, and recommend measures to limit those risks.

(13 marks)

Test your understanding answers

Test your understanding 1

- **Impact on the consumer** – the restriction of free trade will tend to push up prices and restrict the choice of goods available, i.e. the benefits of free trade are lost.

- **Second best solution** – for example, tariffs may be used to protect old, inefficient industries from competition in order to prevent unemployment in this area. However, as a result of this inefficiency, consumers will face higher prices. A better solution would be to subsidise training and investment in new, efficient industries. This should avoid unemployment and the consumer won't suffer.

- **Retaliation** – if one country imposes restrictions on imports, then other countries will tend to retaliate and do the same to them. As a result, the benefits of free trade are lost.

Test your understanding 2

- Technological innovation

- Advances in transportation

- Convergence of lifestyles and tastes

- Increasing travel creating global networks

- Establishment of world brands

- Government drivers such as a reduction in trade barriers

- Increases in ownership of organisations by foreign acquirers

- Globalisation of financial markets

Test your understanding 3

Accountancy services are often outsourced in smaller companies, but it could be argued that they are critical to the performance of the organisation and may well drive the future of the company. Also there should be some managerial control in this area.

Test your understanding 4

Cost savings - one of the biggest advantages is cost savings. Companies have been able to reduce the cost of services by 30-40% by offshoring to India. These cost savings are due to:

- Lower wages – Indian workers are paid much lower wages than those in the UK.

- Lower capital expenditure – infrastructure costs are lower in India.

- Improved labour management – labour is only employed as and when it is needed for a project, rather than on a permanent basis, as in the UK.

Large talent pool - India has a large pool of talented and motivated professionals. There are 2.1 million graduates each year and this number is set to grow. As a result, UK companies are able to choose between a number of suitable candidates.

Technology – advances in technology and the falling price of technology has enabled UK companies to carry out activities overseas that would have previously been done in the UK.

Common language – India has the largest English speaking population in the world. This will ease communication between the UK and India.

Fast turnaround time – the time taken to carry out a task can be reduced by between 30-50% when offshoring to India. This is partly due to the efficiency of the Indian professionals but is also due to the zonal time differences, e.g. many IT projects have an onsite and offsite team. The offsite team can work on the project during the day in India. When the Indian team leaves work for the evening the onsite team can take over the project in the UK.

Test your understanding 5

(a) **Before the investment takes place**

- The company should take steps to understand the level and types of political risk.
- A decision to invest should only be taken if the potential economic return is sufficient to compensate for the political risk.
- The company should take out appropriate insurance prior to investment.

(b) **During the period of investment**

- Establish business relations – partnerships with local businesses and suppliers can help the company to learn local business customs and their advice should help to reduce the risks from nationalism and anti-foreign sentiment in the country.
- Set up a local operation – this should be headed by a local manager and should help to reduce risks from nationalist attitudes.
- Borrow in the local currency – the profit from the business can be used to repay loans. This reduces risks from currency conversion or from restrictions on payments out of a country.
- Develop government contacts – winning the support of government should help to reduce the risk of unhelpful political measures such as the refusal of planning permission.
- Split operations between countries – this will reduce the incentive for the government to nationalise the business.
- Set up a joint venture – risk is shared with another partner.

(c) **After the risk has been realised**

- Litigation or retaliation.
- Implementation of a contingency plan.
- Exit from market.
- Insurance claim.

Test your understanding 6

C

Test your understanding 7

Although the points can be debated, and the culture is changing, Great Britain probably:

Individualistic

Small power distance

Masculine roles

Test your understanding 8

Changes in monetary policy will influence a business in a number of ways:

- **The availability of finance**: Credit restrictions will reduce the availability of loans. This can make it difficult for small or medium-sized new businesses to raise finance. The threat of such restrictions in the future will influence financial decisions by companies, making them more likely to seek long-term finance for projects.

- **The cost of finance**: Any restrictions on the stock of money will raise the cost of borrowing, making fewer investment projects worthwhile and discouraging expansion by companies. Also, any increase in the level of interest rates will increase shareholders' required rate of return. Thus, organisations are less likely to borrow money and will probably contract rather than expand operations.

- **The level of consumer demand**: Periods of credit control and high interest rates reduce consumer demand. Individuals find it more difficult and more expensive to borrow to fund consumption, while saving becomes more attractive. This is another reason for organisations to have to contract operations.

- **The level of inflation**: Monetary policy is often used to control inflation. Rising price levels and uncertainty as to future rates of inflation make financial decisions more difficult and more important.

- **The level of exchange rates**: Monetary policy which increases the level of domestic interest rates is likely to increase exchange rates as capital is attracted into the country. Many companies now deal with overseas suppliers and customers and can therefore not afford to ignore the risk associated with exchange rate movements.

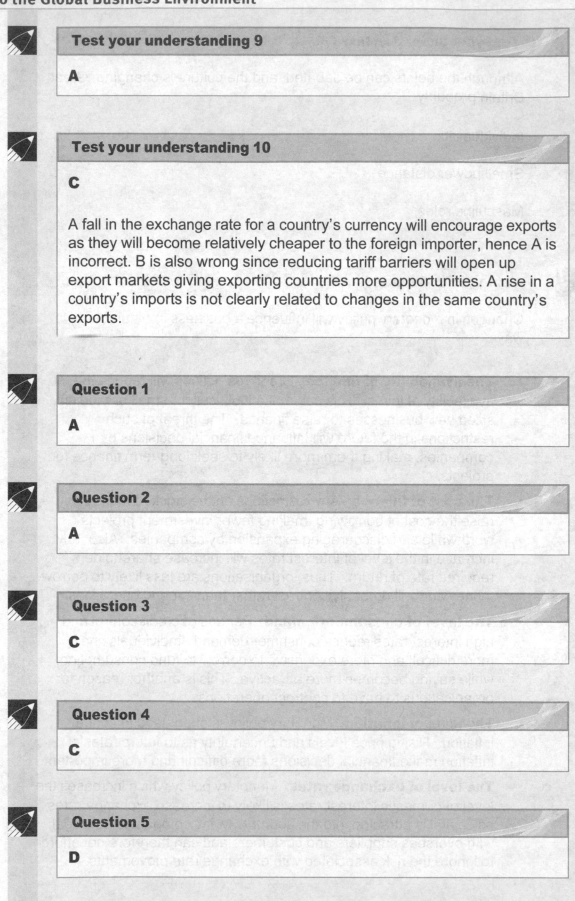

Test your understanding 9

A

Test your understanding 10

C

A fall in the exchange rate for a country's currency will encourage exports as they will become relatively cheaper to the foreign importer, hence A is incorrect. B is also wrong since reducing tariff barriers will open up export markets giving exporting countries more opportunities. A rise in a country's imports is not clearly related to changes in the same country's exports.

Question 1

A

Question 2

A

Question 3

C

Question 4

C

Question 5

D

Question 6

A

Question 7

Job losses – jobs may have to be cut in the UK. This will have associated redundancy costs and may impact employee morale.

Cultural differences – the differences in culture between the UK and India may make offshoring difficult.

Customer reaction – customers may value speaking to someone in a UK call centre and may perceive that the staff in the Indian call centre do not understand their needs or provide a poorer quality service.

Safety of information – there may be concerns that confidential customer information could be lost.

Question 8

The US and the UK both have a mixed economic system. This means that resource allocation is undertaken partly by the government and partly by the private sector. The government will also intervene to influence the behaviour of the private sector.

Although both countries are said to have a mixed economic system, the UK and the US come relatively close to the definition of a free enterprise since there is a limited degree of government intervention.

In the US, the government plays a much smaller role in the provision of services, such as healthcare, than in the UK.

Question 9

There are two areas in which the compatibility of X's culture with that of country Y could be important:

- In assessing the potential for conflict between X and its proposed joint venture partner – it is likely that the partner has many of the cultural norms of county Y. Cultural differences between X and Y could influence the suitability of prospective partners and the management style to be adopted should the joint venture proceed.

- In assessing potential demand for X's products – for example, the way prospective customers view X could influence their buying decisions.

Hofstede has identified five dimensions in which national culture seems to vary:

Power Distance

Power Distance (PD) looks at how much society accepts the unequal distribution of power, for instance the extent to which supervisors see themselves as being above their subordinates. In some cultures, particularly South American ones, disparities of power were tolerated more than in North European cultures.

- High PD means people accept inequality in power.
- Low PD means people expect equality in power.

In countries with high PD, X would have to ensure that managers make autocratic decisions.

Uncertainty Avoidance

Uncertainty avoidance (UA) is the degree to which people feel uncomfortable with risk, uncertainty and unusual situations.

- High UA means people dislike uncertainty and ambiguity.
- Low UA means people have high tolerance for the unstructured and unpredictable.

In countries with high UA, X would have to institute formalised organisational structures, which depend heavily on rules and regulations.

Individualism and Collectivism

Individualism and collectivism examines how much people prefer a tight-knit social framework based on 'loyalty' to an involvement based on individual cost and benefit. Some cultures are more cohesive than others, with Anglo Saxon cultures more individualistic than the collectivist cultures of South America.

- Individualism – individuals are expected to take care of themselves.

- Collectivism – individuals look after one another and organisations protect their members' interests.

If Y has high individualism, then X would have to encourage managers to demonstrate:

- self reliance

- autonomy

- individual achievement not the achievement of the group or community.

Masculinity/Femininity

Masculinity versus femininity looks at the degree to which 'masculine' values predominate: e.g. assertive, domineering, uncaring and competitive, as opposed to 'feminine' values such as sensitivity and concern for others. A masculine culture is one where distinctive roles between genders are large, with the male focus on work, power and success. Such cultures include Japan and Italy. Feminine cultures, such as Finland, have smaller differences in gender roles and success is likely to be regarded as a social, rather than personal activity

- Masculine – value achievement, heroism, assertiveness and material success important.

- Feminine – value relationships, caring for the weak and quality of life.

If Y is a country with high masculinity, then X will seek to motivate staff by:

- recognising that status is often gained through high earnings

- offering the possibility of advancement

- ensuring staff are given challenges.

Long term orientation

This examines how much society values long term standing rather than short term values and traditions.

If Y has a high long term orientation, then X would have to encourage:

* a strong work ethic with a strong emphasis on perseverance.
* education and training.

Should X find that there are significant differences between its own culture and that of Y, then this could seriously undermine the chances of success of the proposed venture.

Question 10

A significant risk in switching from one service provider for accounting services to another is the risk of loss or corruption to data during the change. ITW will be required to supply up-to-date and accurate files at the end of its contract, either to POOL or to the new service provider. During this handover process, records might be lost from files, or entire files might be corrupted. For example, ITW might hand over out-of-date files, missing some recent transactions. POOL needs to be able to check that all the information has been properly transferred.

One way of dealing with this problem might be to arrange for a short period during which both ITW and the new service provider are maintaining accounting records for POOL. An internal (or external) audit can then carry out a check on the files in the two systems, to ensure that they appear identical (e.g. with the same total number of records and same control totals).

There might be technological or software difficulties if the accounts are moved from ITW's computer system to the system of another provider, and there might be difficulties in getting the system to operate properly on the system of the new service provider. The solution to this problem is also to have a period of time during which the two systems are running in parallel, so that any technical problems can be identified and resolved.

There is also a risk of unauthorised retention of files. An individual within the ITW organisation might retain copies of the accounts files of POOL. This would create a risk of file data about customers getting into the possession of another organisation. Alternatively, the individual retaining the file copies might subsequently use the information they contain for fraudulent purposes. POOL needs to check, if possible, that there are no duplicate copies of files that have been retained within ITW without authorisation.

This risk is difficult to deal with. However, ITW should be asked to demonstrate that after the handover of the files, copies have not been retained in ITW's computer system. If ITW is an ethical organisation, it should be willing to comply with this request, and demonstrate that it no longer holds files for POOL.

There could be operational difficulties in changing from ITW to a new service provider, particularly if ITW is unwilling to be helpful. ITW might have no incentive to give assistance to another company that has taken their contract with POOL. Inevitably, operational problems will arise, and the new service provider might need to ask questions. Unless ITW is willing to provide assistance, operating difficulties might arise.

The efficiency and success of the change to the new service provider depends on the goodwill of ITW for a number of reasons, and POOL might wish to consider offering a bonus payment to ITW after the change has taken place, provided this has happened in a satisfactory way, and with the full co-operation and assistance of ITW's staff.

It has been assumed that the same system operated on behalf of POOL by ITW will be used by the new service provider. This is not necessarily the case, and it might be the intention of POOL to switch its accounting system to a different accounting system that is better able to handle the growing volume of transactions and data. If a new system is required, all the risks associated with new system design, development and implementation will arise.

Governance and Regulation in the Global Business Environment

Chapter learning objectives

Lead	Component
A2. Analyse the relationship between the internal governance of a firm and external sources of governance and regulation.	(a) Explain the principles and purpose of social corporate responsibility and the principles of good corporate governance in an international context.
	(b) Analyse relationships between business, society and government in national and regional contexts.
	(d) Discuss the nature of regulation and its impact on the firm.

1 Governance and Social Responsibility

1.1 Stakeholders

A stakeholder is a group or individual, who has an interest in what the organisation does, or an expectation of the organisation. It is important that an organisation understands the needs of the different stakeholders.

An important part of the strategic manager's job is to understand the contribution that relationships with stakeholders can make to the well-being of an organisation. Assessing the expectations of stakeholders enables an organisation to gauge whether its objectives will provide the means of satisfying the demands of the various stakeholders.

Stakeholders can be broadly categorised into three categories; internal, connected and external.

Internal stakeholders

Internal stakeholders are intimately connected to the organisation, and their objectives are likely to have a strong influence on how it is run. Internal stakeholders include:

Stakeholder	Need/ expectation
employees	pay, working conditions and job security
managers/ directors	status, pay, bonus, job security

Connected stakeholders

Connected stakeholders have a direct link with the organisation but function outside of it. They include:

Stakeholder	Need/ expectation
shareholders	dividends and capital growth and the continuation of the business
customers	value-for-money products and services
suppliers	paid promptly
finance providers	repayment of finance

External stakeholders

This group will have quite diverse objectives and have varying ability to ensure that the organisation meets their objectives. They include:

Stakeholder	Need/ expectation
community at large	will not want their lives to be negatively impacted by business decisions
environmental pressure groups	the organisation does not harm the external environment
government	provision of taxes and jobs and compliance with legislation
trade unions	to take an active part in the decision-making process

Further example of stakeholder management

R is a high-class hotel situated in a thriving city. It is part of a worldwide hotel group owned by a large number of shareholders. Individuals hold the majority of shares, each holding a small number, and financial institutions hold the rest. The hotel provides full amenities, including a heated swimming pool, as well as the normal facilities of bars, restaurants and good quality accommodation. There are many other hotels in the city, all of which compete with R. The city in which R is situated is old and attracts many foreign visitors, especially in the summer season.

The main stakeholders with whom relationships need to be established and maintained by management and the importance of maintaining these relationships is as follows:

Internal stakeholders

The employees and the managers of the hotel are the main link with the guests and the service they provide is vital to the quality of the hotel as guests' experience at the hotel will be determined by their attitude and approach.

Managers should ensure that employees deliver the highest level of service and are well trained and committed.

Connected stakeholders

The shareholders of the hotel will be concerned with a steady flow of income, possible capital growth and continuation of the business. Relationships should be developed and maintained with the shareholders, especially those operating on behalf of institutions. Management must try to achieve improvements in their returns by ensuring that customers are satisfied and are willing to return.

Each guest will seek good service and satisfaction. Different types of guest, e.g. business versus tourist, will have different needs and managers should regularly analyse the customer database to ensure that these needs are met.

Suppliers should be selected very carefully to ensure that services and goods provided (e.g. food and laundry) continue to add to the quality of the hotel and to customer satisfaction. They will be concerned with being paid promptly for goods, and maintaining a good relationship with suppliers will ensure their continued support of the hotel.

External stakeholders

The management of the hotel must maintain close relationships with the authorities to ensure they comply with legislation. Failure to do so, could result in the hotel being closed down.

Test your understanding 2

Would competitors be classed as external or connected stakeholders and what are their needs/ expectations?

Stakeholder conflict

The needs/ expectations of the different stakeholder groups may conflict. Some of the typical conflicts are shown below:

Stakeholders	Conflict
Employees versus managers	Jobs/ wages versus bonus
Customers versus shareholders	Product quality/ service levels versus profits/ dividends
General public versus shareholders	Effect on the environment versus profit/ dividends
Managers versus shareholders	Independence versus growth by merger/ takeover

Test your understanding 3

How could conflict arise between shareholders and bankers?

It is important that an organisation meets the needs of the most dominant stakeholders, but the needs of the other stakeholders should also be considered – nearly every decision becomes a compromise. For example, the firm will have to earn a satisfactory return for its shareholders whilst paying reasonable wages.

Mendelow's power-interest matrix

If an organisation is having difficulty deciding who the dominant stakeholder is, they can use Mendelow's power-interest matrix.

Level of interest

		Low	High
Level of power	**Low**	Minimal effort	Keep informed
	High	Keep satisfied	Key players

By plotting each stakeholder according to the power that they have over an organisation and the interest they have in a particular decision, the dominant stakeholder(s), i.e. the key player(s) can be identified. The needs of the key players must be considered during the formulation and evaluation of new strategies.

1.2 Corporate social responsibility

Corporate social responsibility (CSR) refers to the idea that a company should be sensitive to the needs and wants of all the stakeholders in its business operations, not just the shareholders.

A socially responsible company may consider:

- the environmental impact of production or consumption, e.g. due to the use of non-renewable resources or non-recyclable inputs.

- the health impact for consumers of certain products, e.g. tobacco and alcohol

- the fair treatment of employees

- whether it is right to experiment on animals

- the safety of products and production processes.

Different understandings of CSR

A formal definition of CSR has been proposed by the World Business Council for Sustainable Development (WBCSD):

'CSR is the continuous commitment by business to behave ethically and contribute to economic development while improving the quality of life of the workforce and their families as well as the local community and society at large'.

WBSCD meeting in the Netherlands, 1998

From the same source perceptions of CSR from different societies and cultures were given as:

- 'CSR is about capacity building for sustainable livelihoods. It respects cultural differences and finds the business opportunities in building the skills of employees, the community and the government' (Ghana).
- 'CSR is about business giving back to society' (Philippines).

In America there is more emphasis on the philanthropic approach to CSR, where companies will make charitable donations to society or its representatives.

We can contrast the European approach where the emphasis is on business processes which are more socially responsible, complemented by investment in communities for reasons which are supported by good business cases.

It is argued, by Mallen Baker, that the European approach is more sustainable since social responsibility becomes an integral part of the wealth creation process which should enhance the competitiveness of the business and maximise the wealth created from both the business and the society. With a more philanthropic approach when times are hard and the bottom line is under pressure it becomes very easy to cut the size of the donation.

We can see that there is no one definition, or theory, of corporate social responsibility. However, it is certain that there will be increasing pressure on organisations to play an increasing role in the solution to social issues. This will be particularly true of those that have a global presence. This means that multinationals and NGOs will increasingly be looked to take a lead in addressing those issues where a national government or local firm has not been able, or willing, to arrive at a solution. With increasing globalisation, which we discussed earlier, the power of the institutions attached to the nation state (national governments, judiciary and police for example) is declining.

Illustration 1 - British Petroleum (BP)

BP, primarily known as an oil company, launched its 'Beyond Petroleum' initiative in 2000 to address climate change. In 2005, it announced plans to invest $8 billion over the next 10 years in renewable energy. It is already the second largest solar-power producer in the world.

However, a number of incidents have damaged BP's image for CSR:

- In 2005 there was an explosion in its Texas City refinery in which 15 people were killed and over 150 people injured.

- In 2006 there was a serious oil leak from its pipeline in Prudhoe, in Alaska.

- In 2010 the Deepwater Horizon oil disaster spewed 4.1m barrels of oll into the Gulf of Mexico over 87 days, making it the biggest unintentional offshore oil spill in the history of the petroleum industry. The incident fouled hundreds of miles of coastline, cost at least $20bn (£12bn) and turned BP into one of the most hated enterprises in America.

There are accusations that lack of investment in safety, training and inspection were responsible for all of these incidents. Critics of BP have accused it of deflecting blame and 'greenwash', i.e. using environmentally friendly programmes to divert attention from other activities.

Illustration 2 - Responsibilities of businesses to stakeholders

888.com

888.com is an internet gambling site that is listed on the London Stock Exchange. It is headquartered in Gibraltar and operates under a licence granted by the Government of Gibraltar. It has responsibilities to the following stakeholders:

- **Shareholders** – since it is listed on the London Stock Exchange it must comply with the rules of that exchange, including adopting the UK Corporate Governance codes.

- **Employees** – to be a good employer to all its members of staff.

- **Customers** – to offer a fair, regulated and secure environment in which to gamble.

- **Government** – to comply with the terms of its licence granted in Gibraltar.

- **The public** – the company chooses to sponsor several sports teams as part of strengthening its brand. The company also tries to address public concerns about the negative aspects of gambling, e.g. by identifying compulsive gamblers on their site and taking appropriate action.

Test your understanding 4

Voluntarily turning away business

Why should a gambling company like 888.com voluntarily choose to turn away certain business, e.g. known compulsive gamblers, gamblers who may be under-age, gamblers in certain countries, etc?

A closely linked idea is that of **sustainable development**, that companies should make decisions based not only on financial factors, but also on the social and environmental consequences of their actions. This area is explored further in Chapter 5.

The importance of CSR to an organisation's success

Traditionalists argue that companies should operate solely to make money for shareholders and that it is not a company's role to worry about social responsibilities.

The modern view is that a coherent CSR strategy can offer business **benefits** in the following ways:

- Differentiation - the firm's CSR strategy (e.g. with regards to the environment, experimentation on animals or to product safety) can act as a method of differentiation.

- High calibre staff will be attracted and retained due to the firm's CSR policies.

- Brand strengthening - due to the firm's honest approach

- Lower costs - can be achieved in a number of ways, e.g. due to the use of less packaging or energy.

- The identification of new market opportunities and of changing social expectations.

- An overall increase in profitability as a result of the above - project net present values will increase due to increased sales, lower costs, an extended project life and a lower level of risk (which will in turn reduce the cost of capital).

By aligning the company's core values with the values of society, the company can improve its reputation and ensure it has a long-term future.

The single-minded pursuit of short-term profitability will paradoxically always end in reduced profits in the longer-term, as customers drift away from the company if they no longer feel any attachment to it.

There is considerable evidence that the cost of CSR initiatives should be thought of as an investment in an intangible strategic asset rather than as an expense.

Illustration 3 - The importance of CSR

BAA plc

BAA owns and operates seven airports in the UK. BAA recognises that they are responsible, both directly and indirectly, for a variety of environmental, social and economic impacts from their operations.

Positive impacts: employing 12,000 people; allowing business people to travel to meetings, thus supporting the global economy; allowing tourists to enrich their cultural experiences; allowing dispersed families to visit each other.

Negative impacts: large consumption of fossil fuels; emission of greenhouse gases; noise affecting people living close to airports.

BAA sees its CSR programme as managing these operational impacts in order to earn the trust of their stakeholders.

For example, local people living near airports are sensitive to the noise of aircraft approaching and taking off. If BAA did nothing about this issue, local people could complain to politicians who could pass laws to curb the number of flights which would damage the company. As part of its CSR programme, BAA will therefore offer to buy the properties of local people concerned about aircraft noise, or will offer to pay for sound-proofing of the properties.

You should consider whether such expenditure is an expense against the company's profits, or an investment in building up a strategic asset of goodwill among the local community.

The development of CSR over time

Pressures from various stakeholders are likely to increase CSR over time.

The norms of corporate behaviour in Victorian Britain would seem totally unacceptable in Britain today. The long hours, child labour, appalling working conditions, lack of redress for grievances, the filthy conditions of the workplace, the smoke and other pollution pouring from the factories, are not only illegal nowadays, but are totally alien to the norms of society.

Developed countries tend to have a strong sense of CSR although there are differences in approaches. For example:

- America has a more philanthropic approach to CSR, e.g. companies focus on charitable donations to society. The problem with this approach is that donations tend to be one of the first items of expenditure to be cut when the company is facing more challenging times.

- The European approach tends to focus on a combination of responsible business practices and investment in communities. It may be argued that this is a more sustainable approach to CSR.

Many developing countries are still to embrace the practices of CSR, the ruthless forces of globalisation and non-representative governments conniving in the process.

Another factor contributing to the development of CSR is that activities that start as desirable but unprofitable, tend to become profitable as consumers come to expect firms to behave in socially responsible ways and punish firms that do not by boycotting their products. Thus companies such as McDonalds, Nestle and Nike have been very concerned to 'clean up' their corporate image because of adverse publicity.

Illustration 4 - Globalisation and CSR

Nike and Gap, which produce much of their footwear and clothing in South-East Asia, have been accused of operating sweatshops in these countries with low wages and poor working conditions. Nike and Gap reply that, compared with other factories in these countries, pay and conditions are better.

1.3 Corporate governance

The role of government as a stakeholder

In the past the government's role was viewed as:

- a collector of taxes
- a regulator (discussed later in the chapter)
- a supplier of services, e.g. the NHS
- a customer, e.g. for companies such as BAE.

However, their role has now been extended to one of protecting other stakeholders. This resulted in the development of **corporate governance**.

Illustration 5

The huge emphasis that is now placed on good corporate governance was a result of a number of well-publicised financial scandals in Europe and the US, starting with Robert Maxwell at the Mirror Group and extending to Enron, WorldCom and Parmalat.

The separation of ownership and control

The need for corporate governance arises because in all but the smallest of organisations there is a separation of ownership and control.

The separation of ownership and control refers to the situation in a company where the people who own the company (the shareholders) may not be the same people as those who run the company (the board of directors).

Illustration 6 - The separation of ownership and control

The agency problem in a company

The directors of a large quoted company may hold a board meeting and vote themselves huge bonuses and salaries even if only modest profit targets are achieved and may also put contractual terms in place granting them huge compensation payments if they are sacked. Those votes are in the selfish best interests of the directors, and not in the best interests of the shareholders who own the company and whose interests the directors are meant to be working.

Stakeholder theory is an extension of agency theory and recognises that a company should be accountable to all stakeholders and not just shareholders.

The meaning of corporate governance

Corporate governance is the set of processes and policies by which company is directed, administered and controlled. It includes the appropriate role of the board of directors and the auditors of the company.

Corporate governance is concerned with the overall control and direction of a business so that the business's objectives are achieved in an acceptable manner by **ALL** stakeholders.

Different economies have different systems of corporate governance that differ in the relative strength of influence exercised by stakeholders.

Governance should lead to sustainable wealth creation and this should contribute to economic growth. Providing a business case for governance is also important to enlist management support.

Features of UK Corporate Governance codes

The UK model of corporate governance is a **principles-based** one. A principles-based approach requires companies to adhere to the spirit rather than the letter of the code. The company must either comply with the code or explain why it has not. However, since adherence is part of the stock exchange listing requirements it cannot be considered voluntary for large companies.

UK Corporate Governance codes (the Combined Code) include guidance on the use of the AGM, the roles of the Chairman and Chief Executive Officer (CEO), non-executive directors, nomination committees, remuneration committees and audit committees:

Use of the AGM

The board should use the annual general meeting (AGM) to construct a dialogue with shareholders.

Chairman and Chief Executive Officer (CEO)

The positions of the chairman of the board and the CEO (the person in charge of running the company) should be separated. This is to ensure that no one individual has too much power within the company.

Non-executive directors (NEDs)

Directors who are involved in the execution of day-to-day management decisions are called **executive directors**. Those who primarily only attend board meetings (and the meetings of board committees) are known as **NEDs**.

Current guidance is that NEDs should as far as possible be 'independent' so that their oversight role can be effectively and responsibly carried out.

Typical recommendations include:

- At least half of the board (excluding the chairman) should comprise independent NEDs. A smaller company should have at least two independent NEDs.

- One of the NEDs should be appointed the 'senior independent director'. Shareholders can contact them if they wish to raise matters outside the normal executive channels of communication.

Illustration 7 - Sainsbury plc independent NEDs

Among the independent NEDs at Sainsbury's is Anna Ford, a former BBC newsreader. She is well known to the public and of good reputation, so the public at large might see her as 'their' representative on the board and will trust her to put forward their point of view. Anna Ford herself may have little or no experience of big business, but again the public would not see that as a disadvantage in representing them on the board.

Test your understanding 5

Independent NED

Mr X retires from the post of finance director at AB plc. The company is keen to retain his experience, so invite him to become a NED of the company. Can he qualify as an independent non-executive?

Nomination committees

Appointments to the board should be made via a nominations, or appointments, committee. This is to provide some independence from the current board members and to ensure that all appointments are based on merit and suitability.

Remuneration committees

The board of a listed company should establish a remuneration committee of at least three (or two in the case of smaller companies) NEDs.

The remuneration committee should be responsible for setting the remuneration of all the executive directors and the chairman, including pension rights and any compensation payments.

Remuneration committee

Advantages of having a remuneration committee:

- It avoids the agency problem of directors determining their own levels of remuneration.

- It leaves the board free to make strategic decision about the future.

Disadvantages of having a remuneration committee:

- There is a danger that NEDs may recommend high remuneration for the executive directors in the hope that the executives will recommend high remuneration for the NEDs.

- There will be a cost involved in preparing for and holding the meetings.

Test your understanding 6

Remuneration of NEDs

On what basis should NEDs be remunerated for their service to the company?

Audit committees

An audit committee consists of independent NEDs who are responsible for monitoring and reviewing the company's financial controls and the integrity of the financial statements.

Auditors (both internal and external) have long had a problem – the people they report to and liaise with (the board) are often those people whose activities they report on.

The audit committee acts as an interface between the board of directors on one side and the internal and external auditors on the other side.

An audit committee should comprise of three NEDs, and should be the first point of contact for auditors, improving the independence and the overall quality of the audit functions.

The role of the audit committee

- Being available for both sets of auditors (e.g. the audit committee meetings are likely to include both internal and external auditors).

- Executive directors to attend meetings if requested by the audit committee.

- Reviewing accounting policies and financial statements as a whole to ensure that they are appropriate and balanced.

- Reviewing systems of internal controls.

- Agreeing agenda for work for internal audit department.

- Receiving results for internal audit work.

- Short listing firms of external auditors when a change is needed.

- Reviewing independence of external audit firm.

- Considering extent to which external auditors should be allowed to tender for 'other services'.

Test your understanding 7

Composition of audit committee

Why are the members of an audit committee required to be NEDs rather than executive directors?

The US Sarbanes-Oxley Act 2002 (SOX)

The US corporate governance model is a **rules-based** one. A rules-based approach instils the code into the law with appropriate penalties for transgression.

In 2002, following a number of corporate governance scandals such as Enron and WorldCom, tough new corporate governance regulations were introduced in the US by SOX.

SOX is only applicable in the US and for subsidiaries of US-based companies.

2 External Regulation of Business

2.1 Introduction

As mentioned earlier in the chapter, one of the roles of government is to act as a regulator.

Regulation is any form of government interference and is required to ensure that the needs of stakeholders can be met and that businesses act in the public interest.

2.2 Regulation in the UK

Regulation of the level of competition in the market

- The government wants to encourage competition in the market.

- Competition drives down prices, encourages firms to be efficient with the use of their resources and improves quality.

- Therefore, competition is in the best interests of the consumer.

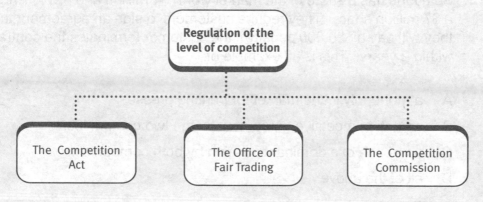

Source of regulation	Powers
The Competition Act	• Prohibits anti-competitive agreements, e.g. illegal cartels who collude to fix prices and production levels. • Prohibits abuse of a dominant position, e.g. a business can be considered dominant if it has at least 40% of the market. It is illegal for a dominant firm to exercise its market power in a way that reduces competition.
The Office of Fair Trading (OFT)	The OFT has powers to investigate businesses suspected of breaching the Competition Act, e.g. OFT officials can enter premises and demand documents. Fines of up to 10% of revenue can be imposed
The Competition Commission	The OFT can refer cases to the Competition Commission for further investigation, e.g. they determine if the structure of an industry is detrimental to competition.

Illustration 8

In 2007, British Airways (BA) was fined £270 million after it admitted collusion in fixing prices of fuel surcharges. BA held illegal talks with rival Virgin Atlantic between 2004 and 2006. During that time, surcharges rose from £5 to £60 per ticket.

Test your understanding 8

The market for industrial printing presses is worth $25 million. Print Solutions has a share of the market worth $4 million and Rapid Print has a $7 million share. They require customers to sign an agreement that they will pay a $20,000 penalty if the customer terminates the contract within 2 years. This is an example of:

A   a monopoly in the market for printing presses.

B   an anti-competitive agreement by the two companies.

C   an abuse of a dominant position by both companies.

D   all of the above.

Regulation of externalities

Externalities are costs or benefits of production experienced by society but not by producers or consumers themselves.

Test your understanding 9

Identify FOUR examples of externalities.

Regulation of externalities can be done in a number of ways:

Method of regulation	Example
Setting maximum or minimum selling prices	Maximum price for prescriptions in the UK.
Taxation	Tax on cigarettes, alcohol and petrol aimed at reducing consumption.
Subsidies	Subsidies given to firms providing training for employees.
Fines and quotas (limits)	Businesses are set quotas for emissions and may be fined if they exceed these quotas.

Test your understanding 10

Explain why the government regulates externalities.

Regulation of people in business

> ### Regulation of people managing the company

> #### To prevent insider trading
> - Criminal offence to use knowledge to make profit or avoid a loss when buying or selling shares

> #### To prevent trading if the company is insolvent (can't pay its debts as they fall due)
> - Fraudulent trading i.e. directors continue to trade when company is insolvent. Directors may be liable for debts
> - Wrongful trading i.e. directors should have known that the company would become insolvent and did not take steps to avoid losses to creditors

---

Test your understanding 11

Explain why the government has taken steps to avoid fraudulent or wrongful trading.

Disqualification of directors

To protect the public interest and creditors in particular, a person may be disqualified from acting as a director or manager of a company for the following reasons:

- Insider trading

- Being a director of an insolvent company

- Breaking company laws

- Making loans from company funds which are unlikely to be repaid
- Being unfit to act as a director or manager

2.3 International regulation

The US Sarbanes-Oxley Act 2002

- The aim of the Act is to stop creative accounting.
- As mentioned in section 1 of this chapter, it was implemented as a result of huge corporate scandals, e.g. Enron and WorldCom.
- It has no impact on a UK company unless they are registered on the US stock exchange as well as the UK stock exchange.
- The main provisions of the Act were reviewed in Section 1 of this chapter.

International regulation of trade

- The benefits of free trade were discussed in chapter 2.
- Free trade is supported by the World Trade Organisation (WTO).
- Regional trading organisations, such as the EU and NAFTA, allow free trade between specific countries.

How firms react to regulations

There are four possible ways in which a firm may react:

- **Entrenchment** – don't respond to regulation. A high risk strategy.
- **Mere compliance** – pass the cost of compliance on to the consumer, e.g. a cigarette manufacturer facing increased taxes may decide to increase the price of a packet of cigarettes.
- **Full compliance** – the company fully changes its behaviour to comply.
- **Innovate** – the company finds ways to save costs that will more than compensate for the cost of compliance, i.e. the firm goes above and beyond what is required.

3 Business/ Government Relations

3.1 Introduction

Corporate political activity refers to the involvement of firms in the political process, with the aim of securing particular policy preferences.

Illustration 9 - Corporate political activity

In the US the protection of domestic trade is among the most popular policies demanded by producers with US politicians being easily influenced by the generous donations made by US firms.

Businesses can try to influence government policies in a number of ways:

- By employing lobbyists, who will put their case to ministers and civil servants and try to obtain their support.

- By giving MPs and retired senior civil servants non-executive directorships, in the hope that they will take an interest in legislation that affects the business and will exercise their influence,

- By influencing public opinion, and hence the legislative agenda, using advertising or other means of marketing communications.

Illustration 10 - President Obama's changes

In January 2009 President Obama implemented some of the toughest lobbying restrictions in US history, seeking to eliminate undue influence in American politics. New rules prohibit presidential appointees from accepting gifts from lobbying organisations and restricts appointees' ability to work on issues on which they recently lobbied while in the private sector. It will take time to see if this new approach has an impact on governance.

Depending on the political regime and the country in question another method may be to make donations to party funds. Obviously this is open to question - it could be seen as a form of bribery.

Illustration 11 - Donations to party funds

The problem of corruption continues to be strong in many developing countries. A cash-for-votes scandal overshadowed the presidential elections in Brazil in 2006.

It is usually in the interest of a government to consult with the business sector when it is forming new policies:

- to widen its perspective

- and so that it can defend its actions politically.

3.2 Business/ government relations in developed and developing countries

In most developed countries there is a strong business lobby consisting of individual companies and business-related organisations.

Very large companies are likely to be in frequent contact with government departments and parliament on an individual basis and many have distinct departments for government liaison.

Such departments will monitor and advise on political and governmental developments, make regular contacts with politicians and senior civil servants, organise representation and undertake lobbying operations in London, Brussels, Washington, Geneva and so on, often assisted by non-executive directors and consultants.

Illustration 12 - Responsible business lobbying
Companies with statements on CSR must align their business activities with social responsibility. For example, mining companies making statements about responsible stewardship to the environment should not be found lobbying to dumb-down environmental legislation.

Business lobbying in the UK
In the UK, the business lobby consists of organisations such as the following: • The Confederation of British Industry (CBI), representing the entire private business sector. • The Federation of Small Businesses (FSB) and local Chambers of Commerce. • The Institute of Directors (IOD). • Several thousand trade associations and employers' organisations, representing particular industries and sectors.

Developing countries do not influence government policies to the same degree. Business lobbying is much weaker but the government can be easily swayed with even small donations to party funds.

Influence of business on international organisations

It may be particularly important to try to influence the drafting process of organisations such as the European Commission and the WTO. Their regulations take priority over national law or more local arrangements and their decisions may be very difficult to change because they are only arrived at after long periods of international negotiation.

- There should be no delay. Firms should monitor the issues that are being dealt with by the governing body and make their views known as early as possible in the process. The governing body will probably publish a 'green paper' discussing proposed changes and inviting comment before issuing a 'white paper' and passing a statute or a treaty or a set of standards.

- Firms should collaborate with others in the same industry and encourage firms in other countries to lobby their own governments. An organisation's opinions will carry more weight if it can show that it is not just self-seeking but that those opinions are shared by others in the industry.

Test your understanding 12

List the possible ways that government can impact on business both as an aid and as an impediment.

3.3 Non governmental organisations (NGOs)

Definitions

The term "non governmental organisation" or NGO can mean different things in different countries. However, NGOs are defined by the World Bank as "private organizations that pursue activities to relieve suffering, promote the interests of the poor, protect the environment, provide basic social services or undertake community development".

The World Association of Non Governmental Organisations (WANGO) states "Whether striving to prevent or treat disease, advance reconciliation, or provide humanitarian aid, at the forefront of an NGO's mission is the recognition of the inherent dignity of each human being."

Given these definitions, NGOs may function at different levels of influence ranging from community, city, country or even internationally. The degree of influence can be significant, particularly for international NGOs. Some of the largest NGOs operate in the humanitarian sphere and include Oxfam, CARE, World Vision and Save the Children. World Vision, for example, had expenditure of over $3.5 billion in 2009, which is more than the GDP of some countries.

Activities

Furthermore, the World Bank identifies two types of NGO:

- Operational NGOs that seek to achieve change directly through projects such as community development.
- Campaigning NGOs that seek to achieve change indirectly through the use of lobbying and public relations (PR) programmes to influence government.

The relationship between businesses and NGOs

In business decisions, a conflict may be encountered between what furthers the firm's interests and what satisfies society. As discussed earlier in this chapter, corporate social responsibility (CSR) is a key element in the management of a firm's relationships with governments, regulatory agencies and civil society. However, to this list we must also add NGOs who could operate as partners with firms in lobbying governments for change or as opponents if the firm's activities are at odds with the NGO's mission.

Companies and NGOs have discovered a number of reasons to partner:

- Creating business value and environmental benefits.
- Raising the bar on environmental performance.
- Gaining skills and perspectives not available in the organisation.
- Building respect and credibility.
- Providing independent validation of a company's claim of environmental and social benefits from a project.

4 Chapter summary

Governance and regulation in the global business environment

Governance and social responsibility
- Stakeholders
- Corporate governance
- Corporate social responsibility

External regulation of business
Regulation in the UK:
- level of competition
- externalities
- people in business
International regulation:
- Sarbanes-Oxley Act
- Regulation of trade

Business/government relations
- How businesses influence government
- Relations in developed and developing countries

5 Practice questions

Question 1

Which of the following is NOT a method of regulating externalities?

A   setting a maximum price

B   taxation

C   subsides

D   administrative legislation

(2 marks)

Question 2

Anti-monopoly laws are based on the idea that the best way to achieve efficiency and to avoid excessive prices is through:

A   corporate governance.

B   increased public ownership.

C   regulation.

D   an increase in corporate social responsibility.

(2 marks)

Question 3

What is the definition of corporate governance?

A   The system by which companies are directed and controlled.

B   The definition in the Sarbanes-Oxley Act 2002.

C   A set of rules that a company must follow to continue being listed on the London Stock Exchange.

D   A set of rules introduced as a result of several high-profile corporate collapses.

(2 marks)

Question 4

Which of the following is NOT the job of a NED (non executive director)?

A   Contribution to the development of strategy.

B   Scrutiny of management performance.

C   Decisions on which suppliers to use for the company's raw materials purchases.

D   Determination of executives' remuneration packages.

(2 marks)

Question 5

Identify FOUR benefits of corporate governance.

(4 marks)

Question 6

JV limited manufactures cleaning chemicals at its factory in a small town in the Lake District. It employs 300 people, and is the largest employer within a 20 mile radius.

The factory is located on the side of a lake, at the end of a single track road.

Required:

Identify FOUR social responsibilities of this company.

(4 marks)

Question 7

An increasing number of companies have expressed their willingness to consider their wider social responsibilities. This often involves them voluntarily undertaking extra responsibilities and costs, for example:

- In order to reduce pollution, they may decide to treat waste products to a higher standard than required by legislation.

- They may decline to trade with countries whose governments they find objectionable.

- They may pay wages above minimum levels.

Required:

(a) Explain:

  (i)   whether the pursuit of a policy of social responsibility necessarily involves a conflict with the objective of shareholder wealth-maximisation

  (ii) the extent to which the existence of a conflict between a company's objectives is acceptable.

(8 marks)

(b) Explain how you can encourage staff, particularly managers, to pursue and implement socially responsible policies.

(5 marks)

(c) Explain to what extent you can include the requirements of all stakeholders when creating a plan for corporate social responsibility.

(7 marks)

(Total: 20 marks)

Question 8

Eastborough is a large region with a rugged, beautiful coastline where rare birds have recently settled on undisturbed cliffs. Since mining ceased 150 years ago, its main industries have been agriculture and fishing. However, today, many communities in Eastborough suffer high unemployment. Government initiatives for regeneration through tourism have met with little success as the area has poor road networks, unsightly derelict buildings and dirty beaches.

Digwell Explorations, a listed company, has a reputation for maximising shareholder returns and has discovered substantial tin reserves in Eastborough. With new technology, mining could be profitable, provide jobs and boost the economy. A number of interest and pressure groups have, however, been vocal in opposing the scheme.

Digwell Explorations, after much lobbying, has just received government permission to undertake mining. It could face difficulties in proceeding because of the likely activity of a group called the Eastborough Protection Alliance. This group includes wildlife protection representatives, villagers worried about the potential increase in traffic congestion and noise, environmentalists, and anti-capitalism groups.

Required:

Discuss the ethical issues that should have been considered by the government when granting permission for mining to go ahead. Explain the conflicts between the main stakeholder groups.

(15 marks)

Test your understanding answers

Test your understanding 1

No, for example, a strategy to mechanise a department could result in increased efficiency, resulting in a higher bonus for a manager, but job losses for employees.

Test your understanding 2

Competitors are connected stakeholders. Their needs/ expectations will be to remain competitive and to ensure customers are not poached.

Test your understanding 3

The shareholders may be willing to take more risks in return for higher profits/ returns, whereas the bankers will be more concerned with low risk/ security.

Test your understanding 4

Either you could argue that such action was ethically correct (with the company wanting to 'do the right thing'), or you could argue that a concentration on short-term profits is likely to store up problems in the longer term. If under-age gamblers are seen to be easily gambling on a particular website, then the public reputation of that site will be damaged and its long term profitability could be in jeopardy if governments or customers turn against it.

Test your understanding 5

It is very unlikely that Mr X can be independent since he has been an employee of the company within the last five years. If the board believes that Mr X is independent despite his recent employment then they must state the reasons for this determination.

Test your understanding 6

NEDs should be paid fees that reflect the time commitment and the responsibilities of the role, e.g. a fixed daily rate for when they work for the company. Share options should not be granted to the NEDs since this could detract from their independent judgement.

Test your understanding 7

NEDS have no day-to-day operating responsibilities, so they are able to view the company's affairs in a detached and independent way and liaise effectively between the main board and both sets of auditors.

Test your understanding 8

B. Neither company owns 40% of the market so would not be classed as dominant.

Test your understanding 9

Costs experienced by society	Benefits experienced by society
Cigarettes	Training of employees by firms
Pollution from cars	Vaccinations

Test your understanding 10

The government wants to encourage certain externalities, e.g. vaccinations due to the positive health benefits for society as a whole. However, it wants to discourage other externalities, e.g. smoking due to the negative health implications for society as a whole.

Test your understanding 11

A director should cease trade as soon as he or she knows that the company is insolvent/ will become insolvent. This should help to minimise losses to creditors.

Test your understanding 12

An aid to business:

- as large buyer
- as sponsor for research and development
- as the champion of free trade (or as protector against unfair trade in certain circumstances)
- as a controller of inflation, and inflationary influences
- by providing help for wealth creation, including skill training
- by providing assistance for the start up of businesses.

An impediment to business:

- as defender of the interest of the consumer
- as the guarantor of health and safety at work
- as the protector of the environment
- as regulator of business practices
- as the protector of minority groupings.

Question 1

D

Question 2

C

Question 3

A

Question 4

C

Question 5

Benefits of corporate governance include:

- reduced risk for shareholders and other stakeholders
- improved leadership
- improved accountability
- enhanced performance
- better image with providers of finance thus making raising finance easier
- greater transparency.

(**Note:** only four benefits are required)

Question 6

Many points can be included, such as:

- not polluting the lake with waste chemicals
- making sure employees use adequate protection when working with the chemicals
- complying with legislation regarding the use of hazardous chemicals
- minimising the impact of traffic on local roads
- minimising the visual impact of the factory on the area.

Question 7

(a)

   (i) About 20 or so years ago, the idea that profitability was overwhelmingly the principal objective of a business would have been uncontroversial. Today's climate is different: increased public awareness of the social impact of large organisations has broadened the range of objectives which businesses must aim to achieve. New factors to be considered include pollution control, conservation of natural resources and avoidance of environmental damage.

      In the short term, the measures described in the question would reduce profits; all of them involve increased profits or revenue foregone. And reduced profits imply reduced shareholders' wealth in the form of dividends and capital growth.

      However, this analysis, though relatively straightforward in the short term, may not be so clear-cut in the long term. Many commentators argue that the reputation and image of corporations will suffer if they do not respond to heightened awareness of social responsibility amongst consumers. Given that many companies are already taking steps along this path, and making good public relations out of their efforts, there is pressure on other companies to follow suit. Failure to do so may lead to long-term decline.

  (ii) A conflict between company objectives implies a picture of managers pulling in opposite directions, some trying to meet criteria of social responsibility, others hell-bent on maximising profit. Given that all of the managers in a company are drawing on the same pool of resources this is a recipe for disaster.

      However, this does not mean that companies are doomed to fail if they pursue more than one objective. The idea is to agree on a balance between conflicting objectives, and to settle on a strategy which satisfies both sets of objectives, to the extent that they can be reconciled.

(b) Part of the difficulty in pursuing aspirations towards social responsibility lies in the relative novelty of the concept. Managers brought up in a culture of profit maximisation may find it hard to appreciate the importance of other objectives, and to adapt their behaviour accordingly. To encourage managers to pursue and implement social responsibility involves, as a first step, making managers aware of the need for it. This may be achieved by:

    – appropriate training

- dissemination of targets and measures related to social objectives

- formal incorporation of social objectives into the decision-making process

- collaboration with other organisations to launch a common approach

- appointment of external consultants to assess existing performance in this area and to recommend improvements

- monitoring achievement by logging and publishing of performance indicators

- appointment of a committee to review and implement social and ethical policies.

(c) An organisation's stakeholders include:

- owners/shareholders

- employees

- business contacts, such as customers and suppliers

- the general public

- the government.

Owners/shareholders will be interested primarily in profitability, but the analysis in Part(a) above suggests that long-term profitability may depend at least in part on the adoption of social objectives.

Employees obviously have a very direct interest in at least some social objectives: for example, the question mentions a policy of paying wages above national minimum levels.

Business contacts have a less direct interest in this issue. However, as a minimum, creditors will be impressed with an ethical policy of paying debts on time, and customers who themselves have social and ethical interests may exert pressure on their suppliers to conform as well.

The general public, as already mentioned, have shown themselves increasingly aware of these issues, and prepared to back their principles with direct action (such as refusing to invest in companies whose objectives they disapprove of).

The government must meet international obligations as well as satisfying the demands of their own electorate. Both factors mean that they will take an interest in the social and ethical policies of organisations.

Question 8

Ethics

Ethics are a code of moral principles that people follow with respect to what is right or wrong. General examples might include staying within the law, not engaging in bribery or theft or endangering other people.

Also a part of ethics is social responsibility; the duty towards the wider community or society in general which includes environmental issues, public safety, employment and exploitation of third world workers.

In this case ethical issues which the government should have considered when granting permission for mining include:

- **Employment in the local area** - the government has a duty toward people to provide them with jobs. In Eastborough there is significant unemployment so it is particularly important to the government to generate jobs in the area. The effect of the mining on employment levels should therefore be considered.

- **The local economy** - the government has an obligation to the people of Eastborough to improve the wealth of the people there. This largely depends on a successful economy. The local economy of Eastborough has been performing badly despite various initiatives based around tourism. The effect of mining on the local economy generally must be considered (i.e. jobs create income which is then spent in local shops, demand for property increases and prices rise for all in the area).

- **Environmental concerns** - Eastborough has a beautiful coastline with rare birds nesting there. The government has a debt towards society generally to preserve areas of natural beauty for all to appreciate and enjoy, and a moral obligation towards other species on the planet to protect them from extinction. The effects of the mining operations on the rare birds, the beauty of the coastline and any pollution caused in the locality should therefore have been considered by the government.

- **Rights of local individuals** - Individuals have the right for their quality of life to remain high. While employment and an improved economy may enrich the quality of life of many, there may also be negative effects for some local people such as increased noise and traffic congestion. These broader effects on villagers is likely to have been considered.

- **Right to free operation of business** - Many capitalist countries believe in free trade and removing barriers to trade. This may be seen as a right of the business, and it may be considered as part of the decision to allow Digwell to open the mining operation.

Conflicts between stakeholder groups

Stakeholders are people who are affected or interested in some way by the mining operations.

In this case stakeholders include:

- national government
- local government
- local people
- wildlife protection groups
- environmental groups
- directors of Digwell
- employees of Digwell
- shareholders of Digwell.

The conflicts which may exist include the following:

- **National vs local government** - local government will be interested in Eastborough and its interests. National government have to balance those needs with the needs of all people of the country. There may be a conflict over the amount of funding available to support local initiatives such as help with starting up the mining operations.

- **Unemployed vs people based near mining operations/working people** - unemployed people in the area will notice a direct benefit from the mining operations through increased jobs and are likely to support it. Other local residents may simply view the operations as disrupting their existing life (noise/congestion) and oppose the idea.

- **Shareholders/directors of Digwell vs environmental/wildlife protection groups** - both shareholders and Directors of Digwell wish to make profits from Digwell's operations. The mining operations will enable them to make full use of an asset they own (tin reserves) and hence increase profit. They will wish it to go ahead, and may have very little interest in the broader impact. Environmental groups aim to protect the environment and are likely to oppose any part of the mining operation which will affect the environment irrespective of profitability.

Information Systems

Chapter learning objectives

Lead	Component
B1. Discuss the wider business context within which information systems operate.	(a) Identify the value of information and information systems organisations.
	(b) Discuss the reasons for organisations' increased dependence on information systems.
	(c) Discuss the transformation of organisations through technology.
B2. Analyse how information systems can be implemented in support of the organisation's strategy.	(a) Discuss ways for overcoming problems in information system implementation.
	(b) Discuss ways for organising and managing information system activities in the context of the wider organisation.

1 Information

1.1 Introduction

Information is different from data.

Data consists of numbers, letters, symbols, raw facts, events and transactions which have been recorded but not yet processed into a form that is not suitable for making decisions.

Information is data that has been processed in such a way that it has a meaning to the person who receives it, who may then use it to improve the quality of decision-making.

1.2 Uses of information

Internal uses	External uses
Management requires information: • to provide records, both current and historical • to analyse what is happening within the business • to provide the basis of decision making in the short-term and long-term • to monitor the performance of the business by comparing actual results with planned results.	Third parties require information about the business, including: • shareholders - to monitor their investment • customers - to assist with product choices • employees - to assist them in their role • government - to monitor employment levels and tax receipts.

1.3 The value of information

- Collecting and processing information for use by managers has a cost.

- The value of the information to the business must be greater than the cost.

Value of Information	Cost of information
Information may: - reduce unnecessary costs; - eliminate losses; - result in better marketing strategies; - assist in attaining competitive advantage.	- Design and development costs, e.g. system design, testing, capital cost of equipment. - Running costs, e.g. staff salaries, security. - Storage costs, e.g. for hardware.

Converting data into information

The process of turning data into information may include the following stages:

(1) Data *collection*: raw data is collected from both the internal and the external environment.

(2) Data *evaluation*: collected data is filtered for relevance.

(3) Data *analysis*: different dimensions of the data are analysed, e.g. comparison with budget, with the historical record, with industry best.

(4) Data *interpretation*: meaning added to the data

(5) Data *reporting*: information is disseminated to users.

Levels of information

Within an organisation, management information requirements can be classified into three different levels:

Strategic information is mainly used by directors and senior managers to choose between alternative courses of action, to plan the organisation's overall objectives and strategy and to measure whether these are being achieved. For example:

- profitability of main business segments

- prospects for present and potential markets.

Tactical information is used by managers at all levels, but mainly at the middle level for tactical planning and management control activities, such as pricing, purchasing, distribution and stocking. For example:

- sales analysis

- stock levels

- productivity measures.

Operational information is used mainly by managers on the operational level such as foremen and section heads who have to ensure that routine tasks are properly planned and controlled. For example:

- listings of debtors and creditors

- payroll details

- raw materials requirements and usage.

2 The Role of Information Systems within Organisations

 Information systems (IS) refer to the provision and management of information to support the running of the organisation.

Information technology (IT) is the supporting equipment (hardware) that provides the infrastructure to run the information systems.

Use of IS/ IT in an organisation

Use	Example
Forecasting	Identify trends, based on historic data.
Analysing	Data collected can assist an organisation in assessing the actions of competitors in response to actions taken by the organisation.
Scenario planning	A model of the organisation is developed using a specialist program. Once completed, the different inputs (internal and external factors) can be varied to model the potential outputs.
Competitive advantage	For example, IS/ IT changes the balance of power in supplier relationships or can be used to generate new products.
Improving performance	Reduce costs or add product value.
Measuring performance	Information systems can provide vast amounts of detail on the activities carried out by the organisation.
Cost reduction	By automating manual tasks.
Improved service	For example, provision of real-time stock levels or web based ordering systems.
Sales performance	Customer relationship management systems can be used (see section 5) or loyalty schemes.

Many of the uses mentioned can be included under the general heading of **'decision making'**. Good decision making is vital to organisational success. A hierarchy of decision making systems can assist in this process. These include:

- **Transaction Processing Systems (TPS)** - These major applications carry out the essential, routine processing of day-to-day transactional data.

- **Management Information Systems (MIS)** - These deliver routine and ad hoc formal reports to management. Such services are used extensively by operational users.

- **Decision Support Systems (DSS)** - A combination of technology used to support the decision-making process of tactical and strategic management.

- **Expert systems** - Expert related DSSs provide expert knowledge and advice. These include a database of decision rules that define expertise in a given area.

- **Executive Information Systems (EIS)** - These are used in large organisations to draw together data from various, usually global, sources. Powerful forecasting and data analysis tools are then used prior to communicating decisions.

Examples of IS/IT in the workplace

Within the factory, computer aided design (CAD) and computer aided (or automated) manufacturing (CAM) offer integrated solutions in product design and control of machinery. This allows flexibility and the elimination of waste factors integral to a 'lean philosophy' and constant improvement. An integrated approach combining both CAD and CAM can lead to the use of robots and computerised inventory management. The problems of economic machine loading and provision of customer and stockists' requirements is one of the most complex in modern factory management but can be easily facilitated through IS.

The office, like the factory before it, has been subject to huge technological advancements in recent years. 'Office automation' is a term that refers to the use of computers, communications and network technology in managing the organisation's operations and information resources. In recent years this has resulted in the combination of data, text, image and sound into office-built multimedia systems. Many organisations have made use of network technology, specifically electronic data interchange (EDI). EDI is the computer-to-computer transmission of data contained in standard business documents and reports, such as customer invoices and purchase orders. EDI replaces conventional business documentation with structured data transmitted electronically over networks ('paperless trading'). Obvious advantages of EDI include saving cost and speeding of transactions, potentially reducing lead times for material purchases (and stock holding) better customer service and improved responsiveness to changes in customer demands.

Many forms of automation and other technology are commonly found in most office environments including the following:

- e-mail

- Tele-conferencing / video-conferencing / webinars

- Internet based networking such as Ning and Twitter

3 Aligning Information Systems with Business Strategy

3.1 Introduction

A **business strategy** is a major plan of action formulated to achieve the organisation's objectives. It is developed by senior management in response to organisational needs and will be used to guide the company through the next period of activity.

Business planning can be viewed as having three levels:

- corporate strategy (for example, which markets should we be in, which products should we have in our portfolio?)

- business strategy (for example, how to make a particular product more successful) and

- functional strategy. (for example, HR and marketing).

Using this hierarchy, IS/IT would be viewed as a functional strategy designed to support the overriding corporate and business strategies. However, developments in IT/IS can also be the trigger for new corporate and business strategy, such as the growth in e-trading, so the relationship is more than simply one of support.

Illustration 1 - How the internet has affected travel agents

Demand for the services of a traditional high-street travel agent have declined due to growth in use of the internet. Travel agents have been cut out of many transactions as the public can book directly with hotels, airlines and rail companies.

However there has been growth in online travel agents such as companies like lastminute.com and expedia.com, who make the online experience easier for customers, presenting a wide choice of products and services.

Another interesting example is Opodo.com, set up by a collaboration of European airlines to encourage customers to book flights directly with them rather than using cost comparison intermediaries such as lastminute.com.

3.2 Information systems and competitive advantage

Competitive advantage means having those factors, which lead customers to consistently prefer your products or services.

IT does not guarantee an enhanced competitive ability because any advantage due to IT alone is likely to be temporary because competitors can use it and it will not necessarily lead to better decision making.

Porter's generic strategies

Porter suggested three overall competitive strategies that an organisation can implement:

- **Cost leadership** - this strategy seeks to achieve the position of the lowest-cost producer in the industry as a whole.
    - Information systems can reduce staff time spent on clerical work and thus increase time spent on business development.
    - Information systems might allow a company to tie up its purchasing services directly with its suppliers, reducing stock-holding costs or delays in processing orders.

Test your understanding 1

Explain how IT might help a car manufacturer to reduce its unit costs.

- **Differentiation** – this strategy assumes that competitive advantage can be gained through particular characteristics of a product or service. The organisation seeks to become different to its competitors in a way that its customers value, e.g. brand, design, customer service.
    - IS can enhance an organisation's ability to compete by providing it with up-to-the minute information on customer needs allowing it to differentiate its products on factors other than price.

Illustration 2

A bank, with a strategy of being a differentiated company focused on banking to high net worth individuals, can use IT to help it to achieve its strategy by:

- Enabling the search and selection criteria of databases for marketing to concentrate on high net-worth customers.

- Provide very high quality banking information with monthly account summaries, portfolio tracking, new investment possibilities provided automatically and by a variety of different mediums (e-mail, post, web site).

- Customers get provided with direct email access to a personal banker so that instructions or communication can be carried out easily.

- Integration of the banks systems to other banking networks to allow the use of things such as cash machines.

- Internet and telephone banking services at all times.

- A facility to allow the bank to communicate with agents of the customer (e.g. accountant, stock broker).

- Banking systems to provide monthly allocation of interest as opposed to six-monthly or annual allocation.

- **Focus** - this involves the restriction of activities to only part of the market.

  IT can facilitate the collection of sales and customer information that identifies targetable market segments

  – It may enable a more customised product/ service to be produced.

3.3 Benefits of IS/ IT strategy

- **Competitive advantage** - for example, travel agents can choose and reserve a holiday in much less time and more conveniently when they are on-line to the suppliers.

- **Improved productivity and performance** - IT/ IS can be used as a strategic weapon to improve productivity and performance. CAD and CAM are two examples where this might be the case.

- **Development of new business** - for example, large supermarket's sales can use IT/ IS to identify trends in product purchasing.

- **Structural change** - Computers with modems enable people to work from home, reducing the cost of travel and office space. Teleconferencing and video conferencing are available to managers, reducing the necessity for them to travel to meetings and making their time more productive.

- **Goal congruence** - the IT/ IS objectives will be in-line with the corporate objectives.

4 IT Enabled Transformation

4.1 Business transformation

Business transformation is the process of translating a high level vision for the business into new services.

A plan will:

- set out new ways of working;
- show how components fit together to deliver strategic objectives;
- show how customer's needs will be met;
- show how IS/ IT will be used to support the business.

Test your understanding 2
Explain the ways in which IT developments have altered the structure of organisations.

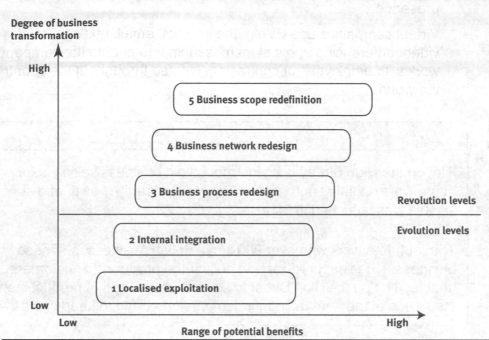

Different degrees of transformation

The diagram below shows the different degrees of transformation in relation to IT-enabled change.

Level of transformation	Characteristics
Localised exploitation (automation)	Use existing IT functionality to reengineer individual, high-value areas of business operation.
Internal integration	Use the capabilities inherent in IT to integrate business operations: reflects a seamless process.
Business process reengineering	Redesign key processes to provide business capabilities for the future: use IT as an enabler.
Business network redesign	Strategic logic used to provide products and services from partners: exploitation of IT for learning.
Business scope redefinition	Redefinition of corporate scope: what you do, what partners do, and what is enabled by IT.

IT has a significant role in business transformation and has resulted in the emergence of new forms of organisation. These include:

- Virtual organisations and virtual teams.
- E-commerce organisations – i.e. trading using the internet.

4.2 Virtual companies

There is no formal definition of a virtual company but characteristics include:

- A virtual company is a business that operates with very little physical presence.

- Virtual companies use IT, e.g. the internet, email, faxes, videoconferencing and instant messaging, to enable the company to work with employees or contractors located throughout the country or the world.

Illustration 3

'Not on the High Street' is an internet based business selling luxury home ware, clothing and gifts. It has enjoyed rapid growth and success since it was launched in 2006.

The founders work with over 900 small British businesses. These businesses design, produce and deliver the products to customers. This enables Not on the High Street to sell a unique range of products to fulfil the needs of the demanding modern customer and to keep costs low.

- Virtual companies enable executives, scientists, writers, researchers and other professionals to collaborate on new products and services without ever meeting face to face.

- The important issue that these organisations feel 'real' to the client, and meet their needs at least as adequately as the more 'traditional' organisations.

- A virtual company will outsource most or all of its functions.

Illustration 4

A firm manufactures wedding dresses. It could outsource:

- the design to a wedding dress designer;
- marketing to a specialist marketing firm;
- manufacture to a sub-contractor;
- delivery to a specialist logistics firm;
- collection of money from customers to a specialist debt collection company;
- tax returns and accounts to a specialist accountancy firm.

Test your understanding 3

Discuss the benefits of adopting a virtual company strategy.

Drawbacks of virtual companies

- It may be difficult to negotiate a revenue sharing agreement between the different partners.

- Loss of control may result in a fall in quality.

- The partners may also work for competitors thus reducing any competitive advantage.

4.3 Virtual teams

A virtual team is a group of people who interact through independent tasks guided by a common purpose and work across space, time and organisational boundaries with links strengthened by IT.

They are essentially teams of people who are not present in the same office or organisation.

The role of IT/ IS in virtual teams

IT/ IS has enabled the formation of virtual teams:

Challenges for virtual teams

The following challenges will face virtual teams:

- **Forming a team** – it may be difficult to establish a cohesive and trusting team.

- **Knowledge sharing** – sharing of knowledge may prove more difficult due to the absence of face to face contact.

- **Processes and goals** – it may be more difficult to establish clear decision making processes and goals.

- **Leadership** – this may be more difficult since employees will be working at different times, in different locations and in different ways.

- **Cultural differences** – team members will be from different backgrounds and cultural differences may make working together more difficult.

- **Morale** – some team members may find this way of working isolating.

Test your understanding 4

Identify the ways in which the challenges faced by virtual teams can be overcome.

Test your understanding 5

IT has enabled employees to work at home, rather than being based in an office. This is known as **'teleworking'.** Discuss the advantages and disadvantages to an organisation of teleworking.

E-commerce

E-commerce refers to conducting business electronically via some form of communication link.

The effects of e-commerce on the organisation
- Access to a much larger market.
- Reduced costs, e.g. less staff, fewer buildings, lower transaction costs.

- Elimination of intermediary organisations, e.g. Dell use the internet to sell their computers directly to customers.

- Reduced use of cash – reliance on debit and credit card transactions.

- Individualised marketing – information can be collected about individual customers which will allow marketing to take place at an individual customer level.

Investment in data collection and retrieval systems will be required.

5 Emerging IS Trends in Organisations

This section explores emerging IS trends in organisations including:

- enterprise-wide systems such as area networks and databases,
- knowledge management systems,
- customer relationship management systems such as e-business and Web 2.0 tools.

5.1 Enterprise-wide systems

In early computer systems many organisations consolidated their information systems into one centralised data processing system. However, as companies become more diverse and distributed across large geographical areas, it was recognised that information systems were required that could meet the specific processing requirements of these distributed locations, but still retain communication to a central computer facility. This is known as distributed data processing (DDP), where the individual processing centres are linked to a centralised computer but have individual processing capabilities at each location. The use of DDP in the modern business environment is increasing and, as a result, large volumes of data transmission over wide area networks (WANs) are increasingly common.

An enterprise-wide system enables:

- communication between different geographical regions, e.g. between divisions located in different parts of the country or world
- the individual divisions to meet their specific processing requirements.

Examples include networks and databases:

Networks

A network is where a number of computers and other devices are linked in such a way that any one device can communicate with any other so enabling resource sharing between a number of users.

A local area network (LAN) links computers in a limited geographical area whereas a wide area network (WAN) links computers in different geographical locations and even in different organisations.

Where the WAN uses dedicated links it is called a physical network. Where a WAN uses a combination of links that are 'transparent' to the user, the network is called a virtual network.

Databases

A database is a collection of data structured completely independent of any one application. A database could be described as a collection of data files that are integrated to provide one single file system. The main aim of a database file structure is to provide one common dataset for a wide variety of users and their information needs.

A database management system (DBMS) is a set of integrated programs designed to organise and simplify the creation, management and access of data held within a database structure. A DBMS represents the way in which an organisation coordinates the complex activities carried out by its department into one data location. A DBMS should enhance the organisation's ability to provide reliable, relevant information to decision makers easily, efficiently and effectively.

When a database is connected to a web server by a database connectivity component, (e.g. Microsoft ADO and Open Database Connectivity) visitors from outside the organisation (such as potential customers) can make enquiries about product and price information, and make orders and view shopping cart items from a web browser.

To be successful, a database system must have the following properties:

*   Data independence – the data must be defined and exist independently of the programs that use it. The logical definition of data in the database is different from the physical organisation and storage on the disks – physical independence. The logical data in an application is viewed from the perspective of that application, this is, different from the logical definition of data in the database – logical independence. As the data and programs are independent of each other, either can be amended without changing the other.

- The database must be capable of being shared. Different users, using different application programs, must be able to access the same data, often at the same time.

- Duplication of data and data redundancy can be reduced as only one entry per record or transaction is needed in the database. Data inputs may also be reduced as data is only required to be input once to update all files.

- Integrity of the data in the database must be maintained. Controls need to be implemented to ensure that the data remains accurate at all times.

- The database should be flexible and able to develop or evolve with the organisation. The database needs to change and develop to meet the future needs of the company.

- The database should be able to connect to web server to support dynamic e-commerce transaction.

Test your understanding 6

Identify the advantages and disadvantages of databases.

Test your understanding 7

Your organisation is considering changing to a database system. List the issues it would need to consider.

5.2 Knowledge management systems

Knowledge management systems help the organisation to create, capture, distribute and share knowledge.

Knowledge resides in:

- **Human capital** - the knowledge, skills and experience possessed by employees.

- **Structural capital** - includes intellectual capital (e.g. patents) and client information (e.g. address lists and client records).

Task	Appropriate knowledge management system
Creating knowledge	Knowledge work systems help knowledge workers (who create knowledge and produce new products) to create and integrate new information into an organisation, e.g. CAD gives engineers precise control over industrial design and manufacturing.
Capturing knowledge	Expert systems hold specialist knowledge and allow non-experts to interrogate the system for information, advice and recommended decisions, e.g. used in medicine for diagnosis of symptoms.
Distributing knowledge	Office technology such as email, faxes and databases.
Sharing knowledge	• Email and databases • Groupware helps work groups to collaborate on projects, e.g. electronic calendars, to do lists, address books and journals. • Intranet (internal internet) • Extranet (intranet extended to customers and suppliers)

5.3 Customer relationship management (CRM) systems

Introduction

CRM systems help the organisation to get to know their customers and to use that knowledge to serve their customers better.

> **CRM systems**
>
> CRM systems can help to manage customer relations in an organised way. For example, a business may build a database about its customers that describes the relationships in sufficient detail so that management, salespeople, employees providing the services, and perhaps customers directly, could access information, match customer needs with product plans and offerings, remind customers of service requirements and know what products a customer has purchased.

Benefits of CRM systems

CRM software integrates the sales, marketing and customer service function making it easier for everyone in the company to share their vital information and work together.

Function	Benefits
Sales	• Elimination of missed opportunities by understanding buying habits. • Real time view of sales activity. • Improved liaison between onsite and offsite staff. • Quoting made easier.
Marketing	• Better identification of prospects. • Rapid access to customer information and reports for analysis.
Customer services	• More communication channels for customers. • Increased satisfaction due to faster response times and better awareness of customer needs. • More options to log, track and deal with queries.

CRM and e-commerce

E-commerce is commonly integrated with CRM leading to improvements in:

- **Marketing** – customer's web experience can be personalised with the most relevant information and products.

Illustration 5 - Amazon and CRM

A number of individualised targeted products will be recommended to customers logging into the Amazon website. These products will be related to previous purchases or searches made by the Amazon customer.

- **Selling** – provides a comprehensive range of selling services, e.g. quote and order management.
- **Service** – provides customers with an intuitive channel to log complaints or register products.
- **Analysis** – analysis can help the organisation to monitor the current online content and to track web behaviour. As a result, customers will be targeted more easily in the future.

CRM and Web 2.0 tools

- Web 2.0 tools, or social networking tools, are changing the way that people share their perspectives, opinions, thoughts and experiences.

- There are two key ways in which the tools can be used by businesses:
    - To listen to customers by monitoring content.
    - To influence customers by writing content.

Test your understanding 8

There are a number of Web 2.0 tools. Identify some of the more popular ones.

Listening to customers – organisations are starting to use CRM systems to harness the information contained in these social networking sites. Areas where customers or potential customers can discuss a product or service can be a powerful tool to a company when trying to understand its customers' needs.

Illustration 6 - Listening to customers

Let's consider how an individual customer or potential customer may use Web 2.0 tools and how these could result in vast amounts of useful information which the organisation can harness.

Podcasting
James is considering buying a new games console. He downloads a podcast (i.e. a video or audio review) about the Nintendo Wii console, from a website such as podcast.net.

Blog
James decides to comment on this podcast on his Blogger blog. This is an online diary which other people can read and write comments on.

Social bookmarking
James decides that he wants more people to see and remark on his blog post. He could submit it to a social bookmarking site such as Digg. This site will organise submissions by allocating 'tags' to them. People searching for say, 'games consoles', could then easily find and read James' submission.

As more people read and comment on the blog, James will be said to be social networking.

How will this benefit Nintendo?

This process will result in a vast amount of information being written in relation to the Nintendo Wii and games consoles that compete with this product. Nintendo can use this to enhance the understanding of their customers' needs.

Generation Y

Addressing the 2008 CIMA Lecturers' Conference, Dr. Melodie de Jager profiled what she believed to be new generation (generation Y) of potential students emerging in many Western countries.

Born between 1980 and 2001, the Y generation are:

- technology savvy (well used to ipods, facebook, blogs and YouTube) but have poor grammar and spelling due to over reliance of text, mms and sms.

- 95% of the generation own a computer and cell phone, and 76% own an instant messaging service: 34% use websites as the primary source of news, 28% author blogs, 44% read blogs and approximately one in two share and download with peers.

The implication of this is that a generation is emerging that is being actively shaped by current technology, possibly more than any other before it. This generation will not only be future customers of existing businesses but also form the workforce. Ignoring technology is not an option for any organisation.

Influencing customers by writing content - companies have started to use a number of Web 2.0 tools to target customers and to demonstrate to customers that they understand their needs

Illustration 7 - Influencing customers by writing content

Blogs

The website for Dove body products includes a number of celebrity blogs. These blogs include diet, fashion and lifestyle information. The writer of each blog and the contents of each blog has been carefully chosen to appeal to Dove's target audience and the blogs have enabled the organisation to serve their customers better.

> **Twitter**
>
> Some companies are using Twitter to post about company accomplishments and to distribute links that take people back to the corporate web page, press releases, and other promotional sites. For example, Starbucks posts new offers and also participates in threaded discussions to these offers with their Twitter followers.
>
> **Facebook**
>
> With over 200 million users worldwide, Facebook represents a huge opportunity for companies to acquire new customers. The company can set up a free Facebook page. This allows the company to interact with users and customers can be incited to join the network. The company can promote company blogs or their website by including extracts on Facebook. In addition to these free tools, the company can also pay for advertising. This advertising can be targeted towards specific customers, whose personal details are recorded when they register.

Cost & benefits analysis for expected costs & benefits

6 The Costs and Benefits of IS

6.1 Introduction

- Cost-benefit analysis (CBA) can be used to assess the expected costs and benefits of the IS.

- The benefits of the new IS should be greater than its cost. If this is the case, the new IS is worth implementing.

- A **post-implementation review** should be carried out to assess the final cost of development and maintenance and to assess whether the proposed benefits have been realised.

Test your understanding 9

Explain why if might be difficult to quantify the costs and benefits of a proposed system.

6.2 Costs

The assessment of costs needs to consider tangible and intangible costs.

Tangible costs	Example
Design and set-up costs	• systems design and development • hardware and software costs • systems testing • installation (new building, wiring, air conditioning) • training
Day-to-day running costs	• staff salaries • supplies (paper, disks, etc) • premises • heating/ power/ insurance • maintenance • finance • ongoing training
Storage costs	• hardware costs • retrieval costs • security costs
Staff disruption	• training will take staff away from their day-to-day work • implementation may lead to downtime
Dysfunctional behaviour	The new system may not achieve goal congruence at first due to resistance to change or initial problems with the system.
Learning curve	Slower operating and/ or an increase in errors until users become more familiar with the system.
Opportunity cost	Organisation foregoes opportunity to invest the money in another area.

6.3 Benefits

The benefits from the new IS must be evaluated. Benefits may be tangible or intangible.

> **Test your understanding 10**
>
> Identify the tangible and intangible benefits that may be achieved with the implementation of a new IS.

Methods of dealing with intangible benefits

Three ways to deal with intangible benefits

Ignore the benefits
– Easy but may result in a negative cash flow and hence a potentially incorrect decision not to invest

Quantify the benefits
– Attempt to include the benefits as part of the cash flow stream. Can be meaningless and misleading

Change in approach
– Use non-qualitative measures, e.g. questionnaires to rate customer satisfaction, increased market share to measure customer satisfaction

> **Cost-benefit analysis**
>
> A sales director is deciding whether to implement a new computer-based sales system. His department has only a few computers, and his sales people are not computer literate. He is aware that computerised sales forces are able to contact more customers and give a higher quality of service to those customers. They are more able to meet commitments, and can work more efficiently with production and delivery staff.
>
> His financial cost/benefit analysis is shown below:
>
> ### Costs
>
> New computer equipment:
>
> - 10 network-ready PCs with supporting software @ $2,000 each
> - 1 server @ $3,000
> - 3 printers @ $1,000 each
> - Cabling & Installation @ $4,000
> - Sales Support Software @ $10,000

Training costs:

- Computer introduction - 8 people @ $300 each
- Keyboard skills - 8 people @ $300 each
- Sales Support System - 12 people @ $500 each

Other costs:

- Lost time: 40 man days @ $150 / day
- Lost sales through disruption: estimate: $10,000
- Lost sales through inefficiency during first months: estimate: $10,000

Total cost: $76,800

Benefits

- Tripling of mail shot capacity: estimate: $30,000 / year
- Ability to sustain telesales campaigns: estimate: $15,000 / year
- Improved efficiency and reliability of follow-up: estimate: $30,000 / year
- Improved customer service and retention: estimate: $20,000 / year
- Improved accuracy of customer information: estimate: $5,000 / year
- More ability to manage sales effort: $20,000 / year

Total Bonofit: $120,000/yoar

Maintenance costs

The costs of maintenance may outstrip the costs of development many times and the quality of the systems development process has a direct impact on the cost of maintenance into the future. There are three types on maintenance:

Corrective maintenance - This relates to the need to correct technical difficulties that have arisen in the operation of the system. These include virus infection, hardware failure and file corruption as well as decaying response times due to systems overload.

Adaptive maintenance - This relates to the need to make changes to the system in order to reflect the changing needs of the organisation over time. Such changes are inevitable given the changing nature of the business environment. Major changes will eventually lead to the need to replace the system entirely.

Perfective maintenance - This relates to general upgrades to both hardware and software in order to maximise the overall speed and functionality of the system, e.g. installing the latest version of an application.

7 System Changeover Methods

7.1 Introduction

System changeover is the change from operating the current system (if there is one) and introducing the new system operationally.

This is a critical phase of system development and implementation because, until a new system 'goes live', there will always be doubts about whether it will work properly.

Difficulties when implementing a new system

- There is a risk that, if the new system does not work properly, the computer user will be unable to do any processing.
- With major new systems, there will inevitably be some initial difficulties and operational problems.
    - Staff might need some time to adapt to the new system.
    - Errors in the software might be discovered, requiring correction by writing a new version of the faulty program.
    - Management might also need to study the impact of the new system, on employees, customers or suppliers.

Illustration 8 - System testing

Before the system is changed over, it should be tested. Types of testing include:

- **Realistic testing** - can the system deal with a realistic example of the environment?
- **Contrived testing** - can the system deal with an unusual or incorrect amount?

- **Volume testing** - can the system handle a large number of transactions?
- **Acceptance testing** - are users satisfied with the new system?

7.2 System changeover methods

There are four approaches to system changeover, and the most appropriate approach will vary according to circumstances.

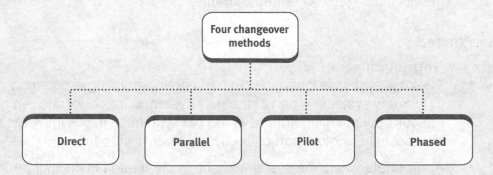

Direct

- The computer user ceases to operate the old system and switches completely to using the new system.

- Appropriate when:
    - The new system has been used elsewhere (for example, an off-the-shelf package) and there is confidence that it will function properly.
    - The problems for the computer user will be tolerable, even if the system fails to function properly.

Parallel

- The old system and the new system are both operated together for a while. If the new system performs to an acceptable level, a decision can be taken to stop operating the old system, and change entirely to the new system.

- Appropriate when:
    - The new system is critical to the business and problems can't be tolerated.
    - The new system has not been used elsewhere, thus implementation is high risk.

Pilot

- The new system is tested operationally within part of the organisation, e.g. a region or a department. The rest of the business continues to operate the old system until the pilot operation has been successfully tested and is operating efficiently. The new system will then be extended gradually (region by region or department by department) to the entire organisation.

- Appropriate when: the system can be operated in different geographical regions or departments.

Phased

- The new system is introduced in parts until everything is changed over to the new system. A part of the new system is introduced to replace the corresponding operations in the old system. If this is implemented successfully, another part of the new system is introduced.

- Appropriate when: the system can be implemented in distinct parts.

> **Illustration 9 - Phased changeover**
>
> If a company introduces a new accounting system by phased conversion, it might begin by introducing the new sales ledger system, followed by the new payables ledger system, followed by the new inventory system, and so on.

> **Test your understanding 11**
>
> Identify the advantages and disadvantages of each of the four changeover methods.

8 IS Implementation - avoiding user resistance and non-usage

8.1 Reasons for project failure

- Insufficient user involvement – the risk of project failure is increased if users are not involved in the implementation. New systems will bring about change, and users reject the system simply because they don't like the change, or the changes have resulted in loss of power. Insufficient user involvement is the major cause for failure.

- Lack of management support – little commitment to implementation or poor problem solving.

- Project is too complex for the organisation to manage.

- Poor planning and scheduling.

- Unrealistic deadlines being set.
- Poor monitoring and control.
- IT staff may have the technical skills but not the management skills required.

Test your understanding 12

Identify **three** reasons why user involvement is so important when implementing a new system.

The 3Cs

Three broad conditions are necessary to implement IT successfully – commitment, coordination and communication.

Commitment

- It is important to get all users that are involved or affected by a project to become committed. The resources of the users will be necessary in the planning, development, testing and implementation stages of any IS project. Gaining their dedication and joint ownership of the project ensures that they are equally responsible for its eventual success or failure.

- Commitment must exist from top management and across all management levels. Commitment from senior management is shown by the allocation of resources in terms of people, money, time, information and technology.

Coordination

- A disorganised project will take considerably longer to achieve success, and normally at a greater cost than an organised one will. This increases the likelihood that such a project will never be completed.

- A disorganised project will have constantly moving targets, which are seldom attained.

- Coordination through planning and control of all the relevant factors will help to ensure that the right people are doing the right things in the right way, using the right resources at the right time.

Communication

- Through good relationships and communication with all interested parties, obstacles within, among and between them can be avoided in the planning and implementation of an information system.

- All stakeholders need to be kept informed and be encouraged to become actively involved throughout the whole process.

- IS projects often suffer severe communication chain problems between the various people involved. The chain is only as strong as its weakest link.

The bigger picture of systems development

It should at this stage be recognised that implementation forms part of a fuller cycle of systems development involving:

- a feasibility study,
- systems analysis,
- systems design,
- implementation, and
- systems review and maintenance.

This can be viewed as a serial process, whereby each stage produces an output which in turn becomes the input for the next stage forming a systems development life cycle (SDLC). The SDLC is characterised by a number of key elements:

- The project is divided into a number of identifiable processes, made up of several activities. This aids project planning and control.

- Specific reports and documentation, known as deliverables, must be produced throughout the stages of the life cycle. These are used to control and monitor procedures.

- Users and managers participate throughout the project.

- The system must be thoroughly tested prior to implementation.

- Training plans are developed for those who will operate and manage the system.

- A post-implementation review is carried out to assess the effectiveness of the new system once in operation.

8.2 User resistance - theories

User resistance can be explained using the theories of **Markus** (1983) and **Davis and Olson** (1985). Resistance falls into one of three categories:

People-orientated theory

Change is resisted because individual users or a group of users do not wish to learn new programs or amend their working practices. This resistance is caused by factors internal to the individual or the group.

System-orientated theory

Resistance to a system is caused by poor usability and functionality, and users find it difficult to make the system work correctly. This resistance is system orientated because it relates to poor system design.

Interaction theory

The system itself is well designed and accepted by some users. However, other users do not accept the system because they fear it will take away some of their power or influence in the organisation. Resistance to the system in this case is caused by poor interaction between people and the system.

8.3 Overcoming user resistance

> **Test your understanding 13**
>
> Explain the strategies that an organisation could put in place to reduce these three types of user resistance.

Kotter and Schlesinger identified six main methods of dealing with resistance:

- Education and communication
- Participation
- Facilitation and support
- Negotiation
- Manipulation and co-optation
- Power/ coercion

Kotter and Schlesinger

Method	Advantages	Disadvantages
Education and communication	• Communication about the benefits of change should result in employees accepting the change.	• Time consuming. • Employees may not agree with benefits. • Usually used to reinforce another approach.
Participation	• Employees are more likely to support the change as they 'own' the change. • Utilises employee expertise.	• Time consuming. • Requires a strong relationship between management and the workforce.
Facilitation and support	• Techniques, such as counselling, will help employees overcome their fears and anxieties about change.	• Can't always address the reason for resistance, e.g. change may threaten job security.
Negotiation	• Conflict dealt with in an orderly fashion, preventing problems such as industrial action. • Since employees agree on the outcome it should encourage commitment and preserve morale.	• Time consuming. • Not always possible to reach a compromise.

Manipulation and co-optation (involves presentation of misleading information or buying off key individuals by giving them positions of authority).	• Quick. • Relatively inexpensive.	• May lead to future problems if individuals realise that they have been manipulated.
Power/ coercion (compulsory approach by management to implement the change).	• Speed. • Managers can implement required changes.	• Poor commitment. • Results in weak motivation. • When employees enjoy a stronger position in the future, e.g. union representation, they are less likely to co-operate.

8.4 Force field analysis (Lewin)

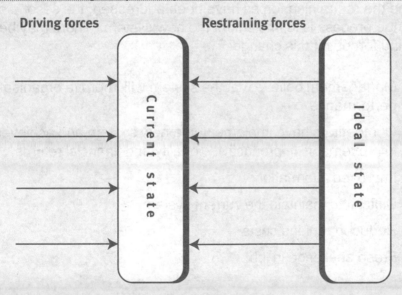

Introduction to force field analysis

Lewin developed a technique for visualising the change process called force field analysis.

Force field analysis maps out the driving forces that are pushing towards a preferred state (i.e. the implementation of the new system) and the restraining forces, which are pushing back to the current state (i.e. continuing to use the old system).

Restraining forces

The first step of any successful change process is to identify the restraining forces and overcome them:

Potential restraining force	Potential method for removing restraining force
Fear of loss of control	Education, participation
Fear that there will not be enough time for training or to attend meetings or that the new system will be too difficult to use	Give employees the time required for training/ meetings and to learn the skills required
Doubt that the initiative will be properly implemented	Participation in the change process, education about benefits
Anxiety about job security	Reassure employees about job security
Employees don't feel the change is needed	Education regarding the benefits of change

Driving forces

Once the restraining forces have been addressed, the second step of the change process is to implement the new system. There may be a number of driving forces for this change:

- Management believe that the system will improve organisational performance.

- Competitors have implemented a new system and achieved significant improvements in productivity, quality and financial returns.

- Improved information.

- Difficult to maintain the current system.

- Reduced running costs.

- Fresh challenge in job.

These forces may be enough to drive the positive change. However, action can be taken to increase the strength of the driving forces, e.g. by providing exact figures regarding the increase in financial returns that could be enjoyed, and to introduce further driving forces, e.g. small rewards may be offered to staff who participate in the implementation of the new system.

Once the new system has been implemented the final step of the change process is to reinforce the new behaviour. This may involve praising and rewarding those employees who embrace the new system.

9 Outsourcing

9.1 Introduction

IT outsourcing involves purchasing from outside the organisation the IS services required to perform business functions.

> ### Illustration 10
>
> In 2008 Shell agreed a $4 billion IT outsourcing deal with three companies; AT&T, EDS and T-systems. In a bid to minimise redundancies for its 3,000 IT staff, Shell negotiated that almost 99% of their staff would be transferred to the three companies.

9.2 Approaches to outsourcing

Total sourcing

- Organisation chooses to outsource more than 70% of its IT capability to a single supplier.

- Includes all aspects of IT, e.g. systems development, maintenance, operations, training.

- Usually involves a long term contract (3-5 years) with a supplier.

- Usually involves transfer by the organisation of most of its IT/ IS staff to the outsourcing company used.

Multiple/ selective sourcing

- Organisation negotiates with a range of suppliers for its services.

- Different suppliers serving the same client may form alliances with each other as well as competing for client business.

- Organisation will usually retain its main IT/ IS staff.

Joint venture/ strategic alliance sourcing

- The organisation enters into a joint venture with a supplier, e.g. to develop new software which is seen as having widespread applications across other organisations.

- The risks and rewards are shared between the organisations and the supplier.

Insourcing

- The organisation retains a large IT department.

- It buys in resources only to accommodate peaks in workload.

- IT contractors are hired for anything between three months and one year.

9.3 Advantages and disadvantages of outsourcing

Test your understanding 14

Many organisations are taking the decision to outsource their non-core activities, such as IT. Identify the advantages and disadvantages of IT outsourcing.

Illustration 11 - Risks of outsourcing

Suppose that a regional hospital authority agrees a contract with a software company. The software company agrees to develop a new system that the hospital will use for maintaining patient records, communicating with patients at home, scheduling operations and charging the patients for services that are not free. After the system has been implemented, the software company will operate the system itself for a contract period of five years, and the hospital staff will only be involved with the system to the extent of providing the software company with the data for input.

The risks of the outsourcing agreement for the development and operation of this system include:

- The system might be imperfectly specified when system development work begins. If the hospital authority subsequently changes the specification, the software house might be able to increase its fee substantially.

- Since the software company will operate the system, it could be difficult for the staff of the hospital authority to test it.

- The software company will wish to make a profit from the contract, and will be reluctant to agree to changes, and might even argue against maintenance, unless it is paid extra.

- Once the system becomes operational, the hospital authority might have very little control over the communications between the software company's staff and the general public (the patients or 'customers').

- If the system creates bad publicity, due to errors in the system relating to scheduling of operations or invoicing, the hospital authority will have no control over the damage to its reputation.

- What happens at the end of five years? Will the hospital authority be forced to renew the contract with the software house because no one else understands the system? Alternatively, will the authority be obliged to abandon the system and buy a new system to replace it?

9.4 Managing the relationship

Nurturing the 'marriage' between the client and the supplier is essential if the outsourcing arrangement is to be successful.

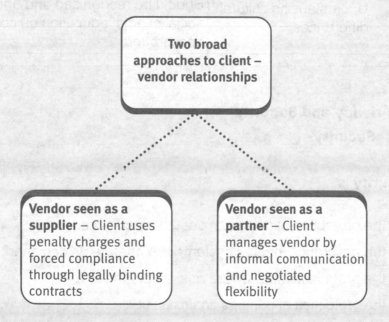

Whilst each organisation may wish to pursue a successful marriage, problems arise when the outsourcing company fails to realise the expectations of the client, e.g. the vendor imposes additional fees for work that were not in the original contract.

A **service level agreement** (SLA), setting out the terms and conditions of the outsourcing arrangement, should be drawn up between the client and the supplier.

Developing successful relationships	
Development point	**Explanation**
• Nurture relationship between key management and personnel	There should be a good understanding and strong working relationship between key personnel of both teams.
• Quantifiable objectives	Allows the client to monitor performance and the vendor will know where they stand.
• Incentives and penalties	Vendor receives incentives for exceeding criteria and penalties when they fall short.
• Periodic review	Regular meetings should ensure that client requirements are understood and that any issues are addressed.
• Training for vendor personnel	Employees of the outsourcing company should be trained so that they can fulfil the specific needs of the client.
• Understanding cultural differences	Should be recognised and bridged, e.g. social events, education on company background.

10 Privacy and Security

10.1 Security

Security is:

- the protection of data from unauthorised access;
- the assurance that the systems can operate as designed;
- the protection of hardware against damage;
- the protection of humans against injury.

Risks to computer systems

Potential threat	Solution
Physical damage - due to fire, flood and physical conditions such as heat or dust.	• Fire procedures - fire alarms, extinguishers, fire doors, staff training and insurance cover. • Location, e.g. not in a basement area liable to flooding. • Physical environment - e.g. air conditioning, dust controls. • Back up procedures - data should be backed up on a regular basis.
Human interference - damage caused by unauthorised access, theft and vandalism.	• Entry systems - secure access to computer room via PIN code or key. • Close circuit television (CCTV). • Security guards. • Hardware alarmed.
Data corruption - e.g. viruses, hackers.	• Virus software - should be run and updated regularly to prevent corruption of the system by viruses. • Firewall software - should provide protection against unauthorised access to the system from the internet. • Passwords and user names - limit unauthorised access to the system. • Back up procedures (as above)
Data theft - e.g. fraud, industrial espionage, loss of confidentiality.	• Data encryption - allows only those individuals with the encryption key, to view data in an understandable form. • Passwords and user names (as above).
Operational problems - such as bugs and user errors.	• Testing - should minimise the risk of software errors (bugs). • Training - adequate staff training and operating procedures.

Human resource risk - e.g. repetitive strain injury (RSI), headaches and eye strain from computer screens, tripping over loose wires.	• Ergonomic design of workstations should reduce problems such as RSI. • Anti-glare screens reduce eye strain. • Cables should be in ducts.

Illustration 12 - Passwords

A user in the Human Resources (HR) department, where there is a requirement to protect data because of its sensitivity, may require passwords to be entered at the following points:

- To boot up the system.
- To gain access to the network.
- To gain access to a particular file.
- To re-enter the system after a period of inactivity.

Viruses and hackers

Hacking

Hacking is the deliberate accessing of on-line systems by unauthorised persons.

Management often requires that the contents of certain files (e.g. payroll) remain confidential and are only available to authorised staff. This may be achieved by keeping tapes or removable disks containing the files in a locked cabinet and issuing them only for authorised use.

The introduction and growth in the use of on-line systems has meant that alternative precautions need to be taken. Security at the terminal should be adequate; the terminal can be locked and/or kept in a locked room. Access and use should be properly recorded and controlled.

As organisations have grown to depend more and more on systems and the data stored on them, individuals and other organisations have become increasingly interested in gaining access to those systems and the data.

Since the 1980s, a class of highly intelligent individuals has emerged. These people use their knowledge of systems to gain unauthorised access to systems for their own purposes. The perpetrators, hackers, often consider hacking to be fun, and it is not necessarily done with malicious intent.

As modems and PCs have become more widespread, the threat of hacking has increased. Due to changing working practices, many systems now have dial-up facilities; this facilitates entry into the system by the hacker after the telephone number has been obtained or by means of an auto dialler. To exacerbate the situation, hackers, having obtained numbers, make these available over the Internet.

Viruses

A further security and control issue, which has been highlighted in recent years, is the growth of computer viruses. A computer virus is a small program that, having been introduced into the system, proliferates; its purpose is to spread extensively, impairing both data and software. As the name suggests, they have the ability to infect a whole computer system. The infected programs may then act as carriers for the computer virus, with the end result that the infection process can have a spiralling effect. The potential for the damage a virus can cause is restricted only by the creativity of the originator. Given the mobility between computerised systems and the sharing of resources and data, the threat posed by a viral attack is considerable.

Viruses can be categorised as:

- trojans – whilst carrying on one program, secretly carry on another

- worms – these replicate themselves within the systems

- trap doors – undocumented entry points to systems allowing normal controls to be bypassed

- logic bombs - triggered on the occurrence of a certain event

- time bombs - which are triggered on a certain date.

Once a virus has been introduced into the system, the only course of action may be to regenerate it from back up. However, some viruses are written so that they lie dormant for a period, which means that the back ups become infected before the existence of the virus has been detected; in these instances restoration of the system becomes impossible.

Test your understanding 15

(a) Identify the sources of viruses within an organisation.

(b) Explain the rules that should be created and then followed to ensure that back up is successfully maintained.

10.2 Privacy

 Privacy is the right of an individual to control the dissemination or use of data that relates to him or her.

Legislation relating to privacy varies considerably from country to country. Within this section we use the example of UK law to illustrate typical principles.

The UK Data Protection Act (DPA) 1998

- Personal information can be misused much more effectively on a computer than on manual systems.

- The DPA gives individuals the right to know what information is held about them (provisions of the Act) and provides a framework to ensure that information is handled properly (principles of the Act).

- Failure by data users to comply with the DPA can result in seizure of data and unlimited fines.

Principles and Provisions of the UK DP Act

The **principles of the Act** make sure that information is:

- Fairly and lawfully processed. For example, data should be collected directly from the individual and they should give their consent for it to be processed.

- Processed for limited purposes. For example, the organisation cannot collect the data for one purpose, such as providing an internet service to a private customer, and then use the data for another purpose, such as marketing other services - unless the organisation has specified those purposes.

- Adequate, relevant and not excessive.

- Accurate and up-to-date. For example, one way the organisation can do this, is to write to individuals periodically asking them to verify the information and to notify the organisation of any changes.

- Not kept for longer than is necessary. For example, when an employee leaves an organisation, the organisation should destroy all records relating to past appraisals of the employee.

- Processed in line with the individual's rights.
- Secure.
- Not transferred to other countries without adequate protection.

The **provisions of the Act**:

- Give individuals the right to ask whether an organisation is holding information about them and is also entitled to receive this information, in a form that can be understood.
- The organisation may charge a nominal fee for providing this information, but is required to reply within a certain time.

Illustration 13 - Criticisms of the UK DPA

Ian Huntley murdered schoolgirls Holly Wells and Jessica Chapman in August 2002. In response to questions that followed his conviction in December 2003, Humberside Police blamed the UK's Data Protection Act for failures in recording and managing information that led to Huntley being appointed as school caretaker, despite there being nine prior allegations against him. Its criticism was that the Act required forces to delete information about suspects that had not led to a conviction.

An inquiry concluded that the DPA was not the problem behind the deletion of Ian Huntley's records but suggested that better guidance was needed on the collection, retention, deletion, use and sharing of information, so that police officers, social workers and other professionals can feel more confident in using information properly.

Privacy and electronic communications regulations

Here we consider an example of UK law derived from EC directives.

The Privacy and Electronic Communications (EC directives) Regulations 2003 is designed to protect consumers and businesses from unsolicited electronic communication, usually known as 'spam'. Marketing via e-mail and SMS (text message) is now permitted only if recipients have given prior consent or 'opted-in' to receive information via these channels. This puts the onus on the sender of the mail.

The regulations state that explicit permission must be obtained from a consumer before contacting them via email or text message for the first time.

The legislation does allow businesses to contact <u>existing customers</u> who have already given their email address or mobile number and also those consumers who have enquired about a product or service via email or SMS. By showing an interest they are deemed to have given permission to be contacted again in the future.

Any form of electronic communication sent to an individual must always contain a clearly stated unsubscribe option which is free for the recipient of the email / SMS. Businesses will be evading the law if they continue to communicate with a consumer once they have opted-out from communications. Breaking the law can result in fines of up to £5,000.

A cookie is a text file or piece of software placed on the user's hard drive by a website that the user has visited. It records details about the user (such as the user's contact details or preferences) so that the user can be recognised on future visits. It is often used by e-commerce sites as a means of memorising items placed on a shopping cart.

The regulations introduce certain limitations on the use of cookies on websites requiring basic information about them e.g. what they store and the consequences of not accepting them, as well as the opportunity to reject them.

Finally, the regulations forbid the use of electronic mail for direct marketing purposes where the identity or address of the sender is concealed or disguised or where a valid reply address has not been provided.

The impact of the regulations is limited because most spam originates from outside the EU, where there are either no laws or the laws are less stringent.

11 Chapter summary

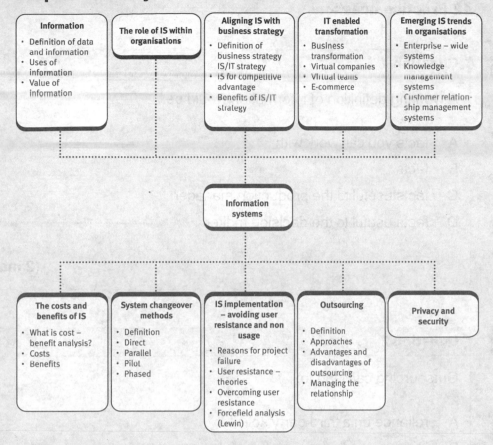

Information
- Definition of data and information
- Uses of information
- Value of information

The role of IS within organisations

Aligning IS with business strategy
- Definition of business strategy IS/IT strategy
- IS for competitive advantage
- Benefits of IS/IT strategy

IT enabled transformation
- Business transformation
- Virtual companies
- Virtual teams
- E-commerce

Emerging IS trends in organisations
- Enterprise – wide systems
- Knowledge management systems
- Customer relation-ship management systems

Information systems

The costs and benefits of IS
- What is cost – benefit analysis?
- Costs
- Benefits

System changeover methods
- Definition
- Direct
- Parallel
- Pilot
- Phased

IS implementation – avoiding user resistance and non usage
- Reasons for project failure
- User resistance – theories
- Overcoming user resistance
- Forcefield analysis (Lewin)

Outsourcing
- Definition
- Approaches
- Advantages and disadvantages of outsourcing
- Managing the relationship

Privacy and security

12 Practice questions

Question 1

A working definition of information would be:

A   facts you can work with

B   facts

C   facts useful to the production manager

D   facts useful to the decision maker

(2 marks)

Question 2

Outsourcing can lead to:

A   reliance on a third party solicitor.

B   increased reliance on internal departments.

C   increasing staff numbers.

D   retaining managers to monitor the contract.

(2 marks)

Question 3

Which of the following is not an approach to changeover?

A   Pivotal running

B   Phased changeover

C   Direct conversion

D   Parallel running

(2 marks)

Question 4

Which of the following is not one of Porter's generic strategies?

A   Cost minimisation

B   Differentiation

C   Cost leadership

D   Focus

(2 marks)

Question 5

Blogs, podcasts and social bookmarking are all examples of:

A   enterprise-wide systems.

B   web 2.0 tools.

C   internet enablers.

D   knowledge management systems.

(2 marks)

Question 6

Which of the following is not an approach to outsourcing?

A   Single sourcing

B   Selective sourcing

C   Total sourcing

D   Insourcing

(2 marks)

Question 7

Explain how FOUR different developments in information technology could assist an organisation with a conventional structure to become a virtual organisation.

(4 marks)

Question 8

Identify FOUR tangible costs and FOUR intangible costs of a new information system.

(4marks)

Question 9

Explain FOUR of the methods recommended by Kotter and Schlesinger for overcoming resistance to a new information system.

(4 marks)

Question 10

Discuss FOUR opportunities that Web 2.0 tools can offer to firms.

(4 marks)

Question 11

A manufacturing company has decided to replace its inventory control system. The current system was implemented 10 years ago but has restricted reporting facilities and a text-based interface. It is to be replaced with a Windows-based package which undertakes the same basic functions, but is easier to use, has flexible reporting facilities and interfaces easily with other Windows-based software. Both systems run on the same hardware.

The manager of the project is now considering the details of implementation. He has been advised that he should consider both 'parallel running' and 'direct changeover/direct conversion'.

Required:

(a) Briefly explain what the terms 'parallel running' and 'direct changeover' mean.

(5 marks)

(b) Briefly describe THREE advantages of 'direct changeover' over 'parallel running'.

(6 marks)

(c) Identify the main risk of direct changeover and suggest how this risk might be reduced for the manufacturing company's inventory control system implementation.

(4 marks)

(Total: 15 marks)

Question 12

The directors of DS are not satisfied with the GDC facilities management company, which was contracted two years ago to run the IT systems of the company. At that time, the existing in-house IT development and support department was disbanded and all control of IT systems handed over to GDC. The appointment of GDC was relatively rushed and, although an outline contract was agreed, no detailed service level agreement was produced.

Over the last few weeks, the number of complaints received from staff regarding the service has been increasing and the provision of essential management reports has not been particularly timely.

A recent exchange of correspondence with GDC failed to resolve the matter. Staff at GDC recognised the fall in standards of service, but insisted that it had met its contractual obligations. DS's lawyers have confirmed that GDC is correct.

Key features of DS's contract with GDC facilities management company:

- The contract can be terminated by either party with three months' notice.

- GDC will provide IT services for DS, the service to include:
  – Purchase of all hardware and software
  – Repair and maintenance of all IT equipment
  – Help desk and other support services for users
  – Writing and maintenance of in-house software
  – Provision of management information
  – Price charged to be renegotiated each year but any increase must not exceed inflation, plus 10%

Required:

(a) Explain, from the point of view of DS, why it might have received poor service from GDC, even though GDC has met the requirements of the contract.

(10 marks)

(b) Explain the courses of action now available to DS relating to the provision of IT services. Comment on the problems involved in each course of action.

(6 marks)

(Total: 16 marks)

Question 13

FP is a local authority that provides a range of public services to its residents. These include school and hospital management, rubbish collection and road maintenance. FP has a large administration centre which supports all of these services from tax collection to payroll services. Although salary levels are lower than the national average, the conditions are generally thought to be good with opportunities for flexible working and child support facilities. Many of the staff have been in service with FP for over 20 years and enjoy the social and expert interaction.

In a recent national local authority comparison FP received one of the poorest evaluations in the country with high costs and low efficiency of service cited as the main problems. FP currently has very low levels of computerisation with only some of its main services being fully computerised, and even these are not compatible and there is little integration of technology as much has been purchased on a piecemeal basis.

A new Head of the Authority has been recruited from a rival authority that scored well in the report. She has decided that it is time for things to change and that staff must 'welcome technology as the way forward'. Staff argue that the IT systems have never been able to meet their requirements and there has been criticism of the non-Windows interfaces and lack of reliability; this has resulted in many staff simply reverting to manual methods to get the job done. As a direct result very few staff have adequate and up-to-date IT skills as training has been a low priority.

The Head of the Authority has agreed the go-ahead of a huge integrated IT project which will take some years to fully implement. It is expected that, as a direct result, customer service will be improved along with the ranking of the authority nationally. In addition it is expected that the new IS will result in a number of job redundancies and flatter departmental structures. Before the project is to commence, an investigation into possible staff resistance has been commissioned. As the IT Manager you have been asked to prepare a paper that covers the following:

Required:

Explain the three types of resistance theory and their application to the current situation at FP. **(6 marks)**

Question 14

The Gort Organisation supplies industrial sewing machines to a variety of clients. Sales of machines and spare parts are made by sales representatives visiting each owner of a Gort machine, checking that machine for maintenance requirements and then ordering the parts upon their return to the office. Requirements for new machines are also discussed during the maintenance visit. While customers are generally happy with the service provided, there can be significant time delays in ordering parts for machines because sales representatives may not return to their office for several days. This delay has resulted in some loss of customer goodwill.

The Board of Gort has recognised the need to develop a new information system to support sales representatives. The new system will allow remote access to the Gort Ordering System via mobile computers, and also provide order status and expected delivery dates for customers who will be able to access the Ordering System via an Extranet connection.

The Gort Organisation has never maintained a large IT department and the Board are seriously considering outsourcing the development of this new system.

Required:

Discuss the benefits and drawbacks of outsourcing the new information system in the Gort Organisation.

(10 marks)

Test your understanding answers

Test your understanding 1

There are a number of ways in which a car manufacturer could use IT to directly reduce its unit costs, including the following:

- Automating the logistics and production activities of the organisation by means of
  - Computerised stock control for raw materials and components, with systems integrated to those of suppliers, to remove administration cost.
  - Computer-aided manufacturing in the production process. to reduce the labour content of the product.
  - Computerised stock control of finished vehicles, to allow staff to locate cars more quickly thus reducing staff time.

- Computer-aided design, to reduce the number of labour hours involved in the production and amendment of technical drawings and improve the productivity of design.

Test your understanding 2

A number of changes in the structure of business organisations arise from IT developments.

- **Greater decentralisation**: Information is power, and as information is spread more widely through the organisation via personal computers the scope of autonomous decision making at local level increases.
- **Increased choice of headquarters location:** Organisations are less tied to the major business centres if much of the workforce is likely to operate from dispersed locations.
- **Greater variety of employment relations**: These developments contribute to the trend by which employees' ties to one particular organisation are loosened. For individuals, communication links enable access to many different 'employing' organisations; for employers, it is no longer necessary to think of a workforce of a certain irreducible size permanently on the payroll.
- **Changes in access to customers**: An often quoted example is the closure (or reduced staffing) of bank branches following the introduction of automated teller machines (ATMs). Shopping by television is also well established.

Test your understanding 3

- **Can exploit opportunities** – a business may not have the time or resources to develop the manufacturing and distribution infrastructure, people competencies and information technology required to exploit new opportunities. Only by forming a virtual company, of all-star partners, can it assemble the components it needs to provide a world-class solution for customers and capture the market opportunity.

- **Look bigger than they are** – virtual companies can be made to look much bigger than they actually are, enabling them to compete with large and successful organisations and to win large and lucrative contracts.

- **Flexibility** – teams of experts can be formed to meet the specific needs of a project. This team can then be dissolved and a new team formed for the next project. The performance of each project team should be much better than those of non-virtual competitors.

- **Lower costs** – one of the main aims of virtual companies is to reduce costs. Investment is assets, e.g. land and buildings, is minimal. This should help to drive competitive advantage.

Test your understanding 4

The challenges faced by virtual teams can be overcome by:

- training in technology and teamwork;

- spending time getting to know each other, e.g. team identity, jokes;

- clear roles and responsibilities;

- detailed and timely feedback between the leader and team members;

- regular and predictable communication matters;

- paying attention to cultural differences;

- choosing dependable and self-reliant people.

Test your understanding 5

Advantages

- Increased employee motivation and productivity
- Increased commitment to the organisation
- Attracting individuals because of the availability of such conditions
- Reduced absenteeism and staff turnover

Disadvantages

- Difficulties in co-ordinating staff
- Loss of control of staff
- Dilution of organisational culture
- Less commitment to the organisation
- Extra labour costs, e.g. providing employees with equipment

Test your understanding 6

Advantages

- Reduced duplication of data in different files.
- Ensures data integrity.
- Wide access to data.
- Improved security and control over data.

Disadvantages

- Systems used in different departments may be incompatible.
- Data will need to be analysed and 'cleansed' before it can be integrated into the database.
- Staff training required.
- Differences between departments may make it difficult to deliver data in all the formats required.
- Ongoing maintenance required.
- Effective back-up essential since data is only held in one location.

Test your understanding 7

- Specialist staff required (in implementing and running the new system, such as a database manager and administrators).

- Set-up costs of new software and possibly new hardware.

- Training costs.

- Security features.

- Possible disruption.

- Responsibilities.

- Contingency and back-up facilities.

Test your understanding 8

Some popular Web 2.0 tools include:

- MySpace
- YouTube
- Blogger
- Facebook
- Twitter
- Digg

Test your understanding 9

Many organisations will want to implement an IS that will help them to gain competitive advantage and will not have a pre-existing IS upon which they can be based or compared.

The costs and benefits (current and future) from these systems will therefore be difficult to quantify precisely in financial terms.

The best cost estimates will tend to be obtained from systems bought from an outside vendor. They will be able to provide cost quotations and quantify the benefits that have been enjoyed by other users of the system.

Test your understanding 10

Tangible benefits

- Improved speed and efficiency.

- Reduced labour time, and therefore lower cost, to carry out an operation.

- Cheaper labour due to lower skill required to carry out a task.

- Inventory – optimum amount of inventory held which reduces obsolescence, lost sales due to stock outs and holding costs.

- Reduction in the number of errors.

- Ability to collect cash more quickly.

Intangible benefits

- Competitive advantage – achieved through product differentiation or improved cost control, e.g. through the use of on-line ordering.

- Improved customer satisfaction due to better service, improved quality or a reduction in delays.

- Better information and decision making.

- Common systems may lead to common standards and consistency.

- Better quality of information, e.g. accuracy, flexibility, robustness, portability, compatibility and maintainability.

	Advantages	**Disadvantages**
Direct	• Quickest and cheapest changeover method.	• High risk - if new system does not function properly, the computer user will have no system at all.
Parallel	• Low risk. • Old and new systems can be compared to verify the output of the new system.	• Cost - additional resources required to operate two systems. • Slower than direct changeover. • Users may feel comfortable with old system and still rely on it.
Pilot	• Less risky than direct changeover since can check new system functions properly and deal with any problems before full implementation. • Less costly than parallel changeover.	• Slow. • Riskier than parallel changeover.
Phased	• Gives staff time to adjust to one part of system before introducing the next. • If new system results in job losses, there will be more time to deal with staff retraining or to prepare them for work elsewhere. • Less risky than direct changeover.	• Slow. • Links between parts of the system may make this difficult.

Test your understanding 12

User involvement:

- Ensures system meets requirements.
- Reduces resistance.
- Incorporates knowledge and expertise into the system.

Test your understanding 13

Strategies for overcoming people-orientated resistance

- Participation – getting users involved in the change process should help them to understand the reasons for the change and buy-in to the change.
- Training and education – to show the benefits of the new system and to help employees to feel comfortable with the change.
- Interviewing users – helps to identify the reasons for not using the system and to then find methods for overcoming those reasons.
- Coercion – by issuing memos or other communications requiring the system to be implemented.
- Threat of dismissal.

Strategies for overcoming system-orientated resistance

- Modify package – to take account of user concerns. May be difficult or expensive.
- Additional user training – to explain the package in more detail.
- Participation – increased user participation in future releases of the package.

Strategies for overcoming interaction resistance.

- Incentives – users are incentivised to use the new system.
- Participation – getting users involved will encourage acceptance and help to demonstrate the benefits of the new system.

Test your understanding 14

Advantages

- Cost reduction: e.g. due to economies of scale since equipment is bought in bulk.

- Improved performance: management can concentrate on core competencies and suppliers used will be IT experts.

- Avoids problem of shortage of IT experts.

- Organisation can keep up with technological change.

- Cost control: creating a formal relationship tends to concentrate the focus on cost control which is sometimes lost when functions are performed internally.

- Flexibility to increase or decrease IT capacity.

- Time to market: outsourcing can accelerate the development and implementation of new IS.

Disadvantages

- Dependent on supplier.

- Loss of confidentiality (outsourcing company may work for competitors).

- Locked into contract.

- Lose expertise.

- Loss of competitive advantage since the outsourcing company may work for competitors.

Test your understanding 15

(a) The following sources of viruses exist:

- External storage media – e.g. disks and memory sticks – probably the biggest source of a virus as they are passed quickly between users and computers.

- Downloading data from the internet – some websites are set up by hackers specifically to infect data with a virus, and anyone visiting this site and downloading data from it will also have a virus attached.

- E-mail – it is possible to transfer a virus by e-mail when there is a document attached. Again the ease of transfer increases the potential risk and damage that the virus can cause.

(Note: The sources of viruses need to be clearly identified by the organisation to ensure that the infection from a virus is reduced. The organisation can never be 100% secure from viruses unless they are prepared to have complete isolation, i.e. no interaction with another computer, which is impossible to achieve with any information system).

(b) Rules for back up include:

- Locate the back-up disk away from the computer – this is because, if the computer is stolen, the disks are also likely to be taken.

- Fireproof safe – if the organisation suffers a fire the back-up will be kept secure.

- Off site – it may even be a good idea to keep at least one set of the data in a completely different location, again to reduce the damage caused by fire and other natural disasters.

- Personnel procedures – a designated member of staff should make the back-ups on a daily basis. This member of staff would probably be high level as it is quite a big responsibility.

Question 1

D

Question 2

D

Question 7

The following developments in IT have made it easier to become a virtual organisation:

- Advanced telephone systems allow features such as call diversion, caller identification and conference calling. This means that individuals can change how they answer the telephone (referring to an organisation or project) and can also participate in 'meetings' without being in the same location.

- Websites allow even very small organisations to appear much larger than they actually are. Customers might visit a website that creates the image of a 'real' organisation, while actually belonging to a virtual one.

- Developments in e-mail mean that individuals can collaborate more easily. Detailed documents and communications can be exchanged almost instantly, so a virtual organisation is no longer at a disadvantage in terms of response times.

- Personal computer (PC) and workstation equipment is so cheap, and takes up so little space, that the individuals within a virtual organisation can each work from home. This reduces premises costs and allows the virtual organisation to be more price-competitive.

- The use of Intranets allows the individuals within a virtual organisation to access and share large volumes of data. There is no requirement to be in the same location as the database, as communication can be via the Internet of a virtual private network (VPN).

- Using the 'desktop publishing' capabilities of modern PC software, a virtual organisation can have many different corporate images or trading styles. These can be generated at relatively low cost, without the need for commercial printing. This allows a group of individuals or small organisations to operate as a large number of apparently different virtual organisations while maintaining a professional appearance.

(**Note:** Only four examples are required. Marks will be awarded for other relevant examples).

Question 8

Tangible costs	Intangible costs
Hardware and software costs	Downtime during implementation
Maintenance costs	Slower operating until users become more familiar with the new system
Training - initial and ongoing	Opportunity cost - money can't be invested elsewhere
Staff salaries	Training will take staff away from their normal work

Question 9

- **Education and communication** – communication about the benefits of the change should result in employees accepting the change.

- **Participation** – employees are more likely to support the change since they have bought into the process and own the change.

- **Negotiation** – conflict is dealt with in an orderly fashion preventing problems such as industrial action. Employees will agree with the outcome which will increase commitment and preserve morale.

- **Power/ coercion** – this is a compulsory approach to implementing the change. This approach may be required if rapid implementation of the change is necessary.

(**Note:** facilitation and support or manipulation and co-optation could also be mentioned).

Question 10

Advertising - for example, Starbucks is tweeting to customers and you can join their Facebook site to find out about its news and promotions.

Brand development - for example, Volkswagen uses Flickr to develop its brand. Individuals are able to post pictures of their Volkswagen Beetle or of their camp-a-van on the site.

To listen to customers - sites where customers and potential customers discuss the products of the company and of its competitors can be vital, e.g. customer ratings on Amazon.com.

Communication - for example, Deloitte Australia have held employee performance reviews in World of Warcraft and BDO uses Second Life as an avenue for meetings, presentations and events for staff and for clients.

Question 11

(a) Parallel running and direct changeover are both methods of systems implementation

With a parallel running approach, the old and the new systems are run together and the results and outputs are compared until the user has sufficient confidence in the new system to switch to it permanently and stop using the old system. Transactions are run through both systems and the outputs of one system are checked against the outputs of the other to check the accuracy and usability of the proposed new system.

With a direct changeover approach the old system is removed on a specific date and operations switched immediately and in full to the new system. There is no period where the systems are operationally used together. The verification of the new system takes place during system and user acceptance testing.

(b) Possible advantages of direct changeover over parallel running include:

Cost and time savings

The direct changeover approach should be cheaper and less time-consuming than the parallel running approach. With parallel running, there is usually a significant cost in entering data twice (staff overtime, temporary staff) and checking the outputs of the two systems against each other. With the direct changeover method, data is entered into the new system only.

Increases commitment to the new system

Users of the system are usually very familiar with the operation and outputs of the current system. During parallel running there may still be a tendency to rely on the old system and not identify properly and investigate the differences between outputs from the current and the new system. As a result, significant problems may only be properly tackled when the parallel running period has ended and the old system is discarded.

> **Proper attention to system and user acceptance testing**
>
> Although the stages of system testing and user acceptance testing are formally recognised in an approach using parallel running, there may be a tendency to underrate their importance because users are aware that the current system will be available as a 'fail-safe' during the implementation stage. The immediate nature of direct changeover means that proper attention has to be paid to both system and user acceptance testing.
>
> (c) The main risk of direct changeover is that the system fails and there is no other system to fall back on to. As a result, the company may not be able to process the transactions required to carry on its business. This places it at considerable business risk and could create an exposure to claims from its customers for consequential damages.
>
> This risk may be reduced in several ways:
>
> - Comprehensive systems and user acceptance testing prior to implementation. Strict testing requirements and acceptance criteria must be laid down and adhered to.
>
> - Effective training of users and operations staff before the new system goes live. Users will need familiarisation with the Windows style of interface with the enhanced reporting facilities, and with interfaces to other software.
>
> - Contingency plans that enable the business to process transactions manually while the new system is corrected and recovered.
>
> - A temporary increase in stock levels to reduce the risk of stock-outs while any problems with the new system are corrected.

Question 12

(a) From the point of view of DS, there are many reasons why it may have received poor service, even though the terms of the contract have been fulfilled. The terms are as follows:

(i) **Purchase of all hardware and software**. GDC may have a preference for hardware and software that they are familiar with and this may not be a suitable fit to the existing system. Unfortunately, hardware and software become obsolete very quickly and GDC may not have been replacing it fast enough to keep up with the demands of the company. It could be that they have bought software to upgrade the system and they have not trained staff sufficiently to maintain it. A similar situation could have occurred with networking and routing equipment. Problems can occur that are very difficult to sort out without available expertise.

(ii) **Repair and maintenance of all IT equipment**. This is a tall order for any company. When the equipment was purchased, DS should have arranged a maintenance service through the manufacturers themselves. There could easily be a misunderstanding over the type of maintenance required from GDC. Are they supposed to fix faults when they occur or do regular maintenance checks to ensure the smooth running of the equipment?

(iii) **Help desk and other support services for users**. Users often have an inadequate understanding of existing systems and develop unrealistic expectations. This means that they may generate unreasonable and unmanageable volumes of requests for change. GDC might suffer from high programmer turnover rates. Their employees may not have the necessary skills or motivation. Many programmers prefer development work to maintenance work and may be reluctant to get involved in help desk support.

(iv) **Writing and maintaining software**. Since the contract is vague and the scope so large, there are bound to be areas of poor service from GDC. Maintenance may be required to:

- correct faults;

- adapt the system to reflect the changing needs of the organisation;

- upgrade the system if product enhancements are released.

(b)   (v)   **Provision of management information**. Unless the type, content and timing of the management report required is specified, then there is ample scope for poor service. A new person at GDC may be responsible for producing the reports and he or she may not know the full routine. The report may have been left in the wrong place, or delivered to the wrong person first. However, the problem may not be due to a fault at GDC. To obtain essential management reports, the information must be kept up to date by the staff at DS. If the employee responsible for maintaining the database is sick or the files containing the data get damaged or corrupted, then the production of reports is likely to be delayed.

(c)   There are several options available to DS:

Re-write contract with the help of GDC
The first is to re-write the contract with the help of GDC so that there is some flexibility but no vague areas and each party knows what is expected from them. This could be done through negotiation while the existing contract is still running. The problems with this course of action is that DS are locked into the current arrangement and GDC will be aware of the problems it could cause by giving three months' notice and leaving DS. They would be in a very strong position to increase the price substantially or restrict their commitment to DS in any negotiations that might take place.

Obtain help in re-writing the contract
The second would be to obtain help in re-writing the contract and, when satisfied, give GDC three months' notice and ask them, and other facilities management companies, to tender for the new contract. The problems with this course of action is that DS might just be trading in one company that is giving poor service for another that they do not know. There is no guarantee that service standards will always be as expected.

End outsourcing agreement
The third option would be to revert to an in-house IT development and support department solution. This would require a lot of effort and expense and, if new staff have to be recruited, there will be a long period before they could understand the system and be in a position to do what GDC are already doing.

Question 13

The three types of resistance theory are:

- – People-oriented resistance.
- – Systems-oriented resistance.
- – Interaction-oriented resistance.

People resistance – people are naturally resistant to change as they would prefer the situation to remain the same. They become accepting of the current system by habit. The staff within FP have all worked in the authority for some time and so, even though there have been problems with the current IS, they perceive that the change in IS will be more problematic than the continued use of the current one.

Systems resistance – this is when the staff perceive the system will be difficult to use; they fear the introduction of new technology and may be concerned about their inability to use the new IS and how this will be viewed by others. There has been limited IT training of staff, implying that the others do not wish to learn the use of IT. They may be basing their perception of technology on the non-Windows based system currently in place which is likely to be difficult to use.

Interaction resistance – this refers to the impact of technology on the social and expert interaction that takes place between the staff in the office environment, in particular the concern that IT will reduce the opportunities for physical contact between staff. Staff spend time socialising both in and out of work – they enjoy swapping ideas and are generally supportive as they are able to move around the office environment.

Question 14

Benefits

The benefits of outsourcing the new Information systems will include the following:

- **Freedom to shop around for the best deal**
  Various suppliers can be asked to tender for the work, with the contract being awarded to the supplier providing value for money and hopefully relevant experience in designing this type of system.

- **Minimum diversion of management time and focus from core business activities**
  The core business of Gort appears to be provision of sewing machines and spares for those machines, not the maintenance or development of IT systems. Outsourcing this development will allow the Board of Gort to remain focused on their core business rather than have to manage an IT project where they lack appropriate knowledge and experience.

- **Advantages of contractual terms and conditions in times of dispute**
  The development of the new system will be governed by the terms of any service contract. If the outsourcing company do not deliver on a part of the contract then they can be asked to complete that phase without additional cost to Gort. Late delivery with in-house systems will normally mean having to allocate additional resources to the project, without any financial remedy from the IT department.

- **Access to the latest programming techniques as in house skills may be out of date**
  As there is only a small IT department in the Gort corporation, it is quite likely that the IT skills will be out-of-date. Any programmers and analysts are also unlikely to have time to take on a significant development project. Outsourcing the contract will therefore provide the Gort corporation with the necessary skills.

- **Shorter delivery time**
  Outsourcing will result in a shorter delivery time because Gort will not have to interview and recruit additional staff to monitor the development.

- **Outsourcer may have experience of developing similar systems**
  Providing a central database with remote access and Extranet access is likely to be a relatively specialised task. However, the outsourcing company may be able to provide relevant experience in this area, which the IT staff at Gort will not have.

Drawbacks

The drawbacks of outsourcing may include the following:

- **Lack of understanding of business objectives**
  The outsourcing company are likely to focus on implementing the IT system. They may not understand fully the business objectives of Gort and so the system may lack some of the required functionality. Care will be required in defining the systems specification to ensure it meets the requirements of Gort.

- **Loss of confidentiality, which could be a source of competitive advantage**
  Provision of an enhanced service to customers may provide Gort with some competitive advantage. The outsourcing company will need to sign appropriate confidentiality agreements to ensure that loss of confidentiality does not happen.

- **Ransom hold of particular supplier for maintenance and upgrades**
  Given that Gort does not have the expertise in-house to implement the system, the outsourcing company will also be required to maintain the system for Gort. This could give rise to increased costs. Details of expected maintenance and service costs for say five years should also be included in the original quote for the system.

Introduction to Operations Management

Chapter learning objectives

Lead	Component
C1. Explain the relationship of operations management to other aspects of the organisation's operations.	(b) Explain the relationship of operations and supply management to the competitiveness of the firm.
	(c) Explain the particular issues surrounding operations management in services.
	(d) Explain the importance of sustainability in operations management.

1 Introduction

Operations – this involves the transformation of inputs to outputs in order to add value.

e.g. materials, labour, capital

e.g. the production department transforms inputs to outputs in a manufacturing organisation

e.g. a product or service

Many of the principles of operations management were developed in a manufacturing context but later adopted by service organisation.

Operations management – refers to the activities required to produce and deliver a product or a service. It includes purchasing, warehousing and transportation.

Operations strategy – as with other aspects of running a business, there is a strategic context to operations management. An organisation can achieve significant competitive advantage over its rivals through superior operating capabilities of its resources, e.g. assets, workforce skills, supplier relationships.

Competitive factors

The objectives for operations should be consistent with the perceived requirements of customers. Various 'competitive factors' can be used to express customer requirements in terms of operational performance requirements. An organisation should establish its priorities for operational performance, and set target levels of achievement as a strategic objective.

- When customers want a low-priced product, the performance objectives in operational strategy should focus mainly on reducing costs and producing a low-cost output.

- When customers want a product or service with certain quality characteristics, and are willing to pay more for better quality, the performance objectives in operational strategy should focus on achieving the required quality standards, subject to a constraint that costs should be kept within certain limits.

- If customers want fast delivery of a product or service, the operational performance objective will concentrate on speed of operations or making the product or service more readily available.

- If customers want reliability, the operational objective should be to set targets for reliability and ensure that these are met. For example, a courier service meets customer requirements by ensuring that packages are delivered within a particular time to their destination, and without loss or damage. The operational target should be to meet these requirements on 100% of occasions.

- When customers want products or services to be designed to their own specification, the operational objective must be to achieve sufficient flexibility to handle the variations in customer requirements, and provide differing products or services accordingly.

- When customers want to alter the timing or delivery of services they receive, the main operational objective will also be flexibility. For example, a training company might have to be sufficiently flexible to deal with changes in the location, timing and duration of the training programmes required by their clients, and the number of delegates to be trained.

Test your understanding 1

The O Company, founded in the early 1970s, manufactures electric pumps.

Required:

Describe the key activities in the operations function of an organisation such as O Company.

2 Mintzberg's effective organisation

Mintzberg suggested that an organisation is made up of five parts:

Operating core

'Operations' is the term covering the central core of the organisation. This central core is known as the 'operating core' and refers to those individuals who perform the task of rendering the product or service.

Strategic apex

Those individuals who formulate and implement strategy in order to serve the owners of the organisation.

Middle line

The hierarchy of authority from strategic apex to front line supervisors.

Technostructure

Concerned with co-ordinating the work by standardising processes, outputs and skills. Includes human resource (HR) managers and accountants.

Support staff

Provide assistance outside of operational workflow such as catering services, legal advice and press relations.

Many organisations are now actively seeking flatter hierarchies, better quality and ways of contracting out of non-core activities.

What are the implications of these developments for the five basic parts of the organisation identified by Mintzberg?

3 Porter's value chain

Infrastructure				
Human Resource Management				
Technology				
Procurement				
Inbound logistics	Operations	Outbound logistics	Marketing and sales	After Sales Service

Margin

Porter developed his value chain to determine whether and how a firm's activities contribute towards its competitive advantage.

"Margin" looks at the difference between the cost of activities and their value. This helps the firm to determine whether or not best value products or services are developed.

The approach involves breaking the firm down into five 'primary' and four 'support' activities, and then looking at each to see if they give a cost advantage or a quality advantage.

'Primary' activities

Activity	Description	Example
Inbound logistics	Receiving, storing and handling raw material inputs.	A just-in-time stock system could give a cost advantage (see chapter 6).
Operations	Transformation of raw materials into finished goods and services.	Using skilled craftsmen could give a quality advantage.

| Marketing and sales | Market research and the marketing mix (see chapter 9). | Sponsorship of a sports celebrity could enhance the image of a product. |
| After sales service | All activities that occur after the point of sale, such as installation, training and repair. | Marks and Spencer's friendly approach to returns gives it a perceived quality advantage. |

'Support' activities

Activity	Description	Example
Firm infrastructure	How the firm is organised.	A firm could have a very "lean" structure at head office in contrast to competitors with more staff and more bureaucracy.
Technology development	How the firm uses technology.	The latest computer-controlled machinery gives greater flexibility to tailor products to customer specifications.
Human resource management	How people contribute to competitive advantage.	Employing expert buyers could enable a supermarket to purchase better wines than competitors.
Procurement	Purchasing, but not just limited to materials.	Buying a building out of town could give a cost advantage over High Street competitors.

Illustration 1 - Value chain

Value chain analysis helps managers to decide how individual activities might be changed to reduce costs of operation or to improve the value of the organisation's offerings. Such changes will increase 'margin' - the residual value created by what customers pay minus the costs.

For example, a clothes manufacturer may spend large amounts on:

- Buying good quality raw materials (inbound logistics)
- Hand-finishing garments (operations)
- Building a successful brand image (marketing)
- Running its own fleet of delivery trucks in order to deliver finished clothes quickly to customers (outbound logistics).

All of these should add value to the product, allowing the company to charge a premium for its clothes.

Another clothes manufacturer may:

- Reduce the cost of its raw materials by buying in cheaper supplies from abroad (inbound logistics)
- Making all its clothes by machinery running 24 hours a day (operations)
- Delaying distribution until delivery trucks can be filled with garments for a particular request (outbound logistics).

All of these should allow the company to be able to gain economies of scale and be able to sell clothes at a cheaper price than its rivals.

Four Vs of operations

All operations involve a transformational process but they can differ in four different ways

Volume

Operations differ in the volume of inputs they process. High-volume operations are likely to be more capital-intensive than low-volume operations, and there is likely to be a greater specialisation of labour skills.

Variety

Some operations handle a wide range of different inputs, or produce a wide range of output products or services. Others are much more restricted in the range of inputs they handle or outputs they produce.

Variation in demand

With some operations, demand might vary significantly from one season of the year to another, or from one time of the day to another, with some periods of peak demand and some periods of low demand. Other operations might handle a fairly constant volume of demand at all times.

Visibility

Visibility refers to the extent to which an organisation is visible to its customers. When an operation is highly visible, the employees will have to show good communication skills and interpersonal skills in dealing with customers.

4 Distinctive features of service organisations

The new approaches to operations management and quality discussed in this chapter have been most widely applied in manufacturing firms. However, modern advanced economies are now dominated by service organisations and future economic growth also depend heavily on this sector.

For service organisations to maintain their competitive advantage they need to embrace management philosophies and techniques that have proven successful in other sectors. Service industries however have certain distinguishing features that may make it difficult to reduce costs and increase quality:

- Services are intangible and it is more difficult to measure their quality than it is for a physical product.

- Services are consumed immediately and cannot be stored.

- Customers participate directly in the delivery process (in contrast to a manufacturing organisation where production and purchase are usually physically separated).

- The customer when evaluating the quality of the service will take into account the face-to-face contact and the social skills of those providing the service.

- Service organisations tend to be more labour intensive.

Despite these difficulties managers of service organisations are now having to come to terms with the requirement 'to do more and better with less' as they face more volatile and competitive markets with better informed and demanding customers.

Some believe that differences between service and manufacturing organisations may be over played. For both types of organisation the operations function provides an agreed volume of products or services within an agreed delivery plan at a pre-planned cost and level of quality. Manufacturing firms also have to achieve targets such as planned return on assets employed, and some of these measures are now starting to take on relevance for service organisations due to changing technologies.

> ### Test your understanding 3
>
> Identify a service that you use and analyse the way in which it has altered over the past ten years.

5 Strategic issues

The operations strategy is an example of a functional strategy and, as such, should be aligned with the overall corporate strategy.

> ### Illustration 2
>
> The UK supermarket, Asda (part of the global Walmart group), has a corporate strategy of cost leadership, i.e. competition through low prices.
>
> Its operations strategy has contributed to the achievement of its corporate strategy. For example:
>
> - Inventory levels are kept low which reduces the storage/ obsolescence costs.
> - Suppliers are located in focused locations, thus reducing delivery times and associated costs.

Strategic decisions in operations include:

New products – innovate or copy competitors?

New services – innovate or copy competitors?

New production technology – introduce leading edge technology?

Vertical integration strategy – operate in how many stages of the supply chain?

Structuring workforce – consider skills/ responsibilities

Capacity/ flexibility strategy – can forecast/ react to demand?

Facilities improvement – how many locations?

Supply strategy – purchase from single/multiple suppliers?

Inventory levels – what is optimum level?

6 Systems used in operations management

A number of manufacturing systems have been developed in an attempt to improve the planning and control of operational capability.

Operations management system

MRP

MRP II

ERP

OPT

6.1 Material requirements planning (MRP)

MRP is a computerised system for planning the requirements for raw materials, work-in-progress and finished items.

Functions include:

- Identifying firm orders and forecasting future orders with confidence.
- Using orders to determine quantities of material required.
- Determining the timing of material requirement.
- Calculating purchase orders based on stock levels.
- Automatically placing purchase orders.
- Scheduling materials for future production.

Benefits of MRP

- Improved forecasting

- Improved ability to meet orders.

- Reduced stock holding.

- The MRP schedule can be amended quickly if demand estimates change since the system is computerised.

- System can warn of purchasing or production problems due to bottlenecks or delays in the supply chain.

- A close relationship tends to be built with suppliers (it is consistent with just-in-time - see chapter 6).

However, MRP will not be suitable if it is not possible to predict sales in advance.

6.2 Manufacturing resource planning II (MRP II)

MRP II is an extension of the MRP system. It integrates into the MRP system other processes that are related to materials planning. For example:

- Financial requirements planning.

- Equipment utilisation scheduling.

- Labour scheduling - particularly important for service operations

MRP II provides a central database that all functions will have access to, thus everyone is working from the same information.

6.3 Enterprise resource planning (ERP)

ERP is an extension of MRP II. It integrates data from all operations within the organisation, e.g. operations, sales and marketing, human resources, purchasing.

- As with MRP II it ensures that everyone is working off the same information.

- Software companies like SAP and Oracle have specialised in the provision of ERP systems across many different industries and types of operation, including both production and service types.

Features of ERP systems

Features of ERP systems include:

- Allowing access to the system to any individual with a terminal linked to the system's central server.

- Decision support features, to assist management with decision-making.

- In many cases, extranet links to the major suppliers and customers, with electronic data interchange facilities for the automated transmission of documentation such as purchase orders and invoices.

Pros and cons of ERP

Advantages

- Can easily share data between departments and across the organisation.

- Better monitoring and forecasting.

- Lower costs.

- Improved customer service.

- Processes can be streamlined.

Disadvantages

- Cost may be prohibitive.

- May be too rigid to fulfil the needs of the organisation.

- Technical support may be inadequate.

5.4 Optimised production technology (OPT)

OPT is another approach to production planning. Production scheduling is based on the capacity of the bottleneck, i.e. the constraint within the system, and the pace of throughput that the bottleneck can handle.

Management should focus on removing the constraint. However, having dealt with one constraint there will be another constraint for the OPT system to deal with.

7 Methods of Managing Operational Capacity

Capacity planning aims to balance customer demand with production capability. There are three possible approaches to capacity planning:

- Level capacity plan - maintains production activity at a constant rate. A simple approach but can result in a build up of inventory or in stock outs.

- Chase demand plan - matches production with demand. Will require a flexible approach to production and a good forecasting system.

- Demand management planning - aims to stabilise demand, e.g. supermarkets may offer discounted ice-cream during the winter period in order to keep demand stable.

A number of methods can be used to help manage operational capacity:

6.1 Flexible manufacturing systems

A **FMS** is a highly automated manufacturing system, which is computer controlled and is capable of producing a large number of parts in a flexible manner.

The main benefit is that dedicated output can be produced quickly in response to specific orders, giving a high level of customer focus and responsiveness.

The main features include:

- The ability to change quickly from one job to another.
- Fast response times.
- Small batch production.

195

The main disadvantage of a FMS is that there is a cost to the enhanced flexibility. Traditional production lines are very efficient at making single products cheaply and benefit from economies of scale and specialisation. However, developments in IT/IS have closed the gap in costs between the two approaches, making FMS more feasible.

6.2 Queuing theory

 Queuing theory is a technique designed to optimise the balance between customer waiting time and idle service capacity.

- It applies in situations where obvious queues form, e.g. shops and bus stops, but it is also applicable in other areas, e.g. call centres, planes that circle before they land and in computing where web servers and print servers are now common.

- Queuing theory concludes that throughput improves and customer satisfaction increases if one long queue is used instead of separate lines.

- The frustrations of getting in a 'slow line' are removed because that one slow transaction does not affect the throughput of the remaining customers.

- Many banks, airport check-ins and large post offices have implemented this system.

6.3 Forecasting

A robust forecasting system will be needed in order to predict customer demand and to balance this with the level of production.

Effective forecasting relies on a mixture of the following:

- Getting accurate information from customers about future purchases and needs. For example, a components manufacturer in the car industry may have a relationship with a major customer that allows it access to the customer's planning system to identify in advance when and how many components will be required. Alternatively the customer may have access to a supplier extranet to make the ordering system quicker.

- Using past demand to accurately forecast future demand, for example through the use of sophisticated modelling techniques.

- Understanding the process well enough to be able to translate customer demand into the relevant aspects for production, such as labour scheduling, inventory management, raw materials purchases and so on. If there is a problem acquiring raw materials for example, then it will be difficult to forecast labour requirements.

Earlier in this chapter we saw how approaches such as MRP, MRP II and ERP often have planning and forecasting modules built into their systems.

8 The Importance of Sustainability in Operations Management

7.1 Introduction

- Companies are beginning to consider how their operations affect the environment and future generations.

- Sustainable development is about meeting the needs of the present without compromising the ability of future generations to meet their own needs.

- It is the practice of doing business in a way that balances economic, environmental and social needs.

7.2 How sustainability impacts operations management

Process design

The process should be designed to minimise waste, reduce energy use and reduce carbon emissions.

Product design

The product design should consider factors such as:

- Use of recycled inputs.
- Use of sustainable inputs.
- Ability to recycle product or dispose of it safely.
- Minimising wastage, e.g. unnecessary packaging.

Supply chain management

- **Purchasing**: Only products from a sustainable and ethical source should be purchased, e.g. a furniture manufacturer may purchase timber from sustainable forests only.

- **Supplier selection**: One of the key criteria to use when choosing between suppliers should be their adoption of sustainable development policies.

- **Location**: The distance between the supplier and the company should be minimised.

Quality management

Higher quality should help to improve efficiency and reduce waste.

Test your understanding 4

Explain the reasons why companies may consider sustainability in operations management.

9 Product/ Service and Process Design

8.1 Introduction

- Companies need to continually look for new or improved products or services, to achieve or maintain competitive advantage in their market.

- Operations managers are not responsible for product/ service design but will offer advice and assistance in the process.

- The design of processes will go hand in hand with the design of new products/ services. Processes may be improved through the operation of methods such as TQM, Kaizen, BPR and improvements in supply chain management (see chapters 6 and 7).

8.2 Stages in product/ service development

Stage 1: Consider customers' needs

The product/ service should satisfy the needs of the customer, e.g. value for money, high quality, cutting edge design.

Stage 2: Concept screening

The new product/ service concept should be vetted. It will only pass through to the design and development process if it meets certain criteria. For example, does the company think that the new product/ service will be profitable?

Stage 3: The design process

This may include procedures such as:

- Building a physical prototype or a virtual prototype (using computer aided design).

- Value engineering, i.e. ensuring that all components/ features add value.

Stage 4: Time-to-market

A short time-to-market is desirable since:

- New product/ service may be released ahead of competitors.

- Developments costs may be lower.

Stage 5: Product testing

The new product should be tested before it is released to the market:

- Does it work proporly?
- Do customers like it?

10 Chapter summary

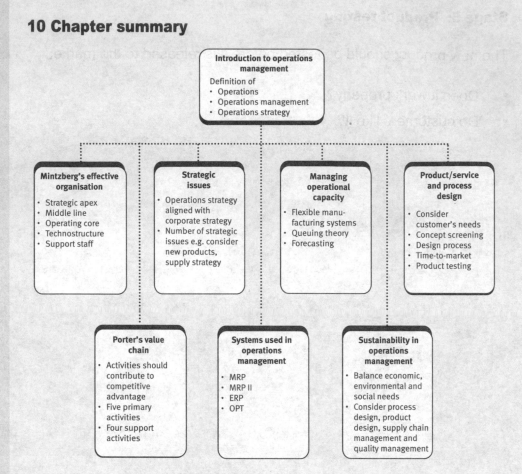

Introduction to operations management

Definition of
- Operations
- Operations management
- Operations strategy

Mintzberg's effective organisation
- Strategic apex
- Middle line
- Operating core
- Technostructure
- Support staff

Strategic issues
- Operations strategy aligned with corporate strategy
- Number of strategic issues e.g. consider new products, supply strategy

Managing operational capacity
- Flexible manufacturing systems
- Queuing theory
- Forecasting

Product/service and process design
- Consider customer's needs
- Concept screening
- Design process
- Time-to-market
- Product testing

Porter's value chain
- Activities should contribute to competitive advantage
- Five primary activities
- Four support activities

Systems used in operations management
- MRP
- MRP II
- ERP
- OPT

Sustainability in operations management
- Balance economic, environmental and social needs
- Consider process design, product design, supply chain management and quality management

11 Practice questions

Question 1

The Technostructure:

A   is dedicated to the technical side of product and process development.

B   is the board of directors who decide on the financial structure and technicalities of a business.

C   are departments such as accounting and personnel which provide support for technical structures by co-ordinating and standardising work.

D   are functions to purchase materials and process them for distribution.

(2 marks)

Question 2

OPT stands for which of the following?

A   Output Production Technology

B   Optimised Planning Techniques

C   Optimised Production Technologies

D   Organising Planning Technology

(2 marks)

Question 3

Which of the following is a value-added activity?

A   Painting a car, if the organisation manufactures cars.

B   Is the board of directors who decide on the financial structure and technicalities of a business.

C   Storing materials.

D   Repairing faulty production work.

(2 marks)

Question 4

Which of the following is an advantage of a flexible manufacturing system?

A   A firm can make bespoke products in response to differing customer needs.

B   The system allows management to identify and remove constraints within the system.

C   The number of employees can be increased or reduced to fit with existing needs.

D   It integrates data from all operations within an organisation.

(2 marks)

Question 5

MRP II:

A   integrates data from all operations within an organisation.

B   schedules production based on the capacity of the bottleneck.

C   is a computerised system for planning the requirements of material.

D   is a system that integrates all processes relating to materials planning.

(2 marks)

Question 6

What is the first stage in product development?

A   Product design.

B   Investigating the product offerings of competitors.

C   Considering customers' needs.

D   Investigating ways to reduce the time-to-market.

(2 marks)

Question 7

Which of the following is not an example of a 'support activity' as described in Porter's Value Chain?

A   Technology development

B   Human resource management

C   Procurement

D   Firm structure

(2 marks)

Question 8

Distinguish strategic decisions from tactical decisions in the context of operations management.

(4 marks)

Question 9

Explain why it might be necessary to involve suppliers in a new product design and development process.

(4 marks)

Question 10

Explain the importance of sustainability in operations.

(4 marks)

Question 11

Woodsy is a garden furniture manufacturing company, which employs 30 people. It buys its timber in uncut form from a local timber merchant, and stores the timber in a covered area to dry out and season before use. Often this takes up to two years, and the wood yard takes up so much space that the production area is restricted.

The product range offered by the company is limited to the manufacture of garden seats and tables because the owner-manager, Bill Thompson, has expanded the business by concentrating on the sale of these items and has given little thought to alternative products. Bill is more of a craftsman than a manager, and the manufacturing area is anything but streamlined. Employees work on individual units at their own pace, using little more than a circular saw and a mallet and wooden pegs to assemble the finished product. The quality of the finished items is generally good but relatively expensive because of the production methods employed.

Marketing has, to date, been felt to be unnecessary because the premises stand on a busy road intersection and the company's products are on permanent display to passing traffic. Also, satisfied customers have passed on their recommendations to new customers. But things have changed. New competitors have entered the marketplace and Bill has found that orders are falling off. Competitors offer a much wider range of garden furniture and Bill is aware that he may need to increase his product range, in order to compete. As the owner-manager, Bill is always very busy and, despite working long hours, finds that there is never enough time in the day to attend to everything. His foreman is a worthy individual but, like Bill, is a craftsman and not very good at man-management. The overall effect is that the workmen are left very much to their own devices. As they are paid by the hour rather than by the piece, they have little incentive to drive themselves very hard.

Required:

(a) Explain what is meant by the terms 'value chain' and 'value chain analysis'?

(5 marks)

(b) Use a diagram to give a brief explanation of the two different categories of activities that Porter describes.

(5 marks)

(c) Analyse the activities in the value chain to identify the key problems facing Woodsy.

(5 marks)

(d) Based on your analysis, prepare a set of recommendations for Bill Thompson to assist in a more efficient and effective operation of his business

(5 marks)

(e) Describe the stages in the development of new garden furniture.

(5 marks)

(f) Explain the different aspects of design that Bill Thompson can consider for his garden furniture.

(5 marks)

(Total: 30 marks)

Test your understanding answers

Test your understanding 1

The operations function in manufacturing electric pumps is concerned with converting raw materials into a finished product and delivering them to the customer. Operations therefore covers the following areas:

- **Purchasing**. The purchasing department are responsible for obtaining raw materials and parts from suppliers.

- **Production**. The production function converts the raw materials and assembles parts and components into finished products. Without more information about the nature of the pumps that the company produces, it is not possible to suggest what type of production process the company uses.

- **Production planning and control**. This function is concerned with scheduling production, and making sure that the materials, labour, machinery and other resources are available to manufacture the pumps. Production control involves monitoring production flow and dealing with any problems, hold-ups and bottlenecks that might arise.

- **Product design or engineering**. There will probably also be a separate section within operations that provides technical expertise. These experts might be responsible for new product design.

- **Inventory management**. Raw materials and finished goods inventory must be stored or warehoused.

- **Logistics**. Manufactured pumps must be distributed to customers. The customers for pumps will be industrial buyers, and the task of delivering them will probably be included within the operations function.

Test your understanding 2

A clearer focus on the core activity and hence further importance attached to operations management.

Test your understanding 3

You may have identified factors such as:

- being less labour intensive
- more extensive use of IT
- being more centralised and global
- communication via the Internet
- trading via the Internet
- other online services.

Test your understanding 4

- **Improved image/ perception**
  - Sustainable development should help the company to portray a positive image.
  - Many customers now view sustainable development as being an important factor in making product choices.
  - Companies can use it as a tool for attracting and retaining the best employees.

- **Compliance with legislation/ regulation**
  - Legislation/ regulation has increased in recent years and has resulted in many companies implementing policies for sustainable development.
  - For example, three new pieces of legislation were introduced in the UK in 2008; the Climate Change Act, the Energy Act and the Planning Act.

- **Economic**
  - Sustainable development in operations management can help the company to seize new markets or market share. Tesco, Toyota and Shell are all viewed as leaders in sustainable development.
  - Costs may be reduced, e.g. due to lower wastage, less energy use, lower resource use.

Question 1

C

Question 2

C

Question 3

A

Question 4

A

Question 5

D

Question 6

C

Question 7

D

Question 8

Strategy deals with how an organisation achieves its objectives. For example:

- Where is the business trying to get to in the long term (direction)?

- Which markets should a business compete in and what kind of activities are involved in such markets (markets; scope)?

- How can the business perform better than the competition in those markets (advantage)?

- What resources (skills, assets, finance, relationships, technical competence, facilities) are required in order to be able to compete (resources)?

- What external, environmental factors affect the business's ability to compete (environment)?

- What are the values and expectations of those who have power in and around the business (stakeholders)?

Tactics are the most efficient deployment of resources in an agreed strategy.

Tactics follow on from strategy.

Question 9

- It is probably not necessary to involve suppliers of standard raw materials or components.

- It might be necessary to check that the supplier is able to produce a part or component to the planned design specification.

- It might be necessary to discuss with the supplier how a part or component might be produced within a target cost limit.

- The supplier might be able to contribute ideas for improving the specification for the product.

Organisations might establish a long-term relationship with some key suppliers, and work together with those suppliers in new product design and development. The supply relationship is then a strategic relationship, with the organisation and the suppliers sharing common strategic business objectives.

Question 10

- It is important for a company to consider how their operations affect the environment and future generations.

- Sustainable development is about meeting the needs of the present without compromising the ability of future generations to meet their own needs.

- Sustainable development will not only benefit the environment but can also benefit the company:

    - The company can use sustainable development as a tool for attracting customers and the best employees.

    - Sustainable development can help the company to reduce costs, e.g. due to lower wastage.

    - Sustainable development can help the company to comply with legislation.

Question 11

(a) **'Value chain'** describes the full range of activities which are required to bring a product or service from conception, through the intermediary of production, delivery to final consumers, and final disposal after use. It is a way of looking at a business as a chain of activities that transform inputs into outputs that customers value. Customer value derives from three basic sources:

- – activities that differentiate the product

- – activities that lower its cost

- – activities that meet the customer's need quickly.

The value chain includes a profit margin since a mark-up above the cost of providing a firm's value-adding activities is normally part of the price paid by the buyer – creating value that exceeds cost so as to generate a return for the effort.

'Value chain analysis' views the organisation as a sequential process of value-creating activities, and attempts to understand how a business creates customer value by examining the contributions of different activities within the business to that value. Value activities are the physically and technologically distinct activities that an organisation performs. Value analysis recognises that an organisation is much more than a random collection of machinery, money and people. These resources are of no value unless they are organised into structures, routines and systems, which ensure that the products or services that are valued by the final consumer are the ones that are produced.

(b) Porter describes two different categories of activities.

Infrastructure				
Human Resource Management				
Technology				
Procurement				
Inbound logistics	Operations	Outbound logistics	Marketing and sales	After Sales Service

Margin

The primary activities, in the lower half of the value chain are grouped into five main areas:

– Inbound logistics are the activities concerned with receiving, storing and handling raw material inputs.

– Operations are concerned with the transformation of the raw material inputs into finished goods or services. The activities include assembly, testing, packing and equipment maintenance.

– Outbound logistics are concerned with the storing, distributing and delivering the finished goods to the customers.

– Marketing and sales are responsible for communication with the customers e.g. advertising, pricing and promotion.

– Service covers all of the activities that occur after the point of sale e.g. installation, repair and maintenance.

Alongside all of these primary activities are the secondary, or support, activities of procurement, technology development, human resource management and firm infrastructure. Each of these cuts across all of the primary activities, as in the case of procurement where at each stage items are acquired to aid the primary functions.

(c) The key problem areas are as follows:

– Inbound logistics – Woodsy has problems with the procurement of the raw materials, labour and machinery. The company is buying its raw materials two years in advance of using it. This must be tying up capital that could be used to purchase new machinery and tools. Storing the timber entails large amounts of money being tied up in stocks, which are prone to damage, restrict the production area and is very slow moving. The workmen are being paid by the hour rather than by the piece and this means that they have little incentive to work harder.

– Operations are concerned with the transformation of the raw material inputs into finished goods or services. At Woodsy, employees work at their own pace on the assembly of the garden seats and tables, using very basic tools. The production methods used make the finished product relatively expensive. The linkages between the support activities are also causing some problems. Both the owner and the foreman have no man-management skills. Technological development is non-existent and the company needs re-structuring.

- Outbound logistics are concerned with storing, distributing and delivering the finished goods to the customers. Woodsy does not seem to have a system for distributing and delivering its goods.

- Marketing and sales are responsible for communication with the customers e.g. advertising, pricing and promotion. This seems to be non-existent at Woodsy as, in the past, satisfied customers have passed on their recommendations to new customers. The company relies on its position on a busy road intersection to displays its products, for customers to carry away themselves.

(d) For Bill Thompson, the main task is to decide how individual activities might be changed to reduce costs of operation or to improve the value of the organisation's offerings. The recommendations would include the following:

- The business needs managing full-time. A new manager, or assistant manager, could encourage Bill to streamline the manufacturing process, introduce new technologies and new production and administrative systems. He or she could also negotiate new payment methods to give the workforce an incentive to work harder.

- To increase the production area the alternative strategies that the company could explore include storing the timber elsewhere, or purchasing it after it has dried out and seasoned.

- Holding high levels of finished goods might give a faster customer response time but will probably add to the total cost of operations.

- The purchase of more expensive power tools and equipment may lead to cost savings and quality improvements in the manufacturing process.

- The company needs a marketing and sales department to research the market, inform the customers about the product, persuade them to buy it and enable them to do so. The product range may need to be extended and alternative outlets for the products sought.

(e) The development stages are as follows:

- Consider customers' needs – the new product should satisfy the needs of the customer. Bill must start by identifying these needs, e.g. value for money, high quality, cutting edge design or a wide product range.

- Concept screening – the new product should be vetted and will only pass through to the design and development stage if it meets certain criteria. For example, does Bill think that a new range of wooden sun loungers would be profitable?

- The design process – Bill may build a prototype and check that all the components add value.

- Time-to-market – Bill should minimise time-to-market in order to reduce development costs and increase competitiveness.

- Product testing – the product should be tested before it is released to the market. For example, do customers like the new sun lounger and does it work properly?

(f) The purpose of design is more than to improve the appearance of a product. It must also satisfy the customer in its performance, durability, simplicity of operation and cheapness. Bill Thompson can consider the following different aspects of design for his garden furniture:

- Design for function – value in use implies quality and reliability: the product must satisfy the customer in its purpose and give long service.

- Design for appearance – although products should please the eye to attract customers, the appeal of the product may not be solely visual. Other senses are also often involved and sometimes characteristics such as texture may predominate.

- Design for production – to ensure component parts are made easily and economically, so that they can be assembled and transported easily and sold at an attractive price.

- Design for distribution – to enable easy packing, reduction of storage space and packing costs.

6

The Supply Chain and Supply Networks

Chapter learning objectives

Lead	Component
C1. Explain the relationship of operations management to other aspects of the organisation's operations.	(a) Explain the shift from price-based to relational procurement and operations. (b) Explain the relationship of operations and supply management to the competitiveness of the firm.
C2. Apply tools and techniques of operations management.	(a) Explain process design. (e) Describe ways to manage relationships with suppliers.

1 Introduction

The supply chain includes the entire process from extracting raw materials to delivering the finished product to the end customer. The supply chain will involve a number of separate companies that will all play a part in satisfying the needs of the end customer.

A **virtual supply chain** is a supply chain that is enabled through e-business links, e.g. the internet.

2 Strategic Supply Chain Management

Supply chain management is the management of all the activities aimed at satisfying the end customer in a way that maximises the effectiveness of the process.

Supply chain management has a strategic role within the organisation and can help the company to achieve competitive advantage.

Illustration 1

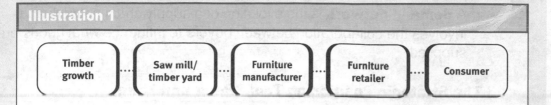

The supply chain for wooden furniture begins with the timber grower, moves on to the saw mill and the timber yard, then to the furniture manufacturer, then to the furniture retailer and finally to the end consumer.

The furniture manufacturer is in the middle of the supply chain. Improvements in the management of the supply chain can help the manufacturer to achieve its strategic objective of achieving and maintaining competitive advantage. For example:

- By reducing supplier lead times from its suppliers, the saw mills.

- By improving the administrative procedures for purchasing wood from suppliers.

- By persuading suppliers to improve their quality.

- By persuading suppliers to provide timber in a form that is better-suited to the production of furniture.

These steps will assist the furniture manufacturer in reducing costs and/or increasing revenue. This will, in turn, improve profitability.

A **supply chain network** is a group of organisations which relate to each other through the linkages between the different processes involved in producing the finished product.

- Traditionally, businesses within the supply chain operated independently.

- However, organisations are recognising that there are benefits associated with establishing links between the different companies in the supply chain.

- Co-ordination of the different firms within the supply chain should lead to better planned production and distribution which may cut costs and give a more attractive final product leading to increased sales and profit for all of the businesses involved.

- Competition is no longer on a company versus company basis but rather takes on a supply chain versus supply chain form.

- A **demand network** is the evolution of a supply chain network and involves the collaboration between buyers to influence what goods are supplied.

3 The Strategic Positioning Tool - Reck and Long

In Illustration 1, all of the steps taken to improve the supply chain involve the relationship between the furniture manufacturer and its suppliers.

In fact, it has been suggested that the largest improvements in profit are often found by improving the interface between the organisation and its suppliers.

The extent to which supply chain management is a strategic issue can be considered through **Reck and Long's** strategic positioning tool.

There are four stages of development that the purchasing function should pass through in order to attain a strategic status:

Stage 1 = The **passive** stage	• Purchasing is seen as an administrative task. • Emphasis is on processing transactions efficiently, in a similar way to, say, payroll processing.
Stage 2 = The **independent** stage	• Greater awareness of the financial importance of purchasing. • Emphasis is on price negotiations.
Stage 3 = The **supportive** stage	• Greater awareness that purchasing can affect the firm's strategic goals. • Emphasis is on better co-ordination between departments involving timely communication about changes in price and availability of materials.
Stage 4 = The **integrative** stage	• Purchasing is seen as a key part of strategic planning. • The emphasis is on developing relationships with suppliers, who are seen as vital partners.

4 The Strategic Supply Wheel - Cousins

Cousins' strategic supply wheel depicts the corporate supply strategy at the hub of the wheel and underlines the need for an integrated approach to supply strategy involving a balancing of all of the spokes of the wheel.

Spoke of wheel	Explanation
Organisation structure	Centralised/ decentralised structure impacts control and interaction.
Relationships	Can be opportunistic or collaborative relationships with suppliers.
Cost/ benefit	The cost of the strategic approach chosen must be less than the benefit.
Competences	Do the skills exist to achieve the strategy? E.g. the development of long term supplier relations may require staff training.
Performance measures	Necessary for monitoring and controlling the strategy chosen.

Relationships

'Cousins' strategic supply wheel depicts the corporate supply strategy at the hub of the wheel since the purchasing director should set goals and policies that are connected to those of the overall firm. For example:

- A firm that is cost focused will expect supply activity to deliver savings. Opportunistic relationships with suppliers will help to achieve short-term price reductions. The firm will not be interested in forming close working relationships with suppliers or implementing complex sourcing strategies.

- A firm that is differentiation focused, e.g. differentiates itself on quality or design, will review supply as strategic to their business. The firm will form close, collaborative relationships with suppliers.

---

5 Relationship-based Supply Chains

Competitive or collaborative partnerships?

Competitive

In the past the supply chain was typically defined by competitive relationships.

- The purchasing function sought out the lowest-price suppliers, often through a process of tendering, the use of 'power' and the constant switching of supply sources to prevent getting too close to any individual source.

- Supplier contracts featured heavy penalty clauses and were drawn up in a spirit of general mistrust of all external providers.

- The knowledge and skills of the supplier could not be exploited effectively: information was deliberately withheld in case the supplier used it to gain power during price negotiations.

Hence, no single supplier ever knew enough about the ultimate customer to suggest ways of improving the cost-effectiveness of the trading relationship, for instance buying additional manufacturing capacity or investing in quality improvement activities.

Collaborative

It is now recognised that successful management of suppliers is based upon collaboration and offers benefits to an organisation's suppliers as well as to the organisation itself. By working together organisations can make a much better job of satisfying the requirements of their end market, and thus both can increase their market share.

- Organisations seek to enter into partnerships with key customers and suppliers so as to better understand how to provide value and customer service.

- Organisations' product design processes include discussions that involve both customers and suppliers. By opening up design departments and supply problems to selected suppliers a synergy results, generating new ideas, solutions, and new innovative products.

- To enhance the nature of collaboration the organisation may reward suppliers with long-term sole sourcing agreements in return for a greater level of support to the business and a commitment to on-going improvements of materials, deliveries and relationships.

6 Supply Networks

A **supply network** is a term used to describe the arrangements made by the organisation to obtain its supplies.

There are four main sourcing strategies available:

Strategy	Explanation
Single sourcing	The organisation chooses one source of supply.
Multiple sourcing	The organisation chooses several sources of supply.
Delegated sourcing	The organisation chooses one supplier (1st tier). This supplier then co-ordinates and works with other suppliers (2nd tier) to ensure the supply requirements are fulfilled.
Parallel sourcing	The organisation uses a mix of the three approaches

Test your understanding 1

State the advantages and disadvantages of:

(i)   Single sourcing

(ii) Multiple sourcing

(iii) Delegated sourcing

(iv) Parallel sourcing

Kyoryoko kai

In most countries, suppliers' associations are organised and run by the suppliers themselves. In Japan, there are supplier associations known as kyoryoku kai, which are organised by a major buyer/customer in the industry. For example, an association of suppliers in the automotive industry might be set up and organised by a major car manufacturer. The first such association was set up by Toyota in 1943. Its original purpose was to provide an assurance of business to suppliers who were suffering from the consequences of the war effort in Japan. Over time, the main focus of interest in these supplier associations has been:

- Improving quality
- Reducing costs by means of efficiency improvements throughout the industry
- Health and safety standards.

The benefit of having a supplier association organised by a major buyer is that the buyer is able to exert strong influence over its suppliers, and encourage the open exchange of ideas and information between suppliers.

7 Process Maps

Process maps can be used to visualise the flow of material and information as the product makes its way through the supply chain.

It builds a flowchart of the process being analysed in order to:

- Standardise the process
- Find areas of improvement, e.g. eliminate unnecessary steps or duplicated steps
- Assist understanding of the process due to the visual representation
- To link the supply chain strategy to the corporate strategy.

Example of a process map

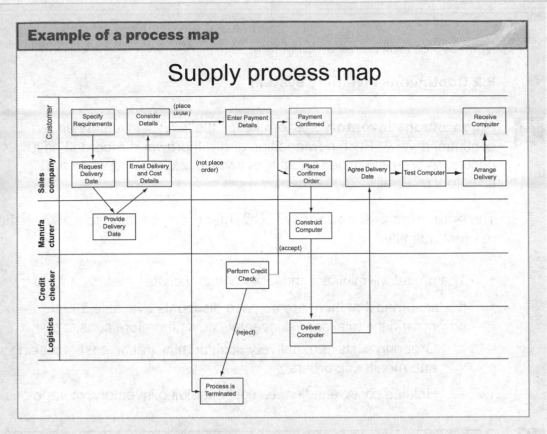

8 Methods of Managing Inventory

8.1 Introduction

The control of inventory is important for a number of reasons:

- Holding costs of inventory may be high
- Production may be delayed if the company runs out of raw materials
- Loss of customer goodwill if demand can't be fulfilled
- Obsolescence if inventory with a short shelf life is not used or sold

Therefore, it is important for a company to choose an appropriate inventory management system. There are four main types of system available:

Each system will be reviewed in turn.

8.2 Continuous inventory system

A **continuous inventory system** keeps the level of inventory under continual review. Each new addition and withdrawal is recorded as it occurs. A pre-determined quantity of inventory is ordered when the inventory level falls to a re-order level.

The **economic order quantity** (EOQ) model can be used to establish the re-order quantity:

- The model will minimise the total inventory costs.

- It is assumed that there are no price discounts available for larger-sized orders, and the total annual inventory costs therefore consist of:
  - Ordering costs, e.g. delivery cost, administration cost of placing and monitoring orders
  - Holding costs, e.g. finance cost of holding inventory, storage costs

EOQ model
Imagine that a firm sells A units a year and sales are constant. If it retails the product at a price p its turnover will be pA. The firm purchases stock at a wholesale price of w, sells it and, when stock has fallen to zero, obtains more stock. If the firm orders an amount Q, the stock level of the firm will follow the profile shown in the diagram below, where Q has been assumed to be 10 and stock usage is one unit a period. From the diagram it follows that the average stock level will be Q/2, in this case five units.

Total inventory costs are minimised when the combined cost of ordering inventory and holding inventory each period (each year) is minimised. To decide what to do, we must look at the demand and costs:

C = ordering cost per order event (fixed cost to place an order, not per unit)
H = holding cost per unit per unit of time e.g, per year
Q = is the reorder quantity
A = total sales per annum

The equation below, which you will not need to derive or use, is the so-called economic order quantity or EOQ

$$Q = \sqrt{\frac{2AC}{H}} = EOQ$$

8.3 Periodic inventory system

The periodic inventory system does not keep inventory levels under continual review. Instead, inventory is checked on a regular basis and a variable order is placed depending on the usage during the period.

8.4 ABC system

The ABC system is based on Pareto's law. This law states that 80% of inventory usage can be accounted for by 20% of inventory items. By dividing a company's inventory into different classifications - A, B or C, managers can focus on items that account for the majority of the inventory.

- Category A – items of high value in terms of usage rate. Close monitoring of these items is vital. A stock-out would result in disappointed customers.

- Category B – items of medium value in terms of usage rate. Less important than category A and therefore require less control.

- Category C – the least used inventory items and require little management control.

8.5 Just-in-time (JIT) system

The inventory management systems reviewed so far assume that it is necessary to hold some inventory. An alternative view is that inventory is wasteful and adds no value to operations.

 Just-in-time (JIT) is a system whose objective it is to produce or procure products or components as they are required by the customer or for use, rather than for inventory. This means that inventory levels of raw materials, work-in-progress and finished goods can be kept to a minimum.

JIT applies to both production within an organisation and to purchasing from external suppliers:

JIT purchasing is a method of purchasing that involves ordering materials only when customers place an order. When the goods are received they go straight into production.

JIT production is a production system that is driven by demand for the finished products (a 'pull' system), whereby each component on a production line is produced only when needed for the next stage.

 Illustration 2

Toyota pioneered the JIT manufacturing system, in which suppliers send parts daily – or several times a day – and are notified electronically when the assembly line is running out.

More than 400 trucks a day come in and out of Toyota's Georgetown plant in the USA, with a separate logistics company organising the shipment from Toyota's 300 suppliers – most located in neighbouring states within half a day's drive of the plant.

Toyota aims to build long-term relationships with its suppliers, many of whom it has a stake in, and says it now produces 80% of its parts within North America.

Requirements for successful operation of a JIT system

- **High quality and reliability** – disruptions create hold ups in the entire system and must be avoided. The emphasis is on getting the work right first time:
  - Highly skilled and well trained staff should be used.
  - Machinery must be fully maintained.
  - Long-term links should be established with suppliers in order to ensure a reliable and high quality service.

- **Elimination of non-value added activities** – value is only being added whilst a product is being processed. For example, value is not added whilst storing the products and therefore inventory levels should be minimised.

- **Speed of throughput** – the speed of production should match the rate at which customers demand the product. Production runs should be shorter with smaller stocks of finished goods.

- **Flexibility** – a flexible production system is needed in order to be able to respond immediately to customer orders:
  - The system should be capable of switching from making one product to making another.
  - The workforce should be dedicated and have the appropriate skills. JIT is an organisational culture and the concept should be adopted by everyone.
  - Management should allow the work teams to use their initiative and to deal with problems as they arise.

- **Lower costs** – another objective of JIT is to reduce costs by:
  - Raising quality and eliminating waste.
    Achieving faster throughput.
  - Minimising inventory levels.

Illustration 3

The Impact of JIT

- Under JIT, a buyer can reduce the number of suppliers. GM reduced their suppliers by 50%.

- Westinghouse has reduced their inventories by 45% and plant stockouts by 95%.

- Warner-Lambert has replaced its costly batch production by a JIT-based controlled process. Suppliers also chosen because of close proximity to the plant. Long-term contracts and single sourcing is advocated to strengthen buyer-supplier relationships and tends to result in a higher quality product. Inventory problems are shifted back onto suppliers, with deliveries being as required.

- Jaguar, when it analysed the cause of its customer complaints, compiled a list of 150 areas of faults. Some 60% of them turned out to be faulty components from suppliers. One month the company returned 22,000 different components to suppliers. Suppliers were brought on to the multi-disciplinary task forces the company established to tackle each of the common faults, establishing and testing a cure and implementing it as quickly as possible. Jaguar directors chaired the task force of the 12 most serious faults, but in one case the task force was chaired by the supplier's representative.

Test your understanding 2

Explain the advantages and disadvantages to an organisation of operating a JIT system.

Kanban

'Kanban' is a Japanese word meaning both 'card' and 'signal'. Within a production system where output moves from one process to another, a system of coloured cards or kanbans can be used to give signals between one stage in the process and the next stage. For example, a card can be used by one stage in the process to give a signal to the previous stage that more output is now required from the previous stage. Details of the parts or materials required can be written on the card. Kanbans are therefore used to authorise a movement of materials within the production system, and without this authorisation there should be no movement.

Variations in the signalling system might be used.

- Colour-coded cards might be used for giving different signals. For example, different colours of card might represent different parts or material items, or differing degrees of urgency.

- When output is transferred from one stage of production to the next in standard batch sizes or container sizes, one card might represent a requirement for one container and two cards might represent a demand for two containers.

- A system might use 'kanban squares'. A kanban square is a physical space marked out on the factory floor. When the space is empty, this acts as a signal to the previous process to produce more output for the next process. When the square contains any items, this acts as a signal that no output from the previous process is required at the moment.

Supplier relationships and JIT

As mentioned previously, many of the steps taken to improve the supply chain (and hence profitability) involve improving the relationship between the manufacturer and its suppliers.

This will be of particular importance in a company operating a JIT system.

The advantages to a JIT company of developing close supplier relationships are as follows:

- **No rejects/ returns** – a strong relationship should help to improve the quality of supplies. This should minimise production delays since there will be less inspection, fewer returns and less reworking of goods.
- **On-time deliveries** – the development of close working relationships should help to guarantee on-time deliveries of supplies.
- **Low inventory** – suppliers can be relied upon for frequent deliveries of small quantities of material to the company, ensuring that each delivery is just enough to meet the immediate production schedule.
- **Close proximity** – the supplier/ portfolio of suppliers will be located close to the manufacturing plant. This will reduce delivery times and costs.

9 Chapter summary

10 Practice questions

Question 1

Reck and Long's strategic positioning tool identifies an organisation's:

A   purchasing approach.

B   sales approach.

C   manufacturing approach.

D   warehousing approach.

(2 marks)

Question 2

An inventory system that records each new addition and withdrawal as it occurs is known as:

A   a Just-In-Time system.

B   an ABC system.

C   a periodic inventory system.

D   a continuous inventory system.

(2 marks)

Question 3

Supply chain partnerships are developed due to:

A   recognising a supply chain and linkages in a value system.

B   a requirement to meet growing demand.

C   the adoption of new information systems.

D   a requirement for quality accreditation.

(2 marks)

Question 4

According to Cousins, which one of the following is a 'spoke' of the 'supply wheel?'

A   Corporate and supply strategy.

B   Organisation culture.

C   Purchasing.

D   Relationships.

(2 marks)

Question 5

An ABC system refers to:

A   an inventory management system that aims to eliminate or minimise inventory levels.

B   accuracy, benefit and cost effectiveness of the inventory management system.

C   an inventory management system that concentrates effort on the most important items.

D   a system used to manage relationships with suppliers.

(2 marks)

Question 6

Explain the relationship between a JIT (Just-in-Time) system and cash flow management.

(4 marks)

Question 7

Explain, using examples, the meaning of JIT (Just-In-Time) purchasing and JIT production.

(4 marks)

Question 8

Identify FOUR reasons why process maps may be used as part of supply chain management.

(4 marks)

Question 9

Overdrive Transmissions and Bearings (Overdrive) is a European manufacturer of gearbox and transmission systems for the car industry. Overdrive was formed in 1949 and is now one of the largest producers of such products in Europe. It has a turnover in excess of 300 million Euros and employs 2,000 staff in three large factories in its home country.

Gearbox and transmission systems are complex products, with each typically containing over 200 parts. Each part must be manufactured to stringent quality standards, as the operating temperatures and stress levels involved are very high. There are also potential safety implications of quality failure in any component supplied to the car industry. Overdrive's customers (the major car manufacturers) demand high standards of quality, reliability and service level. Under the terms of the contracts between Overdrive and their customers, the car manufacturers can charge severe financial penalties for any failure in delivery or quality. Such penalties can amount to many millions of Euro for each incident. Because of this, Overdrive has stringent quality control procedures.

While most of the parts and components used in Overdrive's products are manufactured by Overdrive itself, some components are bought in from other specialist manufacturers. One of these is component G4 – the gearshift selector assembly. Component G4 is used in most of Overdrive's products, and is currently bought from three small suppliers who each make the component to a design supplied by Overdrive. The suppliers are prohibited from supplying component G4 to any other organisation.

In a recent meeting, the purchasing manager of Overdrive said, '… the modern trend in managing inbound logistics is to enter into sole supplier agreements. We should consider this for component G4.'

Required:

(a) Explain what is meant by the 'inbound logistics' in Porter's value chain model.

(5 marks)

(b) Explain the types of decision regarding inventory management that the management of Overdrive need to take?

(5 marks)

(c) Explain the difference between continuous inventory and periodic inventory systems?

(5 marks)

(d) Explain THREE advantages to Overdrive of having a formal agreement with a single preferred supplier for component G4.

(5 marks)

(e) Explain THREE disadvantages to Overdrive of having a formal agreement with a single preferred supplier for component G4.

(5 marks)

(f) Outline the problems of applying the theory of JIT (Just-In-Time) to all industries in practice

(5 marks)
(Total: 30 marks)

Question 10

Operations managers have always been faced with dealing with the two conflicting objectives of inventory management, namely, to provide maximum components availability while keeping inventory investment low. The overall goal of inventory management is to provide the right item, at the right location, at the right time, at the best cost. To meet this goal, managers must work with two major objectives in mind:

(i) maximising customer service, i.e. providing material when the customer needs it, and

(ii) minimising inventory investment, i.e. controlling the money invested in parts and material.

Required:

(a) Explain the main purpose of holding inventory and explain the differing views on inventory levels.

(8 marks)

(b) Describe the common techniques of inventory management

(12 marks)
(Total: 20 marks)

Test your understanding answers

Test your understanding 1

		Advantages	Disadvantages
(i)	**Single sourcing**	• Better communication • Economies of scale • Better production quality, lower variability • Possible source of competitive advantage	• Risk to security of supply since rely on one supplier • Few competitive pressures may reduce incentive for supplier to perform well
(ii)	**Multiple sourcing**	• Greater security of supply • Pressure on suppliers to be competitive • Buyer remains in touch with supply market ·	• Economies of scale may be lost • Suppliers may display less commitment/ quality may be poorer
(iii)	**Delegated sourcing**	• The 1st tier supplier may be able to negotiate economies of scale • May result in the optimum mix of suppliers being used • Organisation delegates responsibility to the 1st tier supplier thus freeing up staff time	• 1st tier supplier is in a powerful position • Organisation may have little knowledge with regards to the 2nd tier suppliers, e.g. quality, work practices.
(iv)	**Parallel sourcing**	• May blend the best bits of each strategy	• Quite difficult to manage

Test your understanding 2

Advantages of JIT

- Lower stock holding costs means a reduction in storage space which saves rent and insurance costs.

- As stock is only obtained when it is needed, less working capital is tied up in stock.

- There is less likelihood of stock perishing, becoming obsolete or out of date.

- Avoids the build-up of unsold finished products that can occur with sudden changes in demand.

- Less time is spent checking and re-working the products as the emphasis is on getting the work right first time.

The result is that costs should fall and quality should increase. This should improve the company's competitive advantage.

Disadvantages of JIT

- There is little room for mistakes as little stock is kept for re-working a faulty product.

- Production is very reliant on suppliers and if stock is not delivered on time or is not of a high enough quality, the whole production schedule can be delayed.

- There is no spare finished product available to meet unexpected orders, because all products are made to meet actual orders.

- It may be difficult for managers to empower employees to embrace the concept and culture.

- It won't be suitable for all companies. For example, supermarkets must have a supply of inventory.

- It can be difficult to apply to the service industry. However, in the service industry a JIT approach may focus on eliminating queues, which are wasteful of customers' time.

Question 1

A

Question 2

D

Question 3

A

Question 4

D

Question 5

C

Question 6

A Just-in-Time (JIT) system involves purchasing items from suppliers and the production of items only when they are needed to meet demand. A consequence of JIT should be a reduction in inventories of raw materials and components, and finished goods. Expenditure will therefore be incurred later than in a traditional operating environment and the 'cash cycle' should be shorter. This is the time between paying for expenses and receiving payments from customers. As a result, working capital should be lower and cash flows should improve.

Question 7

- **JIT purchasing** is a method of purchasing that involves ordering materials only when customers place an order. When the goods are received they go straight into production.

- For example, a customer may place an order for a new car. The materials required to make the car will only be ordered from the suppliers once a firm order is received from the customer.

- **JIT production** is a production system that is driven by demand for the finished products (a 'pull' system), whereby each component on a production line is produced only when needed for the next stage.

- For example, production of a new car will only begin when there is a firm order for the car.

Question 8

Process maps are used to:

- standardise the process.

- find areas of improvement, e.g. eliminate unnecessary steps or duplicated steps.

- assist understanding of the process due to the visual representation.

- to link the supply chain strategy to the corporate strategy.

Question 9

(a) Inbound logistics in the value chain is the systems and procedures relating to the acquisition, movement and storage of inputs to the organisation. The buyer will study commodities, sources of supply, systems and procedures, inventory problems and market trends, methods of delivery, whether maximum discounts are being earned and the amount and use of waste materials. Inbound logistics also includes warehousing, stock control and transport. From the point of view of corporate financial strategy, storing inputs entails vast amounts of money being tied up in stocks, which are prone to damage and shrinkage and are perhaps slow moving. There is also the creation on the shop floor of a mentality that pushes components through to satisfy stocks (just in case) rather than pulling them through made to order (just in time). This means yet more stock is ordered and so on. While the choice of supplier is a 'procurement' function in the value chain, the management of the supplier relationship tends to be classified as inbound logistics, particularly when it comes to more closely integrating the organisation's purchasing systems with the sales systems of the supplier.

(b) There are two main types of decision for inventory management:

– How much to order? When an order is placed with a supplier, what quantity should be ordered?

– When to order? How frequently should inventory be ordered? Should it be ordered at regular intervals, or when the inventory level has fallen to a reorder level?

The trade off is:

Ordering more frequently	**Ordering less frequently**
Higher ordering costs	Lower ordering costs
Smaller average inventory	Larger average inventory

(c) Two methods of inventory control include the periodic review system and the continuous review system. In the **periodic review system**, the inventory position is reviewed at regular intervals (usually at the time of a scheduled re-order). The inventory is counted and the order quantity is calculated by subtracting the amount of stock on hand from the desired maximum inventory. A manager using this system determines the re-supply schedule by establishing a reorder interval (the number of months between orders), and places orders based on this schedule.

In the **continuous review system**, the inventory level is reviewed on an ongoing basis for every transaction in which stock is dispensed. When the amount of stock reaches a predetermined reorder level, an order is initiated. Each time the stock is replenished, it is for a standard quantity (usually for that amount which will raise the stock level backup to the desired maximum level). This system is based on stock levels rather than on time intervals

(d) The main advantages of sole supplier agreements are as follows: (Any three required)

- Overdrive should be able to negotiate lower initial prices due to the increased volume of business to be transacted with the supplier. The suppliers are all currently small organisations, so a trebling of the order quantities from any one of them should allow that supplier to exploit economies of scale.

- Overdrive should be able to gain better control over their inbound logistics through direct involvement with the supplier. Giving the sole supplier more attention and management time should improve the reliability of deliveries and also reduce the risk of quality failure.

- There is an opportunity to integrate the systems of Overdrive with those of the supplier, as mentioned above. For example, Overdrive could give the supplier access to production forecasts, which would allow the supplier to amend production plans for component G4 to meet forecast demand. This would allow a move towards just in time (JIT) logistics, and reduce (or eliminate) finished goods inventory at the supplier and component inventory at Overdrive.

- Overdrive should be able to ensure better quality due to the extent of the supplier's reliance on Overdrive. The supplier would probably not wish to disappoint such a major customer.

(e) The main disadvantages of sole supplier agreements are as follows: (Any three required)

- Once the agreement is signed, there is a risk over future price rises. It could be argued that the sole supplier agreement leads to increased supplier bargaining power over Overdrive, though this will depend on how well the relationship is managed.

- There is a significant risk in relation to possible delivery failure by the supplier. Overdrive has contracts with car manufacturers that include 'liquidated damages' clauses for late delivery. These would have to be written into any contract with a supplier, and a small supplier may not be able to afford the cost of such a high exposure to possible penalties.

- There is a risk of falling quality from the supplier if the relationship with Overdrive becomes too 'comfortable'. Overdrive must continually remind the supplier of its quality expectations. This is a big issue for Overdrive, as they are buying a high technology component that forms a key part of their product. There are also safety implications associated with product failure, and these could lead to legal action against Overdrive.

- If Overdrive only uses one supplier, they might miss out on future innovations in the industry. Overdrive should change their planning process to ensure that they take advantage of any future developments by other suppliers.

(f) Although it might be difficult to argue against the philosophy of JIT, there can be problems with applying the theory of JIT to all industries in practice.

- It is not always easy to predict patterns of demand.

- The concept of zero inventories and make-to-order is inapplicable in some industries. For example, retailing businesses such as supermarkets have got to obtain inventory in anticipation of future customer demand.

- JIT makes the organisation far more vulnerable to disruptions in the supply chain.

- JIT was designed at a time when all of Toyota's manufacturing was done within a 50 km radius of its headquarters. Wide geographical spread, however, makes this difficult.

- It might be difficult for management to apply the principles of JIT because they find the concept of empowering the employee difficult to accept.

Question 10

(a) Holding inventory is cost effective and helps achieve sales at competitive prices. The other objectives of holding inventories are:

- To ensure prompt delivery.
- To obtain quantity discounts.
- To reduce the order cost.
- To avoid production shortage.

Managers will have different views on the levels of inventory to hold:

- The financial manager's view is to keep inventory levels low, to ensure the firm's money is not invested in excess resources.

- The marketing manager's view is to have large inventories of the firm's finished products to ensure all orders could be filled quickly, eliminating the need for back orders.

- The operations manager's view is to keep raw materials inventories high to avoid production delays.

- The purchasing manager's view is to have correct quantities at the desired time at a favourable price.

- An uncoordinated inventory system can allow these competing views to create conflicts and inefficiencies in the firm.

(b) The common techniques of inventory management include:

- **Continuous inventory system:** this keeps the level of inventory under continual review. Each new addition and withdrawal is recorded as it occurs. A pre-determined quantity of inventory can be re-ordered when the inventory level falls to a re-order level. The economic order quantity (EOQ) refers to the optimal ordering quantity that will incur the minimum total cost (order cost and holding cost) for an item of inventory. Order costs include the costs of purchasing, receiving goods, and maintaining inventory records. These costs are fixed regardless of the size of the order. Holding costs include interest, insurance, taxes, handling, warehousing, and shrinkage. If money has been borrowed to purchase inventory, interest payments may consist of a large portion of these costs. With the increase in the order size, the ordering cost decreases but the holding cost increases and the optimal order quantity is determined where these two costs are equal. The company should also keep an eye on the level of safety stock and the lead-time associated with the orders made.

- **The ABC system**: This is founded on the 20/80 concept, where 20% of inventory accounts for 80% of sales. It divides inventory into three groups:

    - A group (the 20%) largest value and is actively managed

    - B group next largest and less actively managed

    - C group smallest and least managed.

The items falling in category A are those that involve the maximum investment. Likewise, the items that require minimum investment are classified into group C.

This approach helps in selective control of inventories. It helps in pinpointing the obsolete stocks, reducing the clerical costs and resulting in better inventory planning.

- **JIT (Just-In-Time) system:** This is an inventory management technique that minimises inventory investment by requiring suppliers to deliver goods to manufacturers just in time to be used in production. It pushes the task of carrying inventory back onto the suppliers. The goal of JIT is manufacturing efficiency. For a JIT system to work, a great deal of faith and extensive coordination must exist between the firm, its suppliers, and shipping companies to ensure that material inputs arrive on time. In addition, the inputs must be of near perfect quality and consistency given the absence of safety stock.

- **Periodic inventory system:** this does not keep inventory levels under continual review. Instead, inventory is checked on a regular basis and a variable order is placed depending on the usage during the period.

Quality Management

Chapter learning objectives

Lead	Component
C2. Apply tools and techniques of operations management.	(a) Apply contemporary thinking in quality management.
	(b) Apply tools and concepts of lean management.
	(d) Illustrate a plan for the implementation of a quality programme.

1 Introduction

Quality management involves planning and controlling activities to ensure the product or service is fit for purpose, meeting design specifications and the needs of customers.

What is quality?

In order to control and improve quality it must first be defined. Most dictionaries define quality as 'the degree of excellence' but this leaves one having to define what is meant by 'excellence'. Who defines what is excellent and by what standards is it measured? In response to this problem, a number of different definitions of quality have been developed.

In an industrial context, quality is defined in a functional way. Here, quality means that a product is made free from errors and according to its design specifications, within an acceptable production tolerance level.

Such an approach also emphasises that every unit produced should meet the design specifications, so the idea of consistency becomes important. Note that consistency is a key aspect of quality standards such as the ISO 9000 series.

This still leaves a problem, however. How should standards and specifications be set? Who decides what an 'acceptable' tolerance level should be?

An alternative approach to defining quality is thus to focus on the user.

* Japanese companies found the definition of quality as 'the degree of conformance to a standard' too narrow and consequently started to use a new definition of quality as 'user satisfaction'.

* Juran defines quality as 'fitness for use' (1988).

In these definitions, customer requirements and customer satisfaction are the main factors. If an organisation can meet the requirements of its customers, customers will presumably be satisfied. The ability to define accurately the needs related to design, performance, price, safety, delivery, and other business activities and processes will place an organisation ahead of its competitors in the market.

Taking these definitions together, Ken Holmes (Total Quality Management) has defined quality as 'the totality of features and characteristics of a product or service which bears on its ability to meet stated or implied needs'.

Quality is also normally seen in relation to price, and customers judge the quality of a product in relation to the price they have to pay. Customers will accept a product of lower design quality provided that the price is lower than the price of a better-quality alternative.

Test your understanding 1

Explain the reasons why quality may be important to an organisation.

2 Quality-related Costs

British quality standard 6143 defines four types of quality cost:

- **Prevention costs** – cost of preventing defects before they occur. For example:
    - Designing products and services with built in quality.
    - Training employees in the best ways to do their job.

- **Appraisal costs** – the cost of quality inspection and testing.

- **Internal failure costs** – the costs arising from a failure to meet quality standards. Occurs <u>before</u> the product/ service reaches the customer. For example:
    - Cost of re-working parts.
    - Re-inspection costs.
    - Lower selling prices for sub-quality goods.

- **External failure costs** – the costs arising from a failure to meet quality standards. Occurs <u>after</u> the product/ service reaches the customer. For example:
    - Costs of recalling and correcting products.
    - Cost of lost goodwill.

3 Traditional Approach to Quality Management

Traditional quality management was associated with the inspection of finished output or goods inward.

Illustration 1

The chocolate manufacturer, Cadbury, had a traditional approach to quality management:

- **Inspection costs** – chocolate was inspected and tested as it came off the production line.

- **Internal failure costs** – any sub-quality goods were sold at a lower price. Mis-shapes were odd shaped chocolates that could not be used in a box of Roses or Milk Tray chocolates.

- **External failure costs** – arose when sub-standard products reached the customer. For example, in 2006 more than one million Cadbury chocolate bars were recalled in the UK after salmonella was found in some Cadbury products.

The traditional approach to quality management allows for built in waste. However, waste reduces profitability.

4 Contemporary Thinking in Quality Management - TQM
4.1 Introduction

Total quality management (TQM) is a philosophy of quality management that originated in Japan in the 1950s.

TQM is the continuous improvement in quality, productivity and effectiveness obtained by establishing management responsibility for processes as well as outputs. In this, every process has an identified process owner and every person in an entity operates within a process and contributes to its improvement.

Illustration 2

A TQM success story

Corning Inc is the world leader in speciality glass and ceramics. This is partly due to the implementation of a TQM approach. In 1983 the CEO announced a $1.6 billion investment in TQM. After several years of intensive training and a decade of applying the TQM approach, all of Corning's employees had bought into the quality concept. They knew the lingo - continuous improvement, empowerment, customer focus, management by prevention and they witnessed the impact of the firm's techniques as profits soared.

An example of TQM failure

British Telecom launched a total quality program in the late 1980s. This resulted in the company getting bogged down in its quality processes and bureaucracy. The company failed to focus on its customers and later decided to dismantle its TQM program. This was at great cost to the company and they have failed to make a full recovery.

4.2 Fundamental features of TQM

Prevention of errors before they occur

The aim of TQM is to get things right first time. This contrasts with the traditional 'UK' approach that less than 100% quality is acceptable. TQM will result in an increase in prevention costs, e.g. quality design of systems and products, but internal and external failure costs will fall.

Continual improvement

Quality management is not a one-off process, but is the continuous examination and improvement of processes.

Real participation by all

The 'total' in TQM means that everyone in the value chain is involved in the process, including:

- Employees – they are expected to seek out, identify and correct quality problems. Teamwork will be vital.

- Suppliers – quality and reliability of suppliers will play a vital role (TQM and JIT often go hand in hand).

- Customers – the goal is to identify and meet the needs of the customer.

Commitment of senior management

Management must be fully committed and encourage everyone else to become quality conscious.

4.3 TQM Tools

Quality circles

 A **quality circle** is a small group of employees, with a range of skills from all levels of the organisation. They meet voluntarily on a regular basis to discuss quality issues and to develop solutions to real problems.

Advantages include:

- Improvements in quality, leading to greater customer satisfaction and improved productivity.

- A culture of continuous improvement is encouraged.

- Employees at operational level will form part of the quality circle. They often have a better understanding of quality problems than their superiors/ managers.

- The group approach helps to foster organisational unity.

Encouraging the development and use of quality circles

Putting the idea of quality circles into practice can be very difficult. Th
are a number of ways in which firms can encourage the development
the use of quality circles:

- Ensuring that there is high profile executive commitment to support the initiative.

- Ensuring that staff members have the training in problem solving and analysis which they need to identify problems and develop workable solutions.

- Ensuring that staff members who are involved in quality circles are free to spend the time necessary away from their day-to-day responsibilities to take part in meetings and activities.

- Reviewing the information system in the organisation to identify the information needs of quality circles, and to ensure that any data required to assess performance and identify problems is available to them.

- Demonstrating that the senior management of the organisation takes the process seriously and takes any action to resolve problems which is identified as necessary by quality circles.

- Developing a culture in the organisation that allows possible changes to be tested out, allowing for the possibility of mistakes.

- Providing training for all staff to increase awareness of the importance and value of quality circles.

Kaizen

Kaizen is a Japanese term for the philosophy of continuous improvement in performance in all areas of an organisation's operations.

Features include:

- Involves all levels of employees.

- Everyone is encouraged to come up with small improvement suggestions on a regular basis.

- Suggestions are not limited to a particular area, such as production or marketing, but look at all areas of the business.

- Kaizen involves setting standards and then continually improving those standards.

- Training and resources should be provided for employees in order for them to meet the standards set.

Illustration 3

Many Japanese companies have introduced a Kaizen approach:

- In companies such as Toyota and Canon, a total of 60-70 suggestions per employee per year are written down and shared.

- It is not unusual for over 90% of those suggestions to be implemented.

- In 1999, in one US plant, 7,000 Toyota employees submitted over 75,000 suggestions, of which 99% were implemented.

Continuous improvement can be described as a never-ending cycle. **Deming** called this the Plan-Do-Check-Act (PDCA) cycle:

- **Plan**: Plan activities
- **Do**: Implement the plan
- **Check**: Check the results
- **Act**: Improve the process

5-S practice

The 5-S practice is an approach to achieving an organised, clean and standardised workplace.

- The 5-S practice is often part of a Kaizen approach.
- The 5Ss are Japanese words but can be translated as follows:

Word	Meaning	Example
Seiri	Sort	Eliminate unnecessary items, e.g. old, unwanted files.
Seiton	Organise	A structured filing system - 'a place for everything and everything in its place'.
Seiso	Clean	Clean work station regularly
Seiketsu	Standardise	Alphabetic filing system
Shitsuke	Discipline	Do not slip back into old habits.

The principle may appear simple, obvious common sense but until the advent of 5-S many businesses ignored these basic principles.

Six sigma

This quality management programme was pioneered in the 1980s by Motorola, a multinational telecommunications company now best known for its mobile phones and tablet pcs,

The aim of the approach is to achieve a reduction in the number of faults that go beyond an accepted tolerance limit through the use of statistical techniques.

The sigma stands for standard deviation. For reasons that need not be explained here, it can be demonstrated that, if the error rate lies beyond the sixth sigma of probability, there will be fewer than 3.4 defects in every one million.

This is almost perfection. Customers will have a reason to complain fewer than four times in a million.

Statistical process control is the method used to continually monitor and chart a process whilst it is operating, to warn when the process is moving away from the predetermined limits.

- As per six sigma, the upper and lower limits will be three standard deviations away from the expected value (mean).

- All points outside the control limits should be investigated and corrective action taken.

For example, the following statistical control chart shows the size of a product (this may be an important aspect of product conformance) against time.

In order to do things right first time with no (or very few defects), a key emphasis of the Six Sigma approach is to identify root problems and address them.

Further aspects of Six Sigma

Key requirements for successful Six Sigma implementation

There are a number of key requirements for the implementation of Six Sigma.

- Six Sigma should be focused on the customer and based on the level of performance acceptable to the customer.

- Six Sigma targets for a process should be related to the main drivers of performance.

- To maximise savings Six Sigma needs to be part of a wider performance management programme which is linked to the strategy of the organisation. It should not be just about doing things better but about doing things differently.

- Senior managers within the organisation have a key role in driving the process.

- Training and education about the process throughout the organisation are essential for success.

- Six Sigma sets a tight target, but accepts some failure – the target is not zero defects.

Some criticisms and limitations of Six Sigma

Literature on Six Sigma contains some criticisms of the process and identifies a number of limitations as follows.

- Six Sigma has been criticised for its focus on current processes and reliance on data. It is suggested that this could become too rigid and limit process innovation.

- Six Sigma is based on the use of models which are by their nature simplifications of real life. Judgement needs to be used in applying the models in the context of business objectives.

- The approach can be very time consuming and expensive. Organisations need to be prepared to put time and effort into its implementation.

- The culture of the organisation must be supportive – not all organisations are ready for such a scientific process.

- The process is heavily data-driven. This can be a strength, but can become over-bureaucratic.

- Six Sigma can give all parts of the organisation a common language for process improvement, but it is important to ensure that this does not become jargon but is expressed in terms specific to the organisation and its business.

- There is an underlying assumption in Six Sigma that the existing business processes meet customers' expectations. It does not ask whether it is the right process.

4.4 Key writers on TQM

Writer	Main contribution
Deming	• Credited with the development of TQM in Japan. • Developed '14 points' to guide companies in quality improvement.
Juran	• Defined quality as 'fit for purpose', i.e. does product/ service fulfil the customer's needs? • Stated that 85% of quality problems are due to the systems that employees work within rather than the employees themselves.
Feigenbaum	• Believed that 'prevention is better than cure'. • Design of systems and procedures should enhance quality.

Crosby	• Introduced the concept of 'zero defects'.
	• Believed that prevention is free and that the importance of quality is measured by the cost of not having quality.
Ouchi	• Showed how American companies could be as successful as Japanese companies.
	• Key tool is a highly effective management style.
	• Recommended certain Japanese management practices such as:
	– Group interaction and consensus decision making.
	– Less hierarchy and more devolved authority/ responsibility.
	– More participative management styles with free flow of information.

4.5 TQM and external quality standards

- TQM is considered to be a management philosophy rather than a set of management practices.

- However, advocates of TQM support the concept of setting standards and monitoring actual performance against these standards.

- In addition to internal quality standards, voluntary external quality standards may be set for an industry.

- The most widely used external quality standards are those published by the International Organisation for Standardisation (ISO).

Introduction to ISO quality standards

- The **ISO 9000** series of quality standards is the most recent set of ISO standards (published in 2000).

Main ISO standards

ISO 9001: contains the quality management standards. Organisations should follow these standards if they want to become registered.

ISO 9000 and 9004: contains guidelines which help organisations to implement quality standards.

- A company registering for ISO 9000 certification is required to submit its quality standards and procedures for external inspection.

- Requirements include:
    - A set of procedures that covers all key business processes.
    - Keeping adequate records.
    - Checking output for defects.
    - Facilitating continuous improvement.

- If the company receives a certificate it can claim to be ISO registered/certified and will be subject to continuing audit.

- In addition, **ISO 14001** is of growing importance to companies. It specifies the process for controlling and improving an organisation's environmental performance, e.g. regarding waste, energy emissions.

Test your understanding 2

Explain the advantages and disadvantages to a fast growing UK based mobile phone company of becoming ISO certified.

4.6 Implementation of a TQM approach

The implementation of a TQM approach may involve the following steps:

Step 1: Senior management consultancy – Managers must be committed to the programme and should undergo quality training

Step 2: Establish a quality steering committee – The committee will guide the company through the process of implementing TQM

Step 3: Presentations and training – The steering committee should communicate the benefits of the change programme to employees in order to gain buy-in

Step 4: Establish quality circles – This will involve employees in the process of quality improvement

Step 5: Documentation – The actions carried out should be clearly documented

Step 6: Monitor progress – Actual results should be monitored against the standard set

4.7 The EFQM Excellence Model

The European Foundation for Quality Management (EFQM) Excellence Model is the most widely-used business excellence framework in Europe, with over 30,000 businesses using the model to improve performance and increase profit. Advocates claim it is a non-prescriptive assessment framework that can be used to gain a holistic overview of any organisation regardless of size, sector or maturity.

A key feature of the Model is its use as a diagnostic tool for self-assessment, where organisations grade themselves against a set of detailed criteria under nine categories grouped into two main headings :

Enablers

- Leadership
- People
- Policy and strategy
- Partnerships and resources
- Processes

Results

- People results
- Customer results
- Society results
- Key performance results

The 'enabler' criteria cover what an organisation does and how it does it. The 'results' criteria cover what an organisation achieves. 'Results' are caused by 'enablers' and 'enablers' are improved using feedback from 'results'. Other tools and standards focus on specific areas of your organisation whereas the Excellence Model follows a holistic approach.

For example, if you conduct a self-assessment via the Excellence Model and determine that an area for improvement is in your "People Results," you may want to use the Investors in People standard to help your organisation improve. Likewise, if your organisation's "Processes" need improving, you may want to consider implementing ISO 9000 or adopting a six-sigma methodology.

Furthermore, there are various recognition schemes based on the Excellence Model. These recognition schemes, known as Levels of Excellence, are standards designed not only to celebrate success but to allow firms to benchmark against the best in Europe.

Illustration 4 - EFQM

In the Basque Country, a region in Northern Spain, experience has been gained over many years into the implementation of the EFQM excellence model in the regional health care service, formed by 31 health organizations.

The project was started in 1995. Until 1999 only self-assessments were done. Since 2000, the most advanced organizations concluded external evaluations and have achieved quality awards from the Basque government.

Scores for most of the EFQM criteria improved, particularly in 'processes'. The overall patients' satisfaction was higher than 89% in all settings, in most of the cases higher than 95%, a significant improvement.

5 Methods of Quality Measurement

5.1 Servqual - measuring service quality

A service company, e.g. a hotel or restaurant, may wish to know more about customers' perceptions of its service, to compare these to what they had expected and to identify trends in perceived quality.

Servqual uses 22 questions to understand a respondent's attitude about service quality. Customers may be asked for their responses both before and after the service is consumed.

These questions are claimed to be reliable indicators of five distinct dimensions:

Dimensions	Examples for a restaurant
Tangibles	Appearance and taste of food
Reliability	Order processed accurately
Responsiveness	Staff response to queries, e.g. information on specials, request for bill
Assurance	Waiting staff inspire confidence
Empathy	Restaurant guests are treated as individuals

Test your understanding 3

Explain how the Servqual dimensions could be applied to an online environment, such as a company using a website to sell its products and to deal with customer concerns and queries.

5.2 Benchmarking

Benchmarking is the process of systematic comparison of a service, practice or process. Its use is to provide a target for action in order to improve competitive position.

Types of benchmarking

- **Competitive benchmarking** – a method of comparing performance in key areas with that of your most successful competitors.

- **Internal benchmarking** - a method of comparing performance in key areas in one part of the organisation with the performance in another part of the organisation, e.g. different divisions or departments.

- **Functional benchmarking** – involves comparing a function with the practices of an organisation known to excel in that area.

Benchmarking process

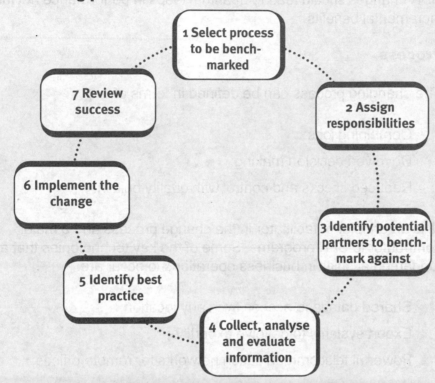

1 Select process to be bench-marked

2 Assign responsibilities

3 Identify potential partners to bench-mark against

4 Collect, analyse and evaluate information

5 Identify best practice

6 Implement the change

7 Review success

Test your understanding 4

Describe the main benefits of benchmarking.

Business process re-engineering (BPR)

Business process re-engineering (BPR) involves focusing attention **inwards** to consider how the business processes could be redesigned or re-engineered to improve efficiency.

Its use contrasts with benchmarking which is an external exercise although the ideas generated through benchmarking may be used here to offer radical solutions.

Hammer and Champy describe BPR in terms of:

Radical and fundamental

BPR assumes nothing; it starts by asking basic questions about why tasks are carried out and challenges traditional methods.

Dramatic

BPR changes should lead to quantum leaps in performance not just incremental benefits.

Process

The changing process can be defined in terms of:

- Combining jobs;
- Devolved decision making;
- Reduced checks and control with quality built in.

IT is an enabler or facilitator in the change process and a major contributor to BPR programs. Some of the key technologies that allow fundamental shifts in business operations to occur are:

- Shared database access from any location;
- Expert systems to devolve expertise;
- Powerful telecommunication networks for remote offices;
- Wireless communication for on-the-spot decision making;
- Tracking technology for warehouse and delivery systems;
- Internet services to re-engineer channels of distribution.

6 Lean Management

As the name suggests, lean management is a philosophy that aims to systematically eliminate waste. In this section we will look first at manufacturing contexts but then we will consider how the same principles can be applied within service organisations.

60 years ago the cars that Toyota was making were uncompetitive in both cost and quality terms. In a bid to catch up with its American competitors it developed lean production. Lean production helped Toyota to become what it is now – the biggest car manufacturer in the world.

6.1 Wastes to be eliminated

- **Inventory** – holding or purchasing unnecessary raw materials, work-in-progress and finished goods.

- **Waiting** – time delays/ idle time when value is not added to the product.

- **Defective units** – production of a part that is scrapped or requires rework.

- **Effort** – actions of people/ equipment that do not add value.

- **Transportation** – delays in transportation or unnecessary handling.

- **Over-processing** – unnecessary steps that do not add value.

6.2 Characteristics of lean production

- **Improved production scheduling** – production is initiated by customer demand rather than ability and capacity to produce, i.e. production is demand-pull, not supply-push.

- **Small batch production or continuous production** – production is based on customer demand resulting in highly flexible and responsive processes.

- **Continuous Improvement** – the company continually finds ways to reduce process times:

    - A multi-skilled, trained workforce provides flexibility.

    - The machines, tools and people used to make an item are located close together.

    - Quality at source reduces re-working.

    - A clean and orderly workplace.

- **Zero inventory** – JIT purchasing eliminates waste.

- **Zero waiting time** – JIT production means that the work performed at each stage of the process is dictated solely by the demand for materials for the next stage; thus reducing lead time.

Illustration 6 - Reverse Engineering

IBM regularly compares part counts, bills of materials, standard versus custom part usage, and estimated processing costs by tearing down competitor products as soon as they are available.

Through such tear-downs during the heyday of the dot matrix printer, IBM learned that the printer made by the Epson, its initial supplier, was exceedingly complicated with more than 150 parts. IBM launched a team with a simplification goal and knocked the part count down to 62, cutting assembly from thirty minutes to only three.

6.3 The six core methods of lean manufacturing

- **JIT** (see earlier discussion)
- **Kaizen** (see earlier discussion)
- **5-S practice** (see earlier discussion)
- **Total productive maintenance (TPM)** - this engages all levels and functions of the organisation in maintenance. Workers are trained to take care of the equipment.

Illustration 7 - TPM

Pulling the cord, called 'andcan', is part of Toyota's lean production system. An employee who notices a problem pulls the cord to stop the production line. This will prompt fellow workers to gather round and to solve the problem.

Workers at the Toyota plant in Georgetown, Kentucky, pull the cord 2,000 times a week and their care is what makes Toyota one of the most desired and reliable brands in the US. In contrast, workers at Ford's plant in Michigan pull the cord only twice a week.

In 1998 it took Ford 50% more hours to make a car than Toyota. Toyota's lean system means that it has been able to produce cars more cheaply, and to a higher quality, than Ford.

- **Cellular manufacturing** - work units are arranged in a sequence that supports a smooth flow of materials and components through the production processes with minimal transport or delay.
- **Six sigma** (see earlier discussion).

6.4 Criticisms and limitations of lean manufacturing

- **High initial outlay** - It might involve a large amount of initial expenditure to switch from 'traditional' production systems to a system based on cellular manufacturing. All the tools and equipment needed to manufacture a product need to be re-located to the same area of the factory floor. Employees need to be trained in multiple skills.

- **Requires a change in culture** - Lean manufacturing, like TQM, is a philosophy or culture of working, and it might be difficult for management and employees to acquire this culture. Employees might not be prepared to give the necessary commitment.

- **Part adoption** - It might be tempting for companies to select some elements of lean manufacturing (such as production based on cellular manufacturing), but not to adopt others (such as empowering employees to make on-the-spot decisions).

- **Cost may exceed benefit** - In practice, the expected benefits of lean manufacturing (lower costs and shorter cycle times) have not always materialised, or might not have been as large as expected.

6.5 Application of lean techniques to services

Toyota pioneered the concept of a 'lean' operating system and it has now been implemented in countless manufacturing companies. Lean techniques can also be applied to service companies. The six core methods will still apply, although the use of the methods will be different.

With service operations a lean approach often focusses on and improving the customer experience.

In chapter 5 we identified certain distinguishing features that may make it difficult for service operators to reduce costs and increase quality. These same factors affect the application of lean techniques to services:

- Service organisations tend to be more labour intensive, so a lean approach to services could involve a mixture of cutting staffing levels, reducing wasted time and reducing mistakes.

  For example, a teller in a bank may spend only 6 out of 8 hours in day in direct customer service, and the remaining 2 hours are wasted in 1-2 minute segments. Rather than let unplanned activities fill the void, a priority list of service support tasks such as restocking supplies, following a standardised procedure, can be used to not only reduce waste but also help eliminate other sources of poor service quality.

- Services are intangible and it is more difficult to measure their quality than it is for a physical product.

  Attempts to improve time efficiency may have an adverse effect on quality that could be difficult to quantify.

- Services are consumed immediately and cannot be stored.

  Matching staff levels to demand for services is critical to avoid wasted time.

- Customers participate directly in the delivery process, so firms must evaluate their services from the customer's perspective.

- The customer when evaluating the quality of the service will take into account the face-to-face contact and the social skills of those providing the service. Again there is a danger that efficiency gains may compromise customer service.

Illustration 8 - Lean management in the NHS

Within the NHS in England lean thinking and Six Sigma have been used to reduce waiting times for patients.

Lean thinking looks to improve the flow in a patient journey and reduce waste while SIx Sigma has been used to uncover root problems to ensure things are done right first time.

NHS leaders and staff previously had not fully understood how patients and their information (referrals, appointments, X-rays, pathology specimens, reports, coding information etc) flowed through their organisations and departments. Managers and clinicians tried to optimise their organisational or departmental activity and costs, with no reference to the bottleneck in the system that governs the rate at which patients and information flow along the system or pathways of care.

Accident and Emergency (A&E)

For example, in A&E, lean management approaches identified the bottleneck as the rate of arrival of patients in ambulances and the rate at which junior doctors could assess them and initiate treatment plans. To address this patient journeys were analysed to identify common processes, skill requirements and cycle times. As a result patients were split into two groups:

- Patients with minor conditions have a huge variety and range of conditions but all require a quick simple process to sort them out by experienced staff with minimal equipment. Processing the majority of patients in less than 20 minutes improves the overall time in A&E for the vast majority of patients.

- The major injury and resuscitation patients are fewer in number, but require different skills and technology and have much longer cycle times.

Mixing minors with majors is like putting a lorry into the fast lane on a motorway. It slows the speed of the whole motorway.

Processing pathology specimens

In 2007, turnaround times in pathology at Hereford Hospital were reduced by 40% in 7 days by improving the flow of the specimens through the department and eliminating wasteful activities, such as unnecessary staff movements like searching and looking for things. A key change here was having dedicated staff man specimen reception. This enabled staff to start processing specimens as soon as they arrived, rather than waiting for someone from a lab to come and see if any had arrived.

The reduction in processing times resulted in estimated savings of £365,000 a year because inpatients could be discharged quicker, shortening length of stay and creating extra capacity in the hospital.

Test your understanding 5

Explain how the six core methods of lean manufacturing can be applied to a call centre.

7 Chapter summary

8 Practice questions

Question 1

Which of the following is not a benefit of quality accredited standards such as ISO 9001?

A   Excellent marketing tool.

B   Better quality.

C   Revenue reduction.

D   Cost reduction.

(2 marks)

Question 2

What are the main benefits of ISO 14001 accreditation?

Question 3

A supermarket providing an internet service for the home-delivery of groceries has recently compared its order processing and delivery system with a company that sells clothing to consumers using catalogues and web-based selling. This type of benchmarking is:

A   internal.

B   competitive.

C   functional.

D   BPR.

(2 marks)

Question 4

What is the likely error rate if it lies beyond the sixth sigma of probability?

A   1 defect in 100,000

B   3.2 defects in 600,000

C   3.4 defects in 1,000,000

D   4 defects in 6,000,000

(2 marks)

Question 5

Which writer on TQM advocated a zero defects philosophy?

A   Deming

B   Peters

C   Crosby

D   Juran

(2 marks)

Question 6

The six core methods of lean manufacturing include cellular manufacturing, six sigma, JIT, Kaizen, TPM and:

A   benchmarking.

B   TQM.

C   MRP.

D   the 5-S practice.

(2 marks)

Question 7

Describe the importance of quality management.

(4 marks)

Question 8

Explain how servqual can be used to measure quality in a hotel.

(4 marks)

Question 9

The Acme Manufacturing Company has successfully produced a limited range of giftware for several years. A major feature of the range has been the simple, uncomplicated mode of design and manufacture. This has meant that there have been very few production problems or complaints from customers, despite the cursory inspection checks carried out. However, a recent variation of one of the products, an electronic version of a trouser press, has brought many problems and complaints.

The managing director of Acme is very worried and has arranged for a small investigative team to be set up to find a solution to the current problem and discuss future projects that Acme is considering. The chairman is the production director, with representatives from design, marketing, purchasing, inspection and accounts. As an accountant with knowledge of product costs, you have been nominated for this committee.

Required:

For the first meeting of the team produce a briefing document that:

(a) explains benchmarking and describes the main types;

(10 marks)

(b) illustrates how benchmarking could be used to improve the management of future projects at Acme

(15 marks)

(Total: 25 marks)

Question 10

The production director in a large manufacturing company wants to introduce quality circles into the company's factories, because he has heard of their success in several Japanese companies. He asks for your advice about introducing a system of quality circles, and he tells you: 'My objectives in wanting to introduce these circles are to arrive at decisions for change in product designs and production methods and to get a maximum degree of acceptance. Quality circles can improve quality, productivity, interdepartmental communication, teamwork, team spirit. They can reduce costs and absenteeism and create more job satisfaction. I want them.'

Required:

The production director asks you to explain whether you can foresee any problems with introducing quality circles, and how you would set about implementing a programme for setting them up and using them.

(10 marks)

Test your understanding answers

Test your understanding 1

Higher quality can help to increase revenue and reduce costs:

- Higher quality improves the perceived image of a product or service. As a result, more customers will be willing to buy the product/ service and may also be willing to pay more for the product/ service.

- A higher volume of sales may result in lower unit costs due to economies of scale.

- Higher quality in manufacturing should result in lower waste and defective rates, which will reduce production costs.

- The need for inspection and testing should be reduced, also reducing costs.

- The volume of customer complaints should fall and warranty claims should be lower. This will reduce costs.

- Better quality in production should lead to shorter processing times. This will reduce costs.

Advantages

- **Recognised standard** – the company's reputation for quality will be enhanced since ISO is a recognised international standard of quality.

- **Marketing** – ISO certification will act as an excellent marketing tool. It will help to differentiate the company, on the grounds of quality, in the customer's eyes.

- **Improved profitability** – fulfilment of the ISO criteria should help the company to improve quality. This, in turn, should reduce costs and increase revenue.

- **International competitiveness** - ISO certification is becoming increasingly useful in international markets and may help the company to compete on a world stage.

Disadvantages

- **Cost** – fees are upwards of £995 depending on the size of the company.

- **Time** – documentation can be time consuming to produce.

- **Bureaucracy** – the scheme encourages bureaucracy with lots of form filling and filing rather than positive actions.

- **Rigid policies** – these may discourage initiative and innovation and may therefore hinder the quality process.

- **Not all embracing** – ISO certification will form a small part of a TQM approach.

Test your understanding 3

Tangibles

- The 'tangibles' heading considers the appearance of physical facilities, equipment, personnel and communications.

- For online quality the key issue is the appearance and appeal of websites - customers will revisit websites that they find appealing.

- This can include factors such as structural and graphic design, quality of content, ease of use, speed to upload and frequency of update.

Reliability

- Reliability is the ability to provide a promised service dependably and accurately and is usually the most important of the different aspects being discussed here.

- For online service quality, reliability is mainly concerned with how easy it is to connect to the website.

- If websites are inaccessible some of the time and/or e-mails are bounced back, then customers will lose confidence in the retailer.

Responsiveness

- Responsiveness looks at the willingness of a firm to help customers and provide prompt service.

- In the context of e-business, excessive delays can cause customers to 'bail-out' of websites and/or transactions and go elsewhere.

- This could relate to how long it takes for e-mails to be answered or even how long it takes for information to be downloaded to a user's browser.

Assurance

- Assurance is the knowledge and courtesy of employees and their ability to inspire trust and confidence.

- For an online retailer, assurance looks at two issues - the quality of responses and the privacy/security of customer information.

- Quality of response includes competence, credibility and courtesy and could involve looking at whether replies to e-mails are automatic or personalised and whether questions have been answered satisfactorily.

Empathy

• Empathy considers the caring, individualised attention a firm gives its customers.

• Most people would assume that empathy can only occur through personal human contact but it can be achieved to some degree through personalising websites and e-mail.

• Key here is whether customers feel understood. For example, being recommended products that they would never dream of buying can erode empathy.

Test your understanding 4

Improved performance and added value
Benchmarking should improve quality, increase customer satisfaction and reduce waste.

Improved understanding of environmental pressures
An understanding of customers' needs and competitors' actions will be key to improving quality.

Eliminate complacency
Benchmarking can help to drive change and quality improvement.

Continuous improvement
Benchmarking can be carried out at regular intervals and therefore drive continuous quality improvement.

Achievability
The methods are already used elsewhere. Therefore, employees should buy-in to the change since it is seen as achievable.

Test your understanding 5

JIT – planning and forecasting can be used to manage demand. This will ensure that there is an appropriate number of staff to minimise queuing times (those waste customer's time but also give them an adverse impression about the quality of the service) but that staff idle time is also kept to a minimum. Well trained staff should be able to meet the customers' needs effectively and efficiently and a well organised work area should be able to reduce the amount of time that customers are on hold for.

Kaizen – this might be used to reduce customer waiting times. Some call centres use electronic wall boards. These show information, such as the number of customers waiting, and can be used to reduce this waiting time for customers.

5-S practice – this model can be used to organise the surroundings of the call centre office. All of the materials the employee uses should be organised and within reach without having to leave the area. This should allow the call centre staff to talk on the phone, access the computer and view any other documents, all without moving from their desk.

TPM – call centre staff should be trained to take care of their equipment and will be able to solve common problems themselves, e.g. with their phone/ computer.

Cellular manufacturing – rather than placing pieces of equipment such as postage machines, photocopiers, fax machines and file drawers throughout the area for everyone to use (and wait on), consider placing these together in a U shaped cell to minimise movement.

Six sigma – It is more difficult to define a fault in a service company but it can be thought of as not fulfilling the needs of the customer. Well trained, experienced staff will have the ability to put the customer first and to achieve the low level of 'faults' required by six sigma.

Question 1

C

Question 2

Benefits of this accreditation are:

- enhancement of environmental awareness within the organisation
- cost savings and reduction in use of resources
- improved compliance with legislation
- potential competitive advantage over companies without accreditation
- demonstration of environmental commitment to stakeholders.

Question 3

C

Question 4

C

Question 5

C

Question 6

D

Question 7

- The management of quality is the function and responsibility of everyone within the organisation.

- Complex products require unique product specifications for demanding customers.

- Customer focus is important, giving value for money and quality and creating competitive value for the price paid. This requires a flexible approach to design procedures and requires supplier involvement at the design and production stages.

- Continuous improvement in both products and internal procedures is a critical factor in maintaining competitive advantage. A Total Quality Management programme (TQM) would instil quality throughout the organisation and ensure that service excellence and value are primary aims for the whole of the company.

Question 8

Servqual will use 22 questions to understand a respondent's attitude about service quality in the hotel. The questions are reliable indicators of five dimensions:

- Tangibles – for example, design of the hotel or cleanliness of the rooms.

- Reliability – for example, booking processed correctly or wake-up call received on time.

- Responsiveness – for example, staff respond to requests for directions.

- Assurance – for example, reception staff inspire confidence.

- Empathy – for example, each hotel guest is treated as an individual.

Question 9

(a) Benchmarking

Benchmarking is the comparison of an organisation's products, services, and work processes with known models of good or best practice in order to improve performance. Through benchmarking, organisations learn about their own business practices and the best practices of others. Benchmarking enables them to identify where they fall short of current best practice and determine action programmes to help them match and surpass it.

Benchmarking focuses on improving key areas and sets targets, which are challenging but 'achievable'. By examining what others have achieved, managers can discover what is really achievable and accept that they are not being asked to perform miracles

Types of benchmarking

The different types of benchmarking include the following:

- **Internal benchmarking** compares an activity with the best that is found elsewhere in the organisation with the aim of improving it to match. It assumes there are differences in the work processes of an organisation as a result of geographical differences, local organisational history, customs, differences among business units, and relationships among managers and employees.

- **Competitive benchmarking** compares an activity with the best that is found elsewhere in the industry. A company tries to identify specific information about a competitor's products, processes or business results and then makes comparisons with those of its own organisation.

- **Functional benchmarking** - make comparisons with organisations in different, non-competing product/service sectors but with similar core operations. They involve the identification of state-of-the-art products, services or processes of an organisation. The objective of this type of benchmarking is to identify best practices in any type of organisation that has established a reputation for excellence in specific business activities such as manufacturing, marketing, engineering, warehousing, fleet management or human resources.

(b) Benchmarking could be used to improve the management of future projects at Acme.

Internal benchmarking - we are not sure whether significant project management expertise exists within Acme. The absence of formal project management procedures suggests that it is not the case. However, there may be individual managers who have experience from earlier employments and are applying project management techniques not used currently in the production department.

It should be possible to contact all staff involved in managing projects, asking them for their views and experiences. This could then be followed up with a 'project management excellence' meeting to build a model that can be used by Acme with procedures being drawn up for the quality assurance staff.

Competitive benchmarking - short of industrial espionage, it is very hard to obtain information about rival companies because they may think that the way they manage capital projects gives them a competitive advantage. However, the practice of 'benchmarking' suggests otherwise. There are several methods by which competitive benchmarking may be made possible.

It can focus on the performance and relative strengths of direct competitors by using information from customer and supplier interviews and published data from any source available. We may find that researchers from a business school or consultancy have studied the project management methodology used by one of our rivals. Often such studies are published, so we may not need to approach the rival directly.

If a rival believes that the management of capital projects is not of significant commercial value, they may be willing to participate in a knowledge-sharing exercise. Although this would benefit us greatly, the rival may feel that they can also learn and improve.

We may find that one (or some) of our employees have been involved in (or had some experience of) project management while employed by one of our rivals. While sharing such an experience has an ethical aspect, staff may be willing to contribute.

Functional benchmarking - an increasing number of companies are turning toward process benchmarking because it is non-competitive. Companies not engaged in direct competition are more open, and so the potential for discovering innovative practices is much higher. It is also very common for best practice organisations to have their activities studied and documented by researchers, making it available from textbooks, academic research papers, business school case studies or the Internet.

Although the techniques of best practice may be in the public domain, it is very difficult to copy the cultural elements of organisations. Such things as beliefs and values depend on individuals and are difficult to record. However, it is often these elements that lead to improved performance.

Models of best practice - it should be possible to find appropriate models of best practice in all areas of project management. The areas that we should attempt to benchmark include the following:

- The authorisation and initiation process;
- Team structure and organisation;
- Using project management tools and software;
- Supplier selection and competitive tendering;
- Reporting of progress and relationship management;
- Sub-contractor management procedures;
- Post-completion audit.

Once the best practices have been identified, the benchmarking team collects the data, analyses it, and then plots our performance against the best practices to help us identify improvement opportunities.

The team then determines the level of effort required to re-engineer the best practices to suit Acme's unique circumstances. The benefits versus the costs involved with eliminating the gaps between current processes and the best practices are evaluated, and then implementation priorities are established.

Question 10

Quality circles are a method of trying to encourage innovative ideas in production, and by involving employees they are likely to improve the prospects for acceptance of changes in products and working methods.

The production director should be advised that the nature of the changes recommended by the quality circle will depend on the range of skills and experience of the circle members. The wider their skills are, and the broader their experience, the more significant and far-reaching will be the changes they might suggest. Groups of workers with similar skills are more likely to make suggestions for limited changes, within the sphere of their own work experience. What range of skills should the circles have?

The 'terms of reference' of the circles should be made clear. Are they to recommend changes to senior management, or will they have the authority to decide changes, and make them?

Since the purpose of quality circles is to encourage innovation, the co-operation of employees will be crucial. The plans for setting up quality circles should therefore be discussed with the employees who will provide membership of the circles.

Possible problems with the introduction of quality circles might be:

(a) not enough support from top management.

(b) no co-operation from middle management.

(c) poor choice of circle leaders.

(d) insufficient training of circle members.

(e) unwillingness to participate among employees.

(f) Individual talkers dominate the circle.

(g) poor communication.

The keys to a successful programme are:

(a) creating a proper atmosphere in which to launch them – a positive approach and good publicity.

(b) giving circle member adequate training in quality circle techniques.

(c) introducing circles slowly, one or two at a time, instead of setting up too many all at once. Learning from experience. Getting employees to accept the value of circles from their experience and observations over time.

(d) full support from top management.

(e) an enthusiastic 'facilitator' – a manager in charge of making the circles a success.

(f)   setting up a good system for following up and evaluating proposals for change.

(g)   giving recognition to circle members – for instance, rewards for successful changes.

Introduction to Marketing

Chapter learning objectives

Lead	Component
D1. Explain developments in marketing.	(a) Explain the marketing concept, and the alternatives to it.
	(b) Describe the marketing environment of a range of organisations.
	(e) Describe theories of consumer behaviour.

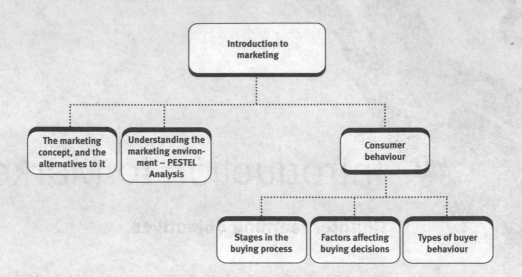

1 Introduction

- Organisations are increasingly recognising the importance of marketing's role and its contribution in achieving sustainable growth and profitability. It can be a key driver of competitive advantage. Marketing is not simply promotion but is a much broader concept.

- This chapter introduces what is meant by marketing. The following two chapters describe the marketing tools that an organisation may use to compete.

2 The Marketing Concept, and the Alternatives to it

A marketing orientated business is one that has adopted a marketing concept. However, a number of other 'orientations' – sales, production and product – may be adopted. Before explaining the marketing concept each of these alternatives will be introduced.

2.1 Sales orientation

- The major task of management is to use persuasive communication and aggressive promotional policies to entice the customer.

- The sales team and the sales manager is the focal point of the business.

- The belief is that a good sales team can sell anything to anybody.

- The organisation sets about increasing demand by investing heavily in sales techniques such as personal selling, advertising and sales promotion in order to emphasise product differentiation and branding.

Test your understanding 1

Explain the types of organisation that adopt a sales orientation.

Drawbacks of the sales orientation

- There is no systematic attempt to identify customer needs, or to create products that satisfy them.

- As a result, the organisation has to rely on intensive sales techniques.

2.2 Production orientation

- The business focuses on making as many units as possible.

- High volume production results in economies of scale and therefore profitability is improved due to a lower unit cost.

- The approach works when the market is growing more rapidly than output.

- A major task of management is to pursue improved production and distribution efficiency.

Illustration 1 - Production orientation

In America and Europe the production orientation was a popular approach until the 1930s. Up until then, there was a general shortage of goods relative to demand, and a lack of competition, resulted in a seller's market.

During periods of shortages, a production orientation sometimes returns to an industry sector. Normally the UK honey industry is typified by a marketing orientation (see below), where customer needs are prioritised. However, a poor summer in the UK in 2008 resulted in a honey shortage since worker bees don't forage as much in the rain or cold weather. This resulted in producers simply trying to harvest and produce as much honey as possible, a production orientation.

Drawbacks of the production orientation

- If production exceeds demand too much may be produced and left unsold.

- The approach does not take account of customer preferences and the low cost may be associated with lower quality.

2.3 Product orientation

The business centres its activities on continually improving and refining its products, assuming that customers simply want the best quality for their money.

Drawbacks of the product orientation

The business concentrates on its products and, as a result, the product may or may not fulfil customer requirements.

Illustration 2 - Product orientation

Sir Clive Sinclair's business adopted a product orientation. Some of his products proved extremely popular. For example, The Spectrum computer released in 1981 was very cheap and powerful for its day.

Other products were not such a success. For example, the Sinclair C5, a road hugging vehicle that could reach speeds of 15mph. When it was released in 1985 it was billed as the last word in futuristic transport. However, it was rumoured to be powered by a washing machine motor and was so small that driving it was dangerous. The product was consigned to the commercial scrapheap after just ten months.

Test your understanding 2

Under which market conditions could product-orientated organisations best succeed?

2.4 Marketing orientation

| Understand customer's needs | .... | Product **benefits and features** should fulfil needs |

All of the approaches reviewed so far have potential drawbacks. The best approach that an organisation can adopt is a marketing orientation.

In the UK, the Chartered Institute of Marketing (CIM) defines marketing as:

"The management process responsible for identifying, anticipating and satisfying customer requirements profitably."

The organisation will first understand the needs of the customer and will then adopt a strategy producing products with the benefits and features to fulfil these needs.

Benefits of the marketing orientation

Where an organisation is able to meet its customers' needs efficiently and effectively, its ability to gain an advantage over its competitors will be increased.

As CIM point out:

"It is all about getting the right product or service to the customer at the right price, in the right place, at the right time. Business history and current practice both remind us that without proper marketing, companies cannot get close to customers and satisfy their needs. And if they don't, a competitor surely will."

Test your understanding 3

Car manufacturers must adapt their strategy to reflect changing customer needs. For example:

- In the 1980's some car manufacturers targeted young upwardly-mobile professionals (yuppies).

- In the early 21st century, car manufacturers targeting families have had to recognise the changing needs of the modern family.

Using the example of a car, explain the needs of the two groups above. Describe what features and benefits manufacturers have included in their cars in order to fulfil the needs of these customers.

Who is responsible for marketing?

Satisfying customers is at the heart of marketing. Who then assumes responsibility for this important function? Possibly the marketing department or the sales force? True, such personnel can have an influence on customer satisfaction, but marketing as a philosophy is wider than this narrow group of employees. Employees outside the marketing department or sales force can also play an important role in determining customer satisfaction.

Marketing is more than a range of techniques that enables the company to determine customer requirements. It can be better understood as a shared business ethos. The marketing concept is a philosophy that places customers central to all organisational activities. The long-term strategies of an organisation might be centred on profit maximisation, market share growth, or growth in real terms but none of this can be achieved without satisfying customers.

Without customers there would be no business.

3 Understanding the Marketing Environment - PESTEL Analysis

Organisational performance will be dependent on the successful management of the opportunities, challenges and risks presented by changes in the external environment. Within the external business environment Johnson, Scholes and Whittington (2008) identify three layers of influence:

- competitors and markets;
- industry or sector; and
- the macro environment

One popular technique for analysing the macro environment is PESTEL analysis.

This analysis divides the business environment into six related sub-systems – Political, Economic, Social, Technical, Ecological factors and Legal. Each of these factors can be applied to the marketing function.

3.1 Political

Political factors can have a direct effect on the way a business operates. Decisions made by government affect our everyday lives.

For example, the instability of many governments in less developed countries has led a number of companies to question the wisdom of marketing in those countries.

3.2 Economic

All businesses are affected by economical factors nationally and globally. For example, within the UK the climate of the economy dictates how consumers may behave within society.

The business cycle

Boom: unemployment is low and job confidence high. This results in high spending by consumers and increased demand for luxury products

Recession: Unemployment is high and job confidence is low resulting in low consumer spending and reduced demand for products

Test your understanding 4

Describe the changes that may be made to the marketing approach of a supermarket if the country goes into recession.

3.3 Social

Forces within society such as family, friends and the media affect our attitude, interests and opinions and in turn will influence our purchases. For example:

- Within the UK people's attitudes are changing towards their diet and health. Over the last 10 years, the UK has seen an increase in the number of people joining fitness clubs and a massive increase in demand for organic food.

- In Japan the fall in the birth rate has had a major impact on the sales of toys, as demand falls competition for the remaining market becomes very intense. If this trend continues it will have an impact on other sectors in the future, i.e. affecting teen products, 20's products and so on.

Social factors

According to Johnson and Scholes the following social influences should be monitored:

- **Population demographics** - a term used to describe the composition of the population in any given area, whether a region, a country or an area within a country.

- **Income distribution** - will provide the marketer with some indication of the size of the target markets. Most developed countries, like the UK, have a relatively even distribution spread. However, this is not the case in other nations.

- **Social mobility** - the marketer should be aware of social classes and the distribution among them. The marketer can use this knowledge to promote products to distinct social classes within the market.

- **Lifestyle changes** - refer to our attitudes and opinions to things like social values, credit, health and women. Our attitudes have changed in recent years and this information is vital for the marketer.

- **Consumerism** - one of the social trends in recent years has been the rise of consumerism. This trend has increased to such an extent that governments have been pressured to design laws that protect the rights of the consumer.

- **Levels of education** - the level of education has increased dramatically over the last few years. There is now a larger proportion of the population in higher education than ever before.

3.4 Technical

This is an area in which change takes place very rapidly and the organisation needs to be constantly aware of what is going on. Technological change can influence the following:

- New technology can result in the production of new products, e.g. hybrid cars have been produced. These cars have improved fuel economy and reduced emissions.

- New technology can allow existing products to be made more cheaply and hence prices can be lowered.

- Technological developments have allowed new methods of distributing goods and services. For example, Amazon's business success is largely due to using the internet as a distribution channel.

- Technology has allowed companies to develop new methods of communicating with their customers, e.g. targeted emails and text messages.

3.5 Ecological

These have become increasingly important in recent years and influence a marketing orientated organisation in a number of ways:

- The general public have become increasingly aware of ecological issues and this has influenced their product choices.

- Pressure on natural resources has influenced the products offered by some industry sectors, e.g. the fishing industry.

3.6 Legal

Regulations governing businesses are widespread; they include those on health and safety, information disclosure, the dismissal of employees, vehicle emissions, the use of pesticides and many more.

For example, the UK smoking ban in public places has resulted in UK tobacco companies exploring new products, such as the legal, electronic cigarette (these simulate the functions of a cigarette but without the harmful chemicals), and new markets outside of the UK.

4 Consumer Behaviour

4.1 Introduction

As discussed, the marketing orientation is about understanding customer's needs. Therefore, an organisation must understand the complex process by which buyers make purchasing decisions. This will assist in driving success in, what may be, a highly competitive environment.

4.2 The stages in the buying process

Research suggests that customers go through a five stage decision-making process in any purchase. This is summarised in the diagram below:

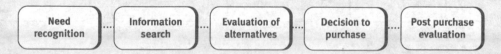

Stage 1: Need recognition

The consumer identifies the need or the problem and the firm must use appropriate promotional tools to convince the customer that their product could be the answer.

Illustration 3

Marketers have recognised that the cheap coffee that was once bought from a supermarket or a cafe is not going to satisfy the needs of increasingly discerning buyers who seek a coffee that suits their particular tastes, lifestyle and budget. In addition, a growing awareness of ethical trading and healthy living has contributed to the development of coffee to cater for these increasingly complex needs.

Starbucks is one company that has successfully understood these needs. Its cafes sell a huge range of coffees and other beverages and the company also sells its own-branded quality coffee in UK supermarkets.

There are a number of theories about how needs influence consumer behaviour. Two of these theories are:

- How society influences needs
- Maslow's hierarchy of needs

How society influences needs

Maslow's hierarchy of needs

Maslow proposed a hierarchy of needs that he used to explain human motivation. Conventionally used to explain the motivation to work, his hierarchy can also be applied to customer motivation.

The five-part hierarchy is arranged in the order in which human needs must be satisfied. Thus, a 'safety' need is a motivating factor only when 'physiological' needs have been satisfied. When the 'safety' need is satisfied, 'love' needs become important, and so on.

Products and services could be considered against this hierarchy, as shown below:

It is the job of the marketing team to persuade the potential customer that the product will satisfy his or her needs.

Stage 2: Information search

Once a need has been recognised buyers will look for information regarding which products may satisfy their needs.

Test your understanding 5

Explain what information sources are likely to be used by a buyer when seeking out information about the alternative ways in which they can satisfy their needs.

Stage 3: Evaluation of alternatives

The total range of products will be filtered down to a manageable number. The alternatives will then be evaluated against an individual's decision criteria.

For example, when buying a new car an individual may gather information on most of the cars available on the market for their budget. They will then filter the alternatives and may decide to visit the showroom or carry out a test drive on a small number of cars.

Stage 4: Decision to purchase

The outcome of the evaluation process may be a decision to:

- buy the product now
- not buy the product at all

- defer the purchase of the product

- start the process again

The final decision to purchase may involve a large number of people, known as the decision-making unit (DMU). The DMU is made up of six groups:

(1) Initiator
e.g. wife identifies need for a second family car

(2) Gatekeeper
e.g. husband starts process by collecting a large number of sample brochures. These are reviewed and a small sample is then chosen for discussion

(6) Buyer
e.g. husband carries out final negotiation and purchase with supplier

DMU

(3) Influencers
e.g. family friend affects product bought due to their expertise

(5) Approvers
e.g. the children may approve of and therefore authorise the final decision

(4) Deciders
e.g. husband makes final decision regarding which product to buy

Stage 5: Post-purchase evaluation

The buyer will evaluate the success of the purchase and add the positive and negative elements to a store of information which will assist further purchasing decisions. The buyer will also be likely to tell his or her friends about the purchase, making either favourable or unfavourable comments.

Satisfied customers will act as one of the best forms of promotion:

For example, a customer spending just $20 in a restaurant on a first visit could be worth thousands of pounds over the next few years.

Evaluation of 5-stage process

The five-stage model implies that customers pass through all stages in every purchase. However, in more routine purchases, customers often skip or reverse some of the stages.

For example, a student buying a favourite hamburger would recognise the need (hunger) and go right to the purchasing decision, skipping information search and evaluation. However, the model is very useful when understanding any purchase that requires some thought and deliberation.

4.3 Factors affecting buying decisions

Some of the factors influencing buying decisions have been discussed above. **Lancaster and Withey** concluded that at each of the five stages there are three key factors that influence the purchasing decision:

Factor	Examples
(1) Socio/cultural influences	• **Reference groups** such as school friends or work colleagues e.g. it is a bold person who reads the Sun in an office full of FT readers • **Role modelling** e.g. a young mother would be influenced to make certain buying decisions, such as a push chair, due to her role • **Family** e.g. the influence of 'pester power' may result in child dominant decisions. • **Culture** e.g. beliefs and values may influence whether or not meat is bought by a household.
(2) Personal influences	• Age • Family status • Occupation • Economic circumstances • Lifestyle e.g. a young single male in his 20s, with a high level of disposable income, is likely to purchase a different type of car to a man in his 30s with a growing family
(3) Psychological influences	• Motivation • Perception • Learning • Beliefs and attitudes e.g. Individuals will be motivated by different needs. Some buyers may be motivated by superb customer service and would not return to a restaurant unless this is received.

Types of buyer behaviour

Buyer behaviour will be influenced by the type of consumer good:

Type of consumer good	Meaning	Factors influencing the purchase
Fast moving consumer good (FMCG)	• Relatively cheap • Purchased on a regular basis E.g. bread, baked beans	• Habitual purchases - often involves very little decision making by buyer
Durable goods	• Relatively expensive • Not purchased on a regular basis E.g. TV, computer, car	• Fashion • New technical features • Old product wearing out

5 Chapter summary

6 Practice questions

Question 1

A company that concentrates on using aggressive promotional policies to entice the customer is referred to as:

A   a production organisation.

B   a learning organisation.

C   a marketing organisation.

D   a sales organisation.

(2 marks)

Question 2

Which of the following is a drawback of the production orientation?

A   The business concentrates on its products but the product may not fulfil the customer's needs.

B   The organisation relies on sales techniques to sell its products.

C   Low cost may be associated with low quality.

D   High volume production results in economies of scale.

(2 marks)

Question 3

Which one of the following is not one of the accepted headings included in PESTEL analysis?

A   Economic

B   Taxation

C   Social

D   Technical

(2 marks)

Question 4

Harry is 12 years old. He is a keen Manchester United supporter and in his spare time he plays football for his local team and is a scout member. Which of the following would be least likely to be a reference group for Harry?

A   His teachers

B   One of the Manchester United players

C   The other members of his local football team

D   The other members of his scout group

(2 marks)

Question 5

Which of the following is an example of a durable good?

A   A games console

B   Milk

C   Tea bags

D   Shampoo

(2 marks)

Question 6

Distinguish socio/ cultural influences from personal influences, giving examples of each.

(4 marks)

Question 7

Explain the relationship between Maslow's hierarchy of needs and marketing.

(4 marks)

Question 8

List FOUR examples of fast moving consumer goods and FOUR examples of durable goods.

(4 marks)

Question 9

M Company began over a century ago as a small family-run business, selling its own-branded clothing, food and drink. The company has grown rapidly over the past 30 years and now has a prominent position on the high street of many of the country's towns and cities.

Until recently, the company had a strong reputation and was well known for quality products at affordable prices. However, the situation has changed dramatically as new entrants have taken market share away from M company.

Sales and profits have fallen over each of the three past consecutive years and there is concern that the company may make a loss in the forthcoming year.

After various attempts failed to improve matters, M company has recently appointed a management consultant to identify the reasons for the declining sales and the loss of customers.

The marketing consultant has concluded that the problem for M company is that it has never moved from being sales orientated to being marketing orientated and that is why it has lost touch with its customers. The consultant has recommended the adoption of a marketing orientation.

Required:

(a) Explain the difference between a company that concentrates on 'selling' its products and one that has adopted a marketing orientation. Explain the benefits to M company of adopting a marketing orientation.

(10 marks)

(b) Explain, using examples, how M company's marketing function may use PESTEL analysis to understand its external environment.

(10 marks)

(Total: 20 marks)

Test your understanding answers

Test your understanding 1

A sales orientation has been adopted by a number of business sectors. For example:

- Organisations selling double glazing
- Organisations selling timeshare holidays

These organisations rely on persuasive and aggressive promotional policies to entice the customer.

Test your understanding 2

Where demand far exceeds supply and the consumer is not discerning due to the shortage of this product or service. Thirty years or so ago this was particularly true within the former Eastern bloc countries where queues formed to buy food and goods irrespective of quality. In some cases those queuing did not know the precise goods they were queuing for!

Test your understanding 3

	Needs of target customer	Product features	Product benefits
1980's - some car manufacturers targeted yuppies	• A fast car • Cutting edge design • Car should enhance image	• Sporty design • Turbo engine • Other features such as an electrically operated roof and leather upholstery	• 0-60 mph in six seconds • Superb road handling
Early 21st century - some car manufacturers target families but have had to recognise their changing needs	• Value for money • Safety • Environmental friendliness • Low fuel consumption	• Air bags • Economical engine • Designed for safety and space	• Good safety record • Low fuel consumption and CO_2 emissions • Room for child seats

Test your understanding 4

The changing needs of the population must be reflected in the product offerings. For example:

• The supermarket may reduce its range of luxury items in favour of lower priced, basic products.

• Special offers may be made on products. For example, discounts, buy one get one free offers, additional loyalty points on products.

• The supermarket may introduce more 'restaurant style' meals to reflect the trend that fewer people are eating out.

Test your understanding 5

- **Personal experience** – the buyer may already have used the company's products.

- **Word-of-mouth** - for example, recommendations from friends regarding a restaurant.

- **Internet** - for example, websites such as Trip Advisor include user feedback on a large number of hotels.

- **Reference groups** - rather than referring to people we know, we may use various other reference groups to guide us. For example, what kind of shoes is our favourite celebrity wearing at the moment?

- **Reviews** - newspapers and consumer review sources such as Which? magazine.

Question 1

D

Question 2

C

Question 3

B

Question 4

A

Question 5

A

Question 6

- Personal influences are specific to the individual and include factors such as age, occupation and family status.

- These personal influences will impact the needs of the individual. For example, a 35 year old professional male, who is married with a young family, may have a need for an estate car.

- However, the manifestation of these needs will be influenced by socio/ cultural factors, e.g. reference groups, role models, family and culture.

- For example, the colleagues of the 35 year old male may influence the model of estate car purchased.

Question 7

- An organisation adopting a marketing approach must first understand the needs of its customers. These needs can be understood by reviewing Maslow's hierarchy.

- Maslow proposed a hierarchy of needs that can be used to explain customer motivation.

- The five-part hierarchy is arranged in the order in which human needs must be satisfied. For example, a 'love' need is a motivating factor only when 'safety' needs have been satisfied.

- The marketing team must persuade the potential customer that the product will satisfy his or her needs.

Question 8

Durable goods	Fast moving consumer goods
Car	Bread
Washing machine	Washing powder
Fridge	Butter
MP3 player	Milk

Question 9

(a) Sales orientation

A company that concentrates on 'selling' its products is said to be sales orientated. M company currently adopts a sales orientation.

The major task of M's management will be to use persuasive communication and aggressive promotional policies to entice the customer to buy its products.

The sales team and the sales manager will be the focal point of M company. There will be huge investment in the sales department, the belief being that a good sales team can sell anything to anybody.

Techniques such as personal selling and product promotion will be used to emphasise product differentiation and branding.

Drawbacks of the sales orientation

M company is losing customers and its sales and profits have fallen for each of the past three consecutive years. These problems may be largely due to the adoption of a sales orientation since:

- There is no systematic attempt by M company to identify customer's needs, or to create products that satisfy these needs.
- As a result, M company is having to rely on intensive sales techniques but these do not appear to be working.

Adoption of a marketing orientation

This orientation addresses the problems highlighted above.

If M company were to adopt a marketing orientation, they would begin by understanding the needs of the customer and would then adopt a strategy producing products with the benefits and features to fulfil these needs.

Benefits of a marketing orientation

If M company adopts a marketing orientation it will put its customer's needs first. If it is able to identify these needs and meet the needs efficiently and effectively, its ability to gain competitive advantage will increase.

(b) If M company is to turn itself around, not only will it have to understand its customer's needs but it will also need to understand the opportunities, challenges and risks presented by changes in the external environment. PESTEL analysis can be used to analyse the external environment. Each of these factors can be applied to M company's marketing function.

Political

Political factors will have a direct effect on the way in which M company operates.

For example, the government in the UK is currently encouraging sustainability in operations and the adoption of a healthy lifestyle by individuals. This may influence a decision by M company to reduce the amount of packaging in its products or to improve product labelling to clearly show the sugar, fat, salt and calorie content of their food products.

Economic

M company will be affected by national and global economic factors.

For example, if the country moves into recession, M company may decide to focus on selling cheaper products rather than luxury products.

Social

Forces within society such as family, friends and the media will influence the choices that individuals make.

For example, within the UK consumer's attitudes, with regards to the source of products, is changing. Ethical sourcing is becoming more important to individuals, e.g. with an increased emphasis on fair trade, a reduction in air miles and fair treatment of suppliers all being considered important. These factors will all influence the decisions taken by M company.

Technical

This is an area in which change takes place very rapidly and it is important for M company to monitor and react to these changes.

For example, new technology may allow existing products to be made more quickly and hence prices can be lowered.

Ecological

These have become increasingly important is recent years and M company must react to any ecological factors. For example, pressure on natural resources may influence the types of fish that M company sell or include in their products.

Legal

Regulations on businesses are widespread, including those on health and safety, information disclosure, the dismissal of employees and many more. For example, M company must clearly display product information on its goods, such as a list of ingredients on its packaged food.

If M company understands its customer's needs as well as its external environment, there is a good opportunity for the business to be turned around.

The Market Planning Process and the Marketing Mix

Chapter learning objectives

Lead	Component
D2. Apply tools and techniques used in support of the organisation's marketing.	(a) Explain the relationships between market research, market segmentation, targeting and positioning.
	(b) Apply tools within each area of the marketing mix.
	(d) Describe the market planning process.
	(e) Explain the role of branding and brand equity.

1 The Market Planning Process

A company may currently have a sales/ production/ product orientation and may want to adopt a marketing orientation. In order to do this it will need to implement a marketing action plan.

The following components should be included in this plan:

Step 1: Situation analysis

A number of techniques can be used:

SWOT analysis – the organisation needs to understand its own strengths and weaknesses together with an appreciation of the wider environment in which it operates (opportunities and threats).

PESTEL analysis – the organisation should review the marketing environment for opportunities that may allow it to further meet their customers' needs. It should also monitor its competitors' strategies.

Step 2: Set its corporate objectives

The organisation may already have a mission statement and a set of corporate objectives in place. However, these should be reviewed to ensure that they are still relevant for the organisation.

Step 3: Set its marketing objectives

The organisation should decide what it wants to achieve based on its business objectives and given its current position.

Marketing objectives should be SMART – specific, measurable, achievable, realistic and time bound, e.g. to achieve a 10% growth in sales in Europe in the next 12 months.

Step 4: Devise an appropriate marketing strategy

The organisation should consider the following:

- Segmentation – the market should be segmented, e.g. by age, social class or income. The needs of each segment should be established using market research.

- Targeting – the most attractive segments in terms of profitability and growth should be targeted using an appropriate marketing mix.

- Positioning – an appropriate positioning strategy, e.g. differentiation or cost leadership should be chosen for each market segment.

- Marketing mix – the organisation should use the marketing mix to determine the correct strategy for product, price, place and promotion.

Note: Each of these ideas will be explored in more detail in the remainder of the chapter.

Step 5: Plan the marketing mix

The organisation must then plan the specific elements of the marketing mix.

Importance of marketing action plan to the business plan

The marketing action plan will form an important component of any business plan. The business plan has many objectives including:

- Securing external funding
- Measuring business success

Step 6: Implementation and control

The marketing plan should then be implemented. The plan should also be monitored to gauge its success and to identify any necessary changes.

2 Segmentation, Targeting and Positioning

2.1 Market segmentation

Market segmentation is the sub-dividing of the market into homogenous groups to whom a separate marketing mix can be focused.

A market segment is a group of consumers with distinct, shared needs.

Why segment the market?

- Market segmentation allows companies to treat similar customers in similar ways.

- Each segment has slightly different needs which can be satisfied by offering each segment a slightly different marketing mix.

- The key objective is to say that people falling into a particular segment are more likely to purchase the product than most.

- The company will choose a particular segment or segments to target.

Criteria for market segments

Kotler suggested that segments must be:

- **Measurable** - It must be possible to identify the number of buyers in each market segment so that their potential profitability can be assessed, e.g. the size of the segment of people aged 30-40, or who are married with children, can be accurately calculated but information about the number of people who are environmentally aware is not readily available.

- **Accessible** - It must be possible to reach the segment, e.g. some buyers in a market may be tied to suppliers by long-term supply contracts. Therefore, this market is not accessible.

- **Substantial** - The cost of targeting a particular segment must be less than the benefit. Small market segments may prove unprofitable.

Bases for segmentation

One form of segmentation may be enough, or a number of variables may be used, to define the target market exactly. Possible bases include:

Bases for segmentation

Demographic

Market segments are frequently based on age, gender, geographical location or family life cycle.

This can be highly relevant with some products. For example, certain brands of breakfast cereal have regular sales to families with young children (e.g. Coco Pops), where as other brands (e.g. Bran Flakes) sell almost entirely to adults.

In other areas, demographic influences seem to have little effect. For instance, own-label products are believed to sell equally to high and low income families and single people and across all age groups.

Family life cycle segmentation divides customers by their position in the family life cycle:

Life cycle stage	Characteristics	Examples of products purchased
Bachelor	Financially well off. Fashion opinion leaders. Recreation orientated.	Cars, holidays, basic furniture, kitchen equipment.
Newly married couple	Still financially well off. Very high purchase rate, especially of durables.	Cars, furniture, houses, holidays, refrigerators.
Full nest (i)	Liquid assets low. Home purchasing at a peak. Little money saving.	Washers, TVs, baby foods, toys, medicines.
Full nest (ii)	Better off. Some partners work. Some children work part time. Less influenced by advertising.	Larger size grocery packs, foods, cleaning materials, bicycles.
Full nest (iii)	Better off still. Purchasing durables.	New furniture, luxury appliances, recreational goods.
Empty nest (i)	Satisfied with financial position.	Travel, luxuries, home improvements.
Empty nest (ii)	Drastic cut in income. Stay at home.	Medicines, health aids.

Socio-economic

One of the most widely used forms of segmentation in the UK is socio-economic.

Class	Social status	Job descriptions
A	Upper middle class	Higher managerial, administrative and professional
B	Middle class	Middle management, administrative and professional
C1	Lower middle class	Supervisory, clerical, junior management, administrative staff
C2	Working class	Semi and unskilled manual jobs
D	Subsistence	Pensioners, widows, lowest grade workers

While such class-based systems may seem out of date, the model is still widely used, especially in advertising. Socio-economic class is closely correlated with press readership and viewing habits, and media planners use this fact to advertise in the most effective way to communicate with their target audience.

Psychological

Lifestyle segmentation may be used because people of similar age and socio-economic status may lead quite different lifestyles. Marketers have segmented the market using terms such as 'Yuppies' (young, upwardly-mobile professionals) and 'Dinkies' (double income, no kids).

Attitudes and values can be harder to measure but can prove to be a useful basis for segmentation, e.g. individuals may have a value based on caution and therefore purchase a safe, reliable car.

Situational

Occasion of use – a product may be bought at different times for different uses. For example, workers may expect a lunchtime meal in a restaurant to be fast and good value for money, whereas those same individuals may be willing to pay more in the evening for a more relaxed dining experience.

Frequency of purchase – frequent buyers may be more demanding with regards to product features and may be more sensitive to price changes.

Test your understanding 1

Explain five variables that you think would be useful as a basis for segmenting the market for cars.

Industrial segmentation

Industrial segmentation is different from that used in consumer marketing. The following factors influence the way industrial customers can be segmented:

Geographic is used as the basis for sales-force organisations.

Purchasing characteristics – is the classification of companies by factors such as average order size or the frequency with which they order.

Benefit – industrial purchasers have different benefit expectations to consumers. They may be orientated towards reliability, durability, versatility, safety, serviceability or ease of operation. They are always concerned with value for money.

Company type – industrial customers can be segmented according to the type of business they are, i.e. what they offer for sale. The range of products and services used in an industry will not vary too much from one company to another.

Company size – it is frequently useful to analyse marketing opportunities in terms of company size. A company supplying canteen foods would investigate size in terms of numbers of employees. Processed parts suppliers are interested in production rate, and lubricants suppliers would segment by numbers of machine tools.

2.2 Targeting

This is the process of selecting the most lucrative market segment(s) for marketing the product.

Having segmented the market, the organisation can now decide how to respond to the differences in customer needs identified. Two questions need answering:

Q1 Which segments are worth investing in?

When evaluating potential target markets, the following issues should be considered:

- Size of segment
- Growth potential
- Profit potential
- Degree of competition
- Accessibility
- Barriers to entry

Q2 Whether / how to vary the marketing strategy between segments

For example, the market for package holidays can be split into a variety of different segments – the family market, the elderly market, the young singles market, the activity holiday market, the budget holiday market, etc.

It would be virtually impossible to provide one single holiday package that would satisfy all people in the above markets. Because the people in the different segments will have different needs and wants, a holiday company has a choice in terms of its marketing approach. It can go for:

- **Concentrated marketing** (sometimes referred to as niche or target marketing) specialises in one or two of the identified markets only, where a company knows it can compete successfully. For example, Saga holidays offers a variety of holidays for the older market niche only.

- **Differentiated marketing** (sometimes called segmented marketing) – the company makes several products each aimed at a separate target segment. For example, Virgin Holidays offers a variety of family holidays, honeymoon packages and city breaks, each of which is targeted at a different group. Many retailers have developed different brand formats to target different groups.

- **Undifferentiated marketing** (sometimes called mass marketing) – this is the delivery of a single product to the entire market. There is little concern for segmentation. The hope is that as many customers as possible will buy the product. When Henry Ford began manufacturing cars he offered any colour 'as long as it's black'.

2.3 Positioning

Positioning involves the formulation of a definitive marketing strategy around which the product would be marketed to the target audience.

After the target market has been chosen, marketers will want to position their products in relation to the competitors for that segment. A variety of techniques are available.

Porter identified a number of potential strategies:

	Low cost	High cost
Broad target	1 Cost leadership	2 Differentiation
Narrow target	3A Cost focus	3B Differentiation focus

Perceptual mapping

Perceptual mapping is used to chart consumers' perceptions of brands currently on offer and to identify opportunities for launching new brands or to reposition an existing brand. Marketers decide upon a competitive position that enables them to distinguish their own products from the offerings of their competition (hence the term 'positioning strategy').

The marketer would draw out the map and decide upon a label for each axis. They could be price (variable one) and quality (variable two), or comfort (variable one) and price (variable two). The individual products are then mapped out next to each other. Any gaps (strategic spaces) could be regarded as possible areas for new products. The analysis below illustrates a local grocery market.

The two critical success factors here are price and quality. Of course, others, such as location, opening hours, marketing expenditure, and so on might be important too under some circumstances.

Group 1 are the price discounters. The business cuts cost wherever it can. Product ranges are restricted and there are few attempts to make the store decorative or service friendly.

Group 2 are the main market retailers. They compete on price, but offer more and better ranges, better customer service, and so on.

Group 3 offer a higher quality range, they do not attempt to compete on price at all.

Group 4 are delicatessens. They offer a superior service and specialist items. Prices are very high.

It is a great strategic mistake to try to position oneself where there are no customer groups. For example, several companies have tried to cross between groups 1 and 2, usually without success.

3 Market Research

Market research is the way in which organisations find out what their customers and potential customers need, want and care about.

It involves a number of data gathering techniques and methods of analysis:

3.1 Data gathering techniques

Primary research

This is collected for the specific purpose of the research in question. Methods include:

- **Questionnaires** – A popular technique and can be done face to face, online, over the telephone or by self completion. Key information about the respondents will be obtained for segmentation purposes.

- **Focus groups** – consist of a group of approximately 8-10 people plus a trained moderator who leads a discussion on an issue about which the company wants to learn more, e.g. feedback on a new product.

- **Observation** – observational techniques can be used to understand behaviour. For example:
  - Many organisations will monitor their competitors through gathering brochures, monitoring websites and obtaining price lists. This will help the organisation to understand how its competitors are aiming to fulfil the needs of its customers
  - In addition, the internet has allowed customer behaviour to be monitored, e.g. how many visits has a customer made to a website, have there been subsequent purchases, which pages did they review and in which order?

- **Interviews** – a similar approach to questionnaires but may be more detailed and open ended and may focus on a smaller group due to the time involved.

- **Experimentation** – similar to focus groups, in so much as users may discuss a product, but it does not require group discussion. For example, triad testing is where people are asked which of a given three items they prefer. If the three are brands of a given type, replies may show a great deal about which features of a product most influence the buying decision.

Secondary research

This is data that is already available and is therefore cheaper and quicker than carrying out primary research. However, the data may not be accurate and may not meet the exact needs of the organisation.

> **Test your understanding 2**
>
> Describe the sources of secondary research that may be available.

3.2 Analysing market research

The method will depend upon whether the data is.

Quantitative - quantifiable from a sample of consumers, or

Qualitative - opinions expressed by a sample of customers.

Methods of analysis - quantitative data

- **Correlation analysis** – marketers will be interested in the strength of the relationship between the two variables, e.g. whether an increase in age resulted in an increase in demand for a product.

- **Regression analysis** – this is used to build a model of cause, e.g. advertising spend, that lead to an effect, e.g. an increase in sales. The model could then be used to predict the level of sales, for any given level of advertising spend.

- **Variance analysis** – this is used to monitor the impact of certain changes on performance. E.g. a supermarket may alter the layout of its store and may monitor the change in sales in order to evaluate the effectiveness of changing the layout.

Methods of analysis - qualitative data

It is much more difficult to analyse the results of a qualitative technique, such as a focus group. Projective techniques such as word association (used when creating a brand name) or sentence completion are commonly used but skill is required to interpret the results.

Forecasting

(Note: forecasting is not in the E1 syllabus but was included as part of a question in the sample paper. Therefore, it has been included here for reference purposes).

The determination of the future profitability of a chosen target segment is the critical element for marketing success. Sales forecasting may utilise a variety of sources, rely on hard facts and subjective views as well as use technology and gut feeling to reveal what is essentially an unknown future to the marketer.

Market demand (total market potential)

This approach uses a combination of variables in simple formulaic structure to determine the future market potential. Variables are:

- Size of customer group;
- Time period;
- Geographical area;
- Market environment.

Area demand (area market potential)

An identical approach but on a smaller geographic scale.

Industry sales and market share

Determination of industry size and the company's relative sales will provide an analysis of market share that can be used to extrapolate income based on projected growth in the marketplace over the future time period.

Survey of buyers' intentions

Survey a small group of potential customers and their reaction to a marketing mix provides some general indication of the likely uptake of a full marketing strategy in the future.

Sales force opinions

Since the sales team is close to the customer they will provide an expert view on the potential future success of a new product.

Expert opinions

Independent experts offer an unbiased view of future environmental conditions particularly economic change that affects consumer confidence and buyer behaviour.

Past sales analysis

Trend analysis including seasonal elements smoothed through time series analysis could be used as the basis for forecasts.

Market tests

There are a variety of market tests including the launch of a trial product in a localised area or the use of market research to elicit possible buyer responses to a new product. This could be the same as a survey of buyers' intentions.

4 The Marketing Mix

4.1 Introduction

Once the positioning strategy has been arrived at, the marketing mix will be formulated.

The marketing mix should focus on satisfying customer's needs profitably.

The traditional marketing mix . (4P's):	Elements
Product	Quality, design, durability, packaging, range of sizes/options, after-sales service, warranties, brand image.
Place	Where to sell the goods, how to transport the goods, intermediaries to use when transferring from manufacturer to final consumer.
Promotion	Advertising, personal selling, public relations, sales promotion, sponsorship, direct marketing, e.g. direct mail and telephone marketing.
Price	Price level, discounts, credit policy, payment methods.
Additional 3P's for the service industry:	
People	Relates to both staff, who will have a high level of customer contact in the service industry, and customer's whose needs must be monitored.
Processes	These are the systems through which the service is delivered, e.g. teaching methods used in a university, speed and friendliness of service in a restaurant.
Physical evidence	Required to make the intangible service more tangible, e.g. brochures, testimonials, appearance of staff and of the environment.

Test your understanding 3

H Company, a High Street clothing retailer, designs and sells clothing. Until recently, the company was well-known for quality clothing at an affordable price, but the situation has changed dramatically as new entrants to the market have rapidly taken market share away from H Company.

One marketing analyst has commented that the problem for H Company is that it has never moved from being sales orientated to being marketing orientated and that this is why it has lost touch with its customers.

Required:

Explain how the management in H Company could make use of the traditional marketing mix to help regain its competitive position in the clothing market.

Link between the marketing mix and positioning

The marketing mix is essentially the working out of the tactical details of the positioning strategy. An organisation should ensure that all of the above elements are consistent with each other.

For example, a firm that decides to go for a strategy of differentiation through high quality knows that it must produce high quality products, charge a relatively high price, distribute through high-class dealers and advertise in high quality magazines.

Each element of the traditional marketing mix will now be reviewed in turn:

4.2 Product

4.2.1 Introduction

A product can be a physical commodity, a service or an experience. It has two important roles in the marketing mix:

- It plays a key role in satisfying the customer's needs.

- Product differentiation is an important part of competitive strategy.

Different ways of defining a product

The product can be viewed or defined in a number of different ways:

The core product – what is the buyer really buying? The core product refers to the use, benefit or problem solving service that the consumer is really buying when purchasing the product, i.e. the need that is being fulfilled.

The actual product is the tangible product or intangible service that serves as the medium for receiving core product benefits.

The augmented product consists of the measures taken to help the consumer put the actual product to sustained use, including installation, delivery and credit, warranties, and after-sales service.

An automobile offers personal transportation (core product), has many different features and attributes (actual product), and may include a manufacturer's warranty or dealer's discounted service contract (augmented product).

A product, therefore, is more than a simple set of tangible features. Consumers tend to see products as complex bundles of benefits that satisfy their needs. Most important is how the customer perceives the product. They are looking at factors such as aesthetics and styling, durability, brand image, packaging, service and warranty, any of which might be enough to set the product apart from its competitors.

4.2.2 The difficulties of marketing services

- **Intangibility** - services cannot be seen, tasted or touched which makes it difficult for a customer to examine a service in advance. Steps can be taken to make the service more tangible, e.g. by using physical evidence such as brochures.

- **Inseparability** - The service is often inseparable from the individual delivering the service, e.g. the reputation of a restaurant may be driven by the waiting staff and the chef. Hence, high quality, well trained individuals are required.

- **Heterogeneity** - As a result of inseparability the service will vary from one occasion to the next and therefore it is difficult to standardise and guarantee the quality.

Test your understanding 4

Explain how the problem of heterogeneity may be overcome by service organisations.

- **Perishability** - services cannot be stored. Steps can be taken to manage this problem, e.g. holiday companies may offer off-peak discounts and temporary staff may be used to solve the problem of fluctuating demand.

- **Ownership** - Consumers may find it hard to value a service since there is no transfer of ownership.

4.2.3 The product life-cycle

Most products go through a number of stages in their existence:

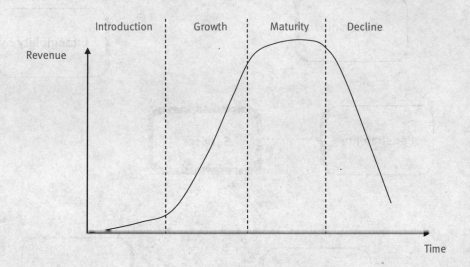

Stage 1: Introduction - A small number of individuals will be prepared to pay a high price for a new, innovative product, e.g. the latest mobile phone model. High marketing costs are likely.

Stage 2: Growth - Revenue grows as production and interest in the product increases. Prices may fall due to economies of scale and increased competitive pressure.

Stage 3: Maturity - Growth slows or halts due to high levels of competition. The price may be cut in order to attract a new group of customers.

Stage 4: Decline - Few people will purchase the product at the end of the life cycle and promotional activity will drop.

Note: An extra stage is sometimes included in the product life-cycle. This stage is called 'market shakeout' and comes between the 'growth' and 'maturity' stages.

A key aspect of product lifecycle analysis is products at different stages in the lifecycle have different implications for resource requirements, risk and strategy. This would emphasise the importance of portfolio management and suggest that a balanced portfolio of products is required. For example,

- Having too many products in the development stage will put a strain on finance as they will all require significant investment in marketing, say.

- On the other hand if all products are at the maturity stage, then there may be a question mark over the firm's long term future - how long will it be before they move into the decline phase?

4.2.4 Product Portfolio Theory – Boston Consulting Group (BCG)

The BCG matrix was developed originally to assist managers in identifying **cash flow** requirements of different products (or SBUs or divisions or businesses) within the portfolio and to help to decide whether change in the mix of products is required.

Products are analysed according to two criteria:

* Relative market share
* Market growth rate

This analysis classifies products into one of four categories with the following implications:

Boston Consulting Group Growth / Share Matrix

Cash cows

* These products have a high market share in a low-growth market. This usually means they have an established, dominant position with few significant rivals and so they are usually a cash generator and profitable.
* Low growth implies a lack of opportunity and therefore the capital requirements are low. Non-current asset investment is not required, hence cash surplus.
* Profits from this area can be used to support other products in their development stage. Therefore a balanced portfolio needs some of these.

Stars

- Stars have a high market share in high growth markets and are usually the market leader;

- However, this does not mean that they are high cash generators. At best they may be cash neutral as significant investment is required to sustain growth and to beat off competitor attack strategies.

- In the longer term they may turn into cash cows when they can be harvested.

Question marks (also known as "problem children")

- These have low market share in high growth industries.

- As such a growth opportunity exists in these areas but they are probably too small to exploit this opportunity. They thus need to invest heavily to secure market share.

- The alternative is not to invest in which case their future is questionable - it may be better to divest.

Dogs

- Dogs have a low market share in a low growth market;

- As a result there are few growth opportunities and the product may be too small to be competitive against any incumbent cash cow competitor.

- As a result these are often divested and the only question is then the speed of the divestment;

- As an alternative, they could be 'niched' and so turned into a success.

As with the product lifecycle analysis above, a key consideration is whether the firm has a balanced portfolio - for example, having cash cows to finance investment in problem children.

The principal benefits of the BCG matrix are that it:

- Provides a convenient way for management to visualise a diverse range of businesses or products.

- Ensures that management will pay attention to cash-flow balances within the product portfolio.

- Can be used to analyse the portfolios of rival firms: to identify which products they may decide to devote resources to spot potential areas for attack such as knocking out a crucial cash cow with an identical product.

4.2.5 Product portfolios and the product mix

After determining the main target markets and the type of product(s) it will offer, the organisation needs to determine the variety and assortment of those products.

The following are the elements of a typical product portfolio:

- **Product item**: This is the individual product, e.g. a specific model of phone or a brand of washing powder. The organisation will usually sell a variety of product items.

- **Product line**: This is a collection of product items that are closely related. For example, The Campbell Soup Company sells many types of soup.

- **Product mix**: This is the total range of product lines that a company has to offer. It consists of:
  - **Width** – the number of product lines. For example, Apple sell computers, i-pods, phones and accessories.
  - **Depth** – the number of product items within each product line. For example, Apple sell a large variety of i-pods.

4.2.6 Brands

A **brand** is a name, symbol, term, mark or design that enables customers to identify and distinguish the products of one supplier from those offered by competitors.

Brands can vary from company names (e.g. Volvo) to logos to product names or even to the people themselves (e.g. David Beckham)

However, brands are much more than corporate symbols, logos and packaging. Successful brands create special relationships with customers because they rely on intangible attributes that provoke strong emotional responses by individuals. The key here is the link between the brand and the assumptions made by the customer about products linked to that brand.

While it may be the case that crash safety testing rates a Jaguar car higher, most potential customers will believe that a Volvo is safer because that is a key attribute associated with the Volvo brand.

Motorcyclists do not so much ride a large bike such as own a Harley Davidson with all the connotations surrounding that brand which once had the strap line 'ride the dream'. Grandparents by comparison insist on only purchasing one type of cough lozenge; something they have bought all their lives. Whether it is the motorcyclist or the grandparent they are showing brand loyalty.

The Chartered Institute of Marketing (CIM) identify certain attributes of brands as follows:

- people use brands to make statements about themselves

- good brands reduce the risk of poor product choice

- brands can be a key asset for a business

- brands are the reason consumers choose one company over another

- although intangible, brands can be of substantial value

- strong brands can positively influence share performance

- brands can command higher prices

Brand equity is the premium that customers are prepared to pay for a brand compared to a similar, generic product.

Illustration 1

The following is a list of the leading brands in the UK in 2008/09:

Brand	Rank	Category
Google	1	Internet - General
Microsoft	2	Technology - Computer hardware and software
Mercedes-Benz	3	Automotive - Vehicle manufacturer
BBC	4	Media - TV stations
British Airways	5	Travel - Airlines
Royal Doulton	6	Household - General
BMW	7	Automotive - Vehicle manufacturer
Bosch	8	Household - Appliances
Nike	9	Sportswear and equipment
Sony	10	Technology - General
Apple	11	Technology - Computer hardware and software
Duracell	12	Household - General consumables
Jaguar	13	Automotive - Vehicle manufacturer
Coca-cola	14	Drinks - Carbonated soft drinks
AA	15	Automotive - General
Lego	16	Leisure and Entertainment - Games & toys
Marks & Spencer	17	Retail - General
Thorntons	18	Food - chocolate and confectionery
Cadbury	19	Food - chocolate and confectionery
Hilton	20	Travel - Hotels and resorts

Characteristics of a strong brand

- **Consistency**: This is crucial to the development of the brand. For example, McDonalds managed to achieve consistency through standardisation.

- **A distinctive name**: The name should have positive associations with the product. For example 'Flash' sounds like it will clean thoroughly whereas the 'Nova' car was very unpopular in Spain since 'Nova', in Spanish, means 'doesn't work'.

- **Distinctive product features**: These will help to prompt instant recognition. For example, the Cadbury Chocolate Orange has a distinctive 'orange shape' design which makes it recognisable and Coca Cola has a distinctive image that is also instantly recognisable.

Brand management

Developing and maintaining a brand can be expensive. However, a strong brand can enhance profitability.

The value of a brand is based on the extent to which it has:

- High loyalty.
- Name awareness.
- Perceived quality.
- Strong personality association.
- Other attributes such as patents and trademarks.

It is very important that brand value is protected:

- Low quality, counterfeit goods can erode the genuine brand's kudos and exclusivity

- There is a risk of some brands becoming a generic term - for example, aspirin and shreaded wheat were once brands but were eventually declared to be generic terms.

- Adverse publicity can seriously undermine the values associated with a brand. For example, Body Shop will vigorously challenge any accusations that its products are not as ethical as they would like you to believe.

- Some firms have made the mistake of using exclusive brands on inferior goods hoping the brand would enhance perceived value. Unfortunately the reverse happened and the value of the brand was compromised.

To maintain a strong brand and increase brand awareness will also involve the rest of the marketing mix, including pricing decisions and choice of promotional methods and messages.

For example, Stella Artois lager still uses its TV adverts to reinforce a quality image through the repeated phrase "reassuringly expensive". Many examples of sponsorship within the promotional mix are attempts to boost brand awareness.

Brand strategies (Kotler)

Kotler identified 5 brand strategies:

(1) Line extensions

- an existing brand is applied to new variants/products within the same product category

- e.g. Ford Fusion and Ford Focus are both small cars

(2) Brand extensions

- an existing brand is applied to products in a new product category

- e.g. Honda cars and motorcycles

(3) Multibrands

- having many different brands in the same product category

- e.g. Kellogs breakfast cereals include Cornflakes, Frosties, Special K, etc

(4) New brands

- new brands are created for new products and/or markets, usually because existing brands are not deemed suitable.

- e.g. when the banking arm of the Prudential expanded into internet banking they created a new brand, Egg Banking

(5) Cobrands

- two brands are combined in an offer so the brands reinforce each other.

- e.g. Dell Computers with Intel Processors

4.3 Pricing

Factors influencing price; the 3 C's

Pricing strategies

The pricing strategy should not be made in isolation. It is important that the company considers:

*   The positioning strategy.
*   The products stage in the product life cycle.

The following pricing strategies are available:

Test your understanding 5

For each of the four stages of the product life cycle describe the pricing considerations.

4.4 Promotion

Promotion includes the tools available to communicate with the customer and potential customers.

The promotion mix comprises the blend of methods that a company uses to promote its products to existing and potential customers.

Test your understanding 6

Identify the advantages and disadvantages of following methods of promotion:

(a) Advertising

(b) Personal selling

(c) Public relations

(d) Sponsorship

(e) Sales promotion, e.g. coupons, freebies

(f) Direct marketing methods, e.g. direct mail and telemarketing

Online marketing

The internet can be used as a method of promotion but can also be used in other parts of the marketing mix, e.g. it can act as a distribution channel in 'place'.

In recent years there has been a huge increase in online marketing and away from traditional media

Advantages of using the internet to sell products	Disadvantages of using the internet to sell products
Global access to customers	Cost of set-up and maintenance
Internet presence not governed by organisational size	Possible credit card fraud
A new method of distribution	Possible virus infection
Information is delivered free to customers	Potential for hacking
Intimate customer relationship possible	Risk of losing confidential customer information
It provides sophisticated segmentation opportunities	Site may fail
	Inability to find site using search engine/ poorly designed site

Illustration 2 - E-marketing

The Amazon.com (or Amazon.co.uk) site provides the following facilities, all of which can be linked to marketing and customer service, and that help Amazon to acquire customers, retain customers and increase income from them.

- Home delivery of books/CDs, etc. (place).

- Customers can write reviews and read other people's reviews of products (promotion).

- Based on previous buying habits, products are recommended (promotion).

- 'Customers who bought this product also bought these products…' (promotion).

- Order tracking

- Prices of new and used items are displayed. Prices of new items are usually lower than conventional shops (price).

- Very smartlooking interface (physical evidence).

- Search facilities (promotion).

- Emails if orders are delayed (processes).

Illustration 3 - Using the internet for promotion

23.5 million people watched an advert on YouTube showing the footballer Ronaldinho spending over two minutes demonstrating the most amazing football skills whilst wearing a new pair of Nike shoes.

Marketing communications

Mass media – primarily serves the purpose of mass advertisers who want to reach the greatest number of viewers

Direct marketing – direct communication with target customer, using direct mail, telemarketing

Interactive media – direct marketing through new media. Technology allows communication between customer and company e.g. interactive TV, internet and mobile phones allow personal messages and customer feeback

Interactive marketing

Prof. John Deighton (1996) first defined interactive marketing as "the ability to address the customer, remember what the customer says and address the customer again in a way that illustrates that we remember what the customer has told us."

For organisations of any size to 'remember' what the customer has said and then 'communicate' with them is realistically only possible by use of the Internet. Thus IT allows customer information to be collected online and communication made either by e-mail or by 'remembering' when a customer logs on to the company website in future.

Developments in other communication technologies, specifically cable, satellite and digital technologies have also provided a platform for another form of home shopping via the television. Advantages over web-based selling include complete user familiarity with the equipment (the TV) and the ability to extensively demonstrate/advertise the products visually on a dedicated channel.

Telephone technology is not new but ownership is more widespread than ever. Within the UK virtually all businesses, most homes and increasingly all teenagers and adults have a telephone. This provides the potential for contact to be made by telemarketing to stimulate product interest, sell directly or arrange for a visit to be made by a salesperson. There has of late been great emphasis in providing specialist training for telesales personnel including coaching on accent and responses to questions raised by customers. A contemporary trend is also the development of large call centres sometimes based overseas. ('M-marketing' refers to the technique being adopted using mobile telephones.)

This type of selling involves the initiative being taken by the vendor and is unsolicited. As such it may be unwelcome, intrusive even and naturally ethical concerns can surface. Impolite approaches or 'pushy' sales techniques being employed are particularly distasteful.

Illustration 4 - Viral, guerrilla and experiential marketing

Three relatively new forms of marketing communication include viral, guerrilla and experiential marketing.

Viral

Individuals are compelled to pass on a message to friends, family or colleagues. It is suited to email or the internet due to its immediate nature. Some examples include news on the latest products, special offers, amusing videos or jokes with a strong product message.

In 2006, shortly before Christmas, Threshers 'leaked' a voucher worth 40% off wine and champagne via the internet. Apparently, the voucher was only intended for suppliers and the belief that Threshers had mistakenly released the voucher made it spread fast around the world via email and social networks.

Guerrilla

This is a way of getting a message through to the target audience when they are least expecting it or in an unusual way.

A good example is when a leading men's magazine projected the image of the model Gail Porter on the Houses of Parliament in London. It was a stunt that was talked about by a huge number of people. It was an attempt to get people to vote for the magazine's 'world's sexiest women' poll and the results were outstanding.

Experiential

An interactive marketing experience aimed at stimulating all the senses, e.g. road shows, street theatre. The next time the consumer sees the product it should trigger a range of positive memories making it the first choice.

For example, Dove body products has a long running campaign for real beauty, challenging the stereotypical model of beauty. This has included building an online sharing community, emotive photography, road shows and in store sampling.

4.5 Place (distribution channels)

Introduction

- The word 'place' is largely used to describe the process of distribution from the producer to the purchaser.

- The process of distribution often involves one or more intermediaries.

- Direct marketing avoids intermediaries, e.g. Dell sells computers directly to consumers.

Types of intermediary

- **Retailers** – a highly visible form of intermediary. Retailers buy the products for the purpose of reselling them to the end consumer. Types include department stores, supermarkets and speciality stores such as HMV and Boots.

- **Wholesalers** – purchase the product in bulk and resell it to other wholesalers or retailers. The retailer will sell to the ultimate customer.

- **Agents** – do not take ownership of the product but arrange the exchange between the buyer and seller in exchange for commission.

- **Internet** - can itself act as an intermediary and allows niche products to reach a target audience.

Distribution strategies

The two best-known distribution strategies are called 'pull' and 'push':

- A '**pull**' strategy means massive advertising to create consumer demand and this demand more or less forces the retailers to include this product in their assortment (not having this product in stock means disgruntled consumers that may go elsewhere to shop).

- A '**push**' strategy means that the producer does not try to create consumer demand through heavy advertising, but instead offers high margins to the trade channel members (retailers and wholesalers) and expects that in return they will actively promote and market the product.

Note: These strategies can also be called push and pull **promotion**.

5 Chapter summary

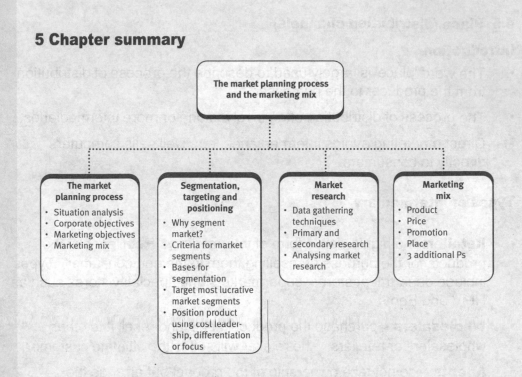

The market planning process and the marketing mix

The market planning process
- Situation analysis
- Corporate objectives
- Marketing objectives
- Marketing mix

Segmentation, targeting and positioning
- Why segment market?
- Criteria for market segments
- Bases for segmentation
- Target most lucrative market segments
- Position product using cost leadership, differentiation or focus

Market research
- Data gatherring techniques
- Primary and secondary research
- Analysing market research

Marketing mix
- Product
- Price
- Promotion
- Place
- 3 additional Ps

6 Practice questions

Question 1

In marketing 'skim pricing' reflects:

A   full recovery of costs only.

B   a promotional device to entice customers into the store.

C   high prices but low profit due to fixed costs.

D   a competitive strategy to deny the competitors opportunities to enter a market.

(2 marks)

Question 2

Undifferentiated marketing involves an organisation in offering:

A   products based on market research.

B   a single product to the market as a whole.

C   multiple products to the market as a whole.

D   single products to segmented markets.

(2 marks)

Question 3

Segmentation involves identifying target market which must be:

A   measurable, accessible and substantial.

B   acceptable, feasible and suitable.

C   undeveloped, undiscovered and undifferentiated.

D   aligned to core competences.

(2 marks)

Question 4

Companies with high costs will find it difficult to compete on the basis of price and would be well advised to:

A   compete on the Internet.

B   develop brand loyalty amongst customers.

C   employ high pressure sales techniques.

D   develop new products.

(2 marks)

Question 5

Which one of the following phrases explains concentrated marketing?

A   The company produces one product for a number of different market segments.

B   The company introduces several versions of the product aimed at several market segments.

C   The company produces one product for a mass market.

D   The company produces one product for a single segment of the marketplace.

(2 marks)

Question 6

A promotional pull policy will lead to:

A   high advertising costs.

B   price reduction to entice customers.

C   a focus on maximising channels of distribution.

D   product breadth and depth decisions.

(2 marks)

Question 7

Quantum pricing relates to:

A a £1.99 price tag.

B a variable price based on timing of use.

C a variable price placed on volume purchased.

D something to do with physics.

(2 marks)

Question 8

(a) Explain the advantages that a company might hope to gain by targeting particular segments of the market.

(5 marks)

(b) Describe three variables you think would be useful as a basis for segmenting the market for clothing sold by a large retail chain, and two variables for segmenting the market in paint sold to other businesses by a paint manufacturer.

Explain your reasons for the choice of all five variables.

(5 marks)

(Total: 10 marks)

Question 9

Johnson, Halifax and Company are a long-established medium-sized training practice operating in a large industrial city, in the country of Wetland. The practice had developed a stable and profitable client base between 20 and 30 years ago providing advice on corporate presentations and media skills, along with the usual steady income stream from general staff training. During this period the practice's main clientele had been owner-managed manufacturing and retail businesses within the city and its suburbs. The partners had never actively sought out business and new clients had arrived on the basis of recommendations and personal contacts. In summary, the practice was seen to be the natural supplier of training services to the small and medium-sized business sector of the city. Over the years Johnson, Halifax and Company have become conservative in approach and inflexible.

The last two recessions led to a massive shake-out in the manufacturing businesses in the city. Many of these businesses closed, and with restructuring in the manufacturing sector there were numerous mergers and acquisitions. Understandably as headquarters were relocated and businesses were taken over, the practice began to lose clients as they moved to larger training practices in order to streamline their training. In addition, many of these companies ran their own training departments.

In response, Johnson, Halifax and Company attempted to attract new business by focusing on the smaller services sector. This approach brought them into direct conflict with the small training companies. The result was not the success they had hoped for. The very wide range of small clients did not present the opportunities for economy of delivery, and the intense fee competition was producing a large amount of smaller profit margin contracts.

By the end of 20X9 the partnership was only just breaking even financially. The long delayed economic recovery was not bringing them the rewards they had hoped for. Although the older partners recognised the problems they were undecided as to the way forward. The younger members of the practice were beginning to voice their discontent.

One in particular, Dominic Gower, was proposing a more proactive role for the firm. His main concern was that the partnership needed to go out and market itself. It was not enough to be technically proficient. It needed new and profitable business, particularly in the current turbulent and competitive environment. The managing partner agreed that something needed to be done urgently if the firm was to see prosperous times again and decided to encourage Gower to develop his ideas.

Required:

(a) Explain the need to adopt a marketing-orientated stance to the management of the partnership and suggest a possible approach to the development of a partnership marketing plan.

(10 marks)

(b) Explain the differences that are likely to arise between the marketing of consumer products and the marketing of services?

(10 marks)

(Total: 20 marks)

Question 10

Vitac Corporation is a medium-sized regional company producing and distributing fruit-flavoured, carbonated drinks. In recent years it has seen a rapid decline in its sales to local stores and supermarkets. There are two main reasons for its poor performance. First, the major corporations who sell cola drinks have developed global brands which are now capturing the youth market in search of 'sophisticated' products. Secondly, the sales outlets are no longer willing to provide shelf space to products which are not brand leaders, or potential leaders, in the product category.

The managing director (MD) of Vitac believes that the company needs a drastic turnaround if it is to survive. The soft drinks industry has become too competitive, and the bottling technology too expensive to warrant new investment. However, the company feels that its greatest strength is its knowledge of and access to distribution channels, and therefore its opinion is that it should stay within the food and drinks industry.

Whilst on a fact-finding mission to the USA the MD was attracted by a new chocolate confectionery product named 'EnerCan' which claims to provide high energy content but low fat. This seems to be a successful combination of attributes for those consumers, mainly active participants in sporting activities, who are concerned with their diet but enjoy an occasional treat. EnerCan has been developed and is owned by a relatively-unknown confectionery company in California. The company has agreed to provide Vitac with a licensing contract for manufacture and sale of the product within Vitac's own country.

The MD is convinced that the secret to success will be in the marketing of the product. The company has suffered in its drinks business because it did not develop a distinctive and successful brand. EnerCan is also unknown in Vitac's own country. In order to get national recognition and acceptance from the major retail outlets, the product will need considerable promotional support. As the company has very little experience or expertise in promotional activity it was decided to use a marketing consultancy to provide guidance in developing a promotional plan.

Vitac, being a medium-sized company, has only a limited budget. It will have to focus upon a new and national market instead of its traditional, regional stronghold. It has to develop a new brand in a product area with which it is not familiar. Before committing itself to a national launch of EnerCan, Vitac has decided to trial the product launch in a test market.

Required:

You have been appointed to act as business consultant in the marketing consultancy team assisting Vitac.

(a) Prepare notes for the management of Vitac recommending and justifying the types of promotional activity that could be used to support the new product launch.

(10 marks)

(b) Explain the factors which need to be considered to ensure that the test market produces results which can be reliably used prior to the national launch?

(10 marks)

(Total: 20 marks)

Test your understanding answers

Test your understanding 1

Gender

It would be useful to segment the market based on gender. Females may prefer a car that is smaller, is available in bright colours and comes with fashionable accessories. Males, on the other hand, may prefer a more masculine looking and powerful car.

Age

The age of the consumer will be of upmost importance. Teenage drivers may prefer a cheaper model whereas drivers in their 20s, with more disposable income, may prefer a more expensive and stylish model.

Lifestyle

There may be a number of different lifestyles that could be targeted. Each group will have quite different needs. E.g. a leisure user may be more interested in the style and design of the car where as a commuter may want a safe, reliable car.

Income

The level of income will impact the make and the model that the user can afford and any optional extras that may be purchased.

Family life cycle

The life cycle stage will be important. E.g. bachelors may prefer a higher priced, sporty, stylish model where as those with a young and growing family may prefer a safe, reliable and family orientated people carrier.

Test your understanding 2

- Market research agency data, e.g. Mintel produce periodic sector reports on market intelligence.
- Companies' Annual Reports and Accounts.
- Professional and trade associations.
- Trade and technical journals.
- National media.

The marketing mix aims to match the products being sold by the company with the needs of the particular market segment that H Company have decided to target. The main elements of the mix are as follows.

Product

If H Company has already carried out some market research into what kind of products its customers want, these products should be available in its stores. For a clothes retailer this will include looking not only at what styles to offer, but also considering things like sizes, colours, fabrics, etc. An additional point is to note that these things are likely to change on a fairly frequent basis, so H Company should always be trying to look ahead.

Price

In the past, H Company has attempted to sell quality clothing at affordable prices. This may now have to be reviewed. The research carried out by the company may lead it to attempt to go upmarket, the higher quality/design of its clothes leading to higher prices, or it may go downmarket, by reducing innovative design/using cheaper fabrics with a consequent reduction in price if customers feel that the company is not offering them anything extra for their money.

Place

The place commonly refers to where the products are available to consumers. For a clothes retailer such as H Company, this would have traditionally been via retail outlets. Based on the results of market research, H Company will have to decide on the best way to retail their clothes. Various possibilities exist, amongst these are:

- Expanding the number of shops in the High Street.

- Expanding the number of shops on retail parks.

- Expanding the number of in-store displays in departments stores (within e.g. Debenhams etc.).

- Setting up an Internet website.

The place must be linked in with the other elements of the marketing mix, for example if H Company is trying to appeal to a more exclusive clientele then having its own range of shops in prestigious locations would be sensible. Alternatively, if the company wants to appeal to a more mainstream customer base then having the clothes sold in department stores would be more appropriate.

Promotion

The promotional part of the mix refers to how the potential customer is made aware of the products. The first consideration is looking at where to advertise. Clothes have traditionally been advertised through magazines and newspapers. If H Company goes down this route, then they should advertise in appropriate publications that are likely to be seen by their target customers. An increasingly popular approach particularly for clothes aimed at the upper end of the market is that of endorsement by celebrities. Clothes might be loaned/given to people in the public eye, thus generating positive publicity.

All of the above elements must be blended together so that the product, price, place and promotion appeal to the market segments identified by H Company.

Test your understanding 4

Steps can be taken to standardise the service. McDonalds is an example of a company that has tried to do this, using methods such as:

Calculability – each meal is identical and standardised. For example, each Big Mac contains the same number of gherkins and the same amount of sauce. The soft drinks are dispensed automatically ensuring that each drink contains the same volume.

Control - the delivery of products involves a known set of materials and a predetermined sequence of tasks. For example, each Big Mac is assembled in the same way and in the same order and customer orders are always taken in the same way.

Test your understanding 5

- **Introduction**.
  High prices might be charged, because the product is new and supply is limited also initial set up costs need to be recovered.

- **Growth**.
  Competition between rival producers intensifies so prices will reduce in the hope of penetrating the existing market and either retaining or increasing market share at the expense of competitors.

- **Maturity**.
  Prices fall mainly in order to beat competitors but the experience curve and scale economies should come into play. Market segments are sought where higher prices can be charged.

- **Decline**.
  The product declines into obsolescence so it may even be sold off below cost price to clear stocks and exit the market.

Two forms of pricing might also be applied particularly in the introduction stage of the product life cycle, namely:

- Skim pricing reflecting high prices but low profit due to high fixed costs.

- Penetration pricing, deliberately entering a market to build market share and pricing so as to deny the competitors those opportunities.

Test your understanding 6

Method	Advantages	Disadvantages
(a) Advertising	• Reach a large number of potential customers. • Low cost for each potential customer.	• Total cost can be very high. • Difficult to evaluate effectiveness.
(b) Personal selling	• Can focus on needs of individual customer. • A talented salesperson can be very persuasive.	• Can be seen as pushy. • High cost per potential customer.
(c) Public relations	• Low or no cost. • Can be targeted. • Unbiased opinion.	• Negative review may damage reputation.
(d) Sponsorship	• Can enhance image. • Audience may match target audience.	• Difficult to evaluate effectiveness.
(e) Sales promotion, e.g. coupons, freebies	• Can help gain new users. • Counteract competition. • Clear out surplus stock.	• Can be costly. • May not win customer loyalty.
(f) Direct marketing, e.g. direct mail and telemarketing	• Personalised targeting of an individual. • Test market before a full roll out. • Less competitor visibility.	• Negative associations. • Can be costly.

Question 1

C

Question 2

B

Question 3

A

Question 4

B

Question 5

D

Question 6

A

Question 7

A

Question 8

(a) There are a number of different ways in which a company can aim marketing at people. One of these is known as undifferentiated marketing, which involves marketing the product in the same way to everybody. The obvious problem with this approach is that a lot of the marketing effort and cost will be wasted, by marketing products to people who are not interested in them.

An alternative would therefore be to market products individually to consumers, the obvious disadvantage here is that this would cost too much money and be impractical (an example of a company successfully carrying this out is Dell computers, which makes computer systems individually to customer specifications).

The solution most companies adopt is to undertake what is referred to as market segmentation. This means dividing the population into a number of segments. The population within each segment will have similar needs and the company can market their product in the same way to this entire segment. This approach should be cost effective as well as achieving desired sales levels.

An additional benefit of this approach is that the company may identify some segments that it is not interested in, or that the company knows will have no interest in the product. These segments can therefore be avoided to reduce wasted expenditure.

A final advantage of segmentation is that segments that are currently not catered for might be identified. The company can then develop products to satisfy the needs of these consumers. A good example is the rise in products and services aimed at young, single, professional people (particularly women) who have a high disposable income.

(b) There are many ways in which a company can segment its market. The variable it chooses will depend on the business it is in.

Clothes retailer

Gender

The first obvious variable is gender, clothes for men and women are clearly different and many shops will specialise in one type or the other (even if they sell both, the departments will be separated).

Use

Many clothes shops specialise in clothes for a particular use; good examples include shops specialising in sports clothes. At a more general level some shops specialise in suits and other 'workplace' clothes whilst others specialise in leisure-wear clothes.

Age

One of the most distinctive differences between clothes shops is in the age group that they cater for. As people grow older their tastes in clothes will change and so retailers can specialise in clothes aimed at different age ranges.

Paint manufacturer

Price

The first thing to bear in mind is that a manufacturer is an industrial company, in other words it does not sell products to consumers, but rather to other businesses. A key variable will therefore be the price the business is prepared to pay. For a construction company painting interior walls a low price might be a key requirement, while a car manufacturer might be prepared to pay a higher amount.

Volume

Another key variable will be the amount of paint that the customer will require. The construction company mentioned above is likely to require a high volume while the car manufacturer may require much smaller amounts. If the manufacturer cannot produce paint in large quantities there is little point in trying to attract the construction company.

Question 9

(a) Adopting a marketing orientation

Johnson, Halifax and Company need to perform better and more cost-effectively than their competitors; forcing them to be more flexible and responsive to client needs. In order to satisfy them, the needs of the clients must be analysed and understood by the partnership.

Marketing plan for the partnership

<u>Step 1: Situation analysis</u> - an initial assessment of the current position of the partnership will be performed as part of the marketing plan. This will involve why and where there has been a deteriorating change in the client base in recent years. One reason is the economic downturn within the region that Johnson operates in.

Another reason may be that they are offering the wrong types of training, i.e. not meeting the demands of their customers. One of the main problems identified by the company is that it appears to be 'stuck in the middle', in other words its services are not priced cheaply enough to appeal to small companies whilst at the same time it does not have the range of services required by larger companies.

<u>Step 2: Set corporate objectives</u> - the partnership did enjoy past success but there is no indication that there is a mission statement or set of corporate objectives in place. Even if there is, these should be reviewed to make sure that they are still relevant.

<u>Step 3: Set marketing objectives</u> - these should be set in relation to the marketing objectives.

<u>Step 4: Devise an appropriate strategy</u> - this will involve:

– Segmentation - the market should be segmented, e.g. by size of client, and the needs of each segment should be established.

– Targeting - the most profitable segment(s) should be targeted using an appropriate marketing mix.

– Positioning - a strategy of differentiation or cost leadership should be chosen for each segment.

<u>Step 5: Marketing mix</u> - a plan for the development of the marketing mix needs to be adopted for Johnson and Halifax to achieve its plans.

Product (i.e. the development of new services)

In the light of newly-established customer requirements, new products or services need to be developed, possibly forced by the changing requirements of the local economy. Johnson will need to carry out some kind of research in order to establish what these needs are and then segment the market to decide which training courses they will provide. These new services will have to be closely monitored and may have to be regularly updated.

Price

Prices charged by the firm will obviously have to be competitive but will equally have to be reflective of the business segment they are operating within, and its specific competitiveness. It may prove necessary to run free 'taster' courses so that potential clients can see what the company is like.

Distribution channel (i.e. place)

If the firm has a great deal of flexibility in its distribution of services, then it should gain a competitive advantage quickly. At the moment Johnson appears to be tied to its current geographical region.

The partnership should take advantage of any available IT systems such as the Internet to help gain a competitive advantage.

Promotional activity

The use of good quality communication will be crucial in an attempt to target appropriate clients. Media considerations are relevant (e.g. where and when to advertise), however it should be remembered that there may only be one person within a company who decides on the company's training needs, these people should be identified and contacted with a view to building a long-term relationship.

Step 6: Implementation and control - The marketing plan should then be implemented. The plan should also be monitored to gauge its success and to identify any necessary changes.

(b) Service industries face different problems to production industries for the following reasons:

Intangibility

In a service industry it is difficult to judge quality because it is difficult to sample a service.

It is difficult for customers to examine a service in advance. However, in a production business, such as the manufacture of cars, the sampling will be achieved by test driving the vehicle. Steps can be taken to make the service more tangible, e.g. physical evidence such as brochures can be used.

Inseparability

The service is often inseparable from the individual delivering the service. Clients could easily become disappointed if they discover that the work carried out on their behalf is not performed by the person with whom the contract was negotiated. Partners therefore need to maintain enough interest in the work performed to ensure that personal contact with the client is maintained. The marketing of a product is different, as the item or goods will be purchased from the seller.

Heterogeneity

As a result of inseparability the service will vary from one occasion to the next. To ensure consistency, the firm needs to maintain the training of personnel as well as ensuring quality standards are adhered to. However, in the production of, say a motor car, each vehicle will conform exactly to its specification.

Perishability

Services cannot be stored; sale and consumption take place at the same time. To ensure that assets are utilised effectively, steps can be taken to manage this problem, e.g. off-peak discounts or using temporary staff to solve the problem of fluctuating demand. Products, on the other hand, can be stored (even if only for a limited period).

Differentiation

As most training firms offer similar services to their clients it is important to gain a competitive advantage by offering a slightly different service which is relevant to the needs of the particular clients served. This could include aspects such as personal involvement by all staff, follow-up contacts, experience and the use of high technology equipment. The differentiation of a product refers to the specific attributes enforced by that firm and therefore is easy to undertake.

Ownership

Consumers may find it difficult to value a service since there is no transfer of ownership.

Question 10

(a) Introduction

The company has acquired an interest in a product that is new to the market, and is proposing to market this product via the major retail outlets to a specific target group, namely sports participants.

Promotional vehicles

The key objective during the trial period is to create awareness within the target market. The focus of the promotion will be on the different types and styles of promotion to be used to obtain the appropriate responses from the target market. These will vary from conventional advertising to sales and public relations.

With a limited promotional budget the company could concentrate on a 'push' strategy which influences the retail outlets to stock and display the products.

In attempting to influence the target consumers a key strategy would be to encourage them to try the product initially.

Due to the inherent high costs, it is not realistic to expect wide-scale consumer advertising on television and through the mass print media. This strategy would not be specifically targeting the chosen market segment.

The preferred choices would include a balanced selection of the following.

– **Advertising**. Dependent upon the budget available, advertising should focus on advertisements or editorials placed in one or two specialist magazines. These magazines would be those that are commonly read by the target market - sports enthusiasts. The advertising should be supported with point-of-sale material to draw potential consumers' attention and encourage trial purchase.

– **Sales promotions** could be both trade and consumer led.

– **Trade promotions**. It is essential that retailers both stock the product and provide excellent shelf display. To generate a 'push' approach to promotion it may be possible to provide retailers with inducements in the form of customer prizes and discounts. Without retailer commitment it is unlikely that the product launch will be successful.

- **Customer promotions**. This will need significant expenditure on sales promotional material which would include a mixture of the following:
  - In-store trials;
  - Coupon offers;
  - Initial price reductions.

All of the above might help to stimulate demand and make the product recognisable. Attractive packaging of the product will in itself help stimulate product interest and create brand awareness. The following could also be tried:

- **Public relations**. It could be beneficial to use one or two well-known sports personalities to recommend the product. Though it might appear to be expensive this could provide exposure significantly cheaper than could otherwise be obtained from conventional media. Additionally the product could be trialled at prestigious sports meetings, international athletics meetings, cycling events, tennis tournaments, etc. The product image would reach the target audience and it would be promoted in a superior environment

- **Sales**. The sales force will need to be sufficiently skilled and committed, being able to operate at a national level to obtain wide geographical coverage. Although this approach may be expensive it will be far more cost effective than attempting a nationwide television campaign. The sales force will have the task of persuading retailers to accept the product, and providing merchandising support. They will handle most of the problems at the product's launch.

Conclusion

With the restrictions of a limited budget, expenditure should be directed at those areas which will accurately reach the target market and encourage participation in the trial.

On this basis, the promotional emphasis should be on a 'push' strategy as opposed to a 'pull' strategy. To measure how well the campaign is progressing, control systems should be implemented. The systems should ensure that the use of the limited money available achieves the desired objectives.

(b) **Definition of a test market**

A test market is often used prior to the launch of fast-moving consumer goods. It enables the company to identify any operational problems that may occur and to fine tune its marketing activities.

The company has the benefit that it can save considerable amounts of money which would have been lost if the mistakes had occurred at the national level.

Factors to consider

The following factors should all be taken into consideration before deciding upon a test market area. If the test is to provide guidance for a future national launch the results should be based upon reliable sets of data.

— **Comparable test areas**. The test market area should provide a good indication as to how the market throughout the whole country will behave. It would be of little use if the results from the test market misrepresented the true state of the total market. The test market area must be representative of the total market in terms of demographics - income, social class, age and any other parameter which would help determine purchase activity.

— **Comparable distribution channels**. The distribution channels, including the sales outlets, should be comparable with the rest of the country. It is pointless if small retailers dominate the test area whereas in the rest of the country the multiple supermarkets are dominant.

— **Isolation of test area**. The area should be reasonably isolated so that outsiders coming into the test area do not influence test results.

— **Comparability of promotional media**. If the national promotional emphasis were to be radio then there ought to be a local radio station available.

— **Control markets**. There should be a control market just in case extraneous activities might falsify the results, e.g. a strike at a major employer within the test area.

— **Test period**. The test period should be long enough to enable reliable results to be obtained, in this case time for a repurchase after the initial trial. However, the test period must not be so long that it alerts competitors.

10

Further Aspects of Marketing

Chapter learning objectives

Lead	Component
D1. Explain developments in marketing.	(c) Explain marketing in a not-for-profit context. (d) Explain the social context of marketing behaviour.
D2. Apply tools and techniques used in support of the organisation's marketing.	(c) Describe the business contexts within which marketing principles can be applied.

1 Business to Business (B2B) and Business to Consumer (B2C) Marketing

1.1 Definitions

- **B2B marketing** – targeting goods and services at businesses that will use the products to produce the goods or services that they sell.

- **B2C marketing** – the market for products and services bought by individuals for their own use or for their family's use.

1.2 Features of B2B marketing

- **Derived demand** - demand for the product is derived from consumer demand.

- **Fewer buyers** - the number of buyers for an industrial good is generally smaller than for a consumer good.

- **High purchasing power** - each industrial buyer tends to have a higher purchasing power than consumers.

- **Closer relationships between buyers and sellers** - this is because there are fewer buyers with higher purchasing power in B2B marketing compared to B2C marketing.

- **Technical complexity** - There is often a greater degree of technical complexity in B2B marketing.

1.3 Buying decisions with B2B

Business-to-business (B2B) marketing differs from business-to-consumer (B2C) marketing in a number of key respects, not least the fact that the purchaser makes buying decisions for organisational rather than personal reasons. In addition, several individuals and groups are involved in the B2B buying decision including:

- **Initiators** who start the buying process. (For example, a department who identifies a need to replace a piece of equipment.)

- **Influencers** who affect the buying decision often based on their particular technical expertise.

- **Buyers** who raise orders and sanction payment and although they may enter into negotiation they may be guided heavily by others in the organisation.

- **Users** who ultimately operate the equipment (using the earlier example).

There may be others (dependent upon the organisation) who will have further roles such as Deciders, Approvers and Gatekeepers.

B2B marketing in different contexts

- **Services marketing** – services may be bought by businesses in order to add value to their own production process, e.g. the services of a courier or management consultant.

- **Direct marketing** – the direct marketing model works for both B2B and B2C applications. In fact Dell's customers range from individuals ordering from home to large corporations such as Barclays Bank.

- **Interactive marketing and e-marketing** – the tools of interactive marketing and e-marketing, e.g. the internet and email, can also be used in the context of B2B marketing.

Test your understanding 1

On what basis are B2B purchasing decisions made?

2 Internal Marketing

This is the means of applying the philosophy and practices of marketing to the people who serve the external customers so that:

- The best possible people can be employed and retained.
- The employees will do the best possible work.

Internal marketing is essentially the process of motivating and training employees so as to support the organisation's external marketing activities.

Implications of internal marketing

- The company may have a strong marketing strategy but without their employee's support it will not be effective.

- If advertising promises are not kept through the services and the products provided, eventually the company's reputation will suffer and the customers will stop coming.

- For the firm to deliver consistently high quality, everyone must practise a customer orientation. This will require investment in employee quality and performance.

- Internal marketing will be of particular importance in service companies which tend to be more customer-facing.

3 Social marketing and social corporate responsibility

3.1 Social marketing

Social marketing uses commercial marketing practices to achieve non-commercial goals. The term social marketing refers to the application of marketing to the solution of social and health problems.

Social marketing is based on the logic that if marketing techniques can encourage people to buy products such as a fizzy drink brand or a particular telephone handset then it can also encourage people to adopt 'beneficial' behaviours for their own good and the good of others

Merit goods are commodities that an individual or society think they should have on the basis that it is 'good' for them. Governments often provide merit goods 'free at the point of use' and then finances them through general taxation (e.g. in the UK access to health care through the National Health Service).

Demerit goods are the exact opposite of merit goods and negative consequences can arise from their consumption for society as a whole. It is human behaviour that causes many of society's problems (e.g. the spread of sexually transmitted diseases, road traffic accidents, smoking tobacco, unwanted pregnancies, etc.).

Social marketing can be applied to promote merit goods and encourage society to avoid demerit goods. Social marketing involves the systematic application of marketing along with other concepts and techniques to achieve specific behavioural goals for the wider good of society. This may include persuading people (for instance) to refrain from smoking in public places, reduce the speed at which they travel in cars or to practice 'safe sex'.

Understanding social marketing

According to the National Social Marketing Centre (2008) the following features and concepts are key to understanding social marketing:

- A strong customer orientation with importance attached to understanding where the customer is starting from, their knowledge, attitudes and beliefs, along with the social context in which they live and work.

- A clear focus on understanding existing behaviour and key influences upon it, and developing clear behavioural goals.

- Using a mix of different methods to achieve a particular behavioural goal.

- Audience segmentation to target efforts more effectively.

- Use of the 'exchange' concept (understanding what is being expected of an individual, and the real cost to them).

- Use of the 'competition' concept (understanding factors that impact on people and that compete for their attention and time).

3.2 Corporate social responsibility in a marketing context

As discussed, a marketing orientated firm will seek to produce and sell products that meet the needs of the customers. However, this policy may result in firms adopting policies which society, as a whole, view as irresponsible.

Test your understanding 2

Explain why a company may be deemed irresponsible for providing customers with products that meet their needs?

Social responsibility is the acceptance of an obligation towards the society in which the organisation exists. In a marketing context the term initially highlights the needs for the organisation to accept that, in the process of pushing products towards individuals, it has the responsibility for the impact of those products on individuals and society overall.

Key questions include the following:

- To whom do we sell?
- Are our products of an appropriate standard, safe and produced to environmental standards?

- How do we advertise: is it fair balanced and truthful?

- Do we have policies that address the concerns of dissatisfied customers?

- Is our pricing or advertising policy exploitive of any groups in society, etc.?

The basis of social responsibility is the premise that an organisation enjoys certain benefits of society and in return should engage in practices that supports rather than exploits society.

Illustration 1

The following are some of the companies that will have a responsibility that goes beyond their own profit motive:

- Tobacco companies

- Alcohol producers and retailers

- Gas and oil companies

- Car manufacturers

- Drug companies

- Media companies

3.3 Advantages to a company for adopting a socially responsible approach

- **Unique selling point** – the market for a particular product may be highly competitive. The support of socially valuable causes may allow a company to develop a unique identity for its products.

  E.g. Starbucks has managed to create a strong brand and a unique selling point in, what is, a saturated market by only using 'Fair Trade' coffee and supporting community projects.

- **Increased sales** – customers may be willing to pay more for a product bought from a responsible company rather than an irresponsible one.

  E.g. in 2008, a UK TV program saw celebrity chefs on a crusade against intensive chicken farming. As a result of this campaign, sales rocketed for the more expensive, free range chickens.

- **Change before new legislation is introduced** – some companies may put new practices in place before new legislation is introduced. This may help the company to gain from positive publicity.

For example, some UK pubs and restaurants introduced a smoking ban before the UK legislation banning smoking in enclosed public spaces was introduced in July 2007.

- **Can reduce company costs** – many companies wrongly believe that social responsibility will increase costs but it can actually reduce them.

Illustration 2 - Marks & Spencer

In May 2008 Marks & Spencer (M&S) introduced a number of initiatives aimed at improving their image as a socially responsible retailer. These included an initiative to reduce the number of plastic carrier bags used by customers:

- The introduction of a 5p charge for its single use carrier bags, in all of its UK stores.

- All profits (1.85p per bag) raised from the sale of the 5p bags will be invested in 'Groundwork', a charity which creates and improves greener living space in the UK.

- Any unwanted or unused M&S carrier bags can be returned by customers to any M&S store for recycling.

- M&S were the first major UK food retailer to use a standard carrier bag made from 100% recycled plastic.

- The steps taken have not only helped M&S's image as a socially responsible retailer but they have also enabled the company to reduce their costs.

4 Marketing in a Not-for-Profit Context

4.1 Introduction

The not-for-profit sector incorporates a diverse range of operations including charities, national and local governments, trusts and so on.

Many such organisations have now adopted a marketing orientation, reflecting the increasingly competitive environments in which they now operate.

4.2 Problems associated with marketing in the not-for-profit sector

Problem 1: Multiple objectives

- The not-for-profit sector may have a number of financial and non-financial social objectives.

- Therefore, its desire to meet its customers' needs is further constrained by its requirement to meet wider social objectives.

- However, sometimes the interests of a marketing orientation and social policy can overlap. For example, an art gallery may set an objective of providing a range of educational and entertaining exhibitions. Charging lower prices for unemployed people to enter the art gallery may provide social benefits for this group, while gaining additional revenue from a segment that might not have otherwise have been able to afford a visit to the gallery.

Problem 2: Absence of markets

- Many not-for-profit organisations have claimed to have introduced marketing when in fact there is no marketplace within which customers can choose competing goods and services.

- However, some not-for-profit organisations have successfully used marketing principles to promote ideas rather than a tangible product or service. For example, in the 1990s the UK labour party rebranded itself as 'New Labour' after careful research of its audiences. This was backed up by an effective advertising campaign and helped labour to win the subsequent general election.

4.3 Marketing for charities

Bruce (2005) believes that charities have to improve their focus on the needs and wants of all different customer groups:

- beneficiaries (users, clients, members, etc.),
- supporters, and
- regulators.

He goes on to argue that commercial marketing concepts can be adapted to suit voluntary and community organisations through relationship marketing, partnership marketing, and cause marketing. (Cause marketing involves the cooperative efforts of a business and a charity for mutual benefit and so goes much further than the organisation merely making a charitable donation.)

With thousands of charities worldwide (there are over 200,000 registered charities in the UK alone), competition for voluntary giving is intense. Those charities employing the most appropriate marketing practices are most likely to lever the generosity of peoples' time and money for their particular cause. Branding in particular is important in communicating a particular charity's core values, and distinguishing it from another.

4.4 Marketing for NGOs

Non-governmental organisations (NGOs) were first conceived as part of a United Nations Charter as a non-profit making international organisation made by members of two or more states. NGOs are (supposed to be) above politics and dedicated to a common cause. (Amnesty International and the International Committee of the Red Cross are examples of NGOs).

NGOs play an important role in international development directing development funds from donors and agencies to the point of need, while setting aside profit or politics.

NGOs use marketing to:

* to find a position for themselves within the market

* to distinguish client and donors needs

* to formulate and communicate NGO requirements

* to gain new supporters.

4.5 Marketing for the public sector

The public sector is a broad category for many different sorts of organisation and functions. Within local government for instance there are very many differing services each using marketing techniques in different ways for leisure, culture and the arts, to regeneration, education and social services, etc.

Proctor (2007) examines the role of marketing in public organisations, and views it from the perspective of creating value for different organisational stakeholders through a philosophy based on setting a vision, creating and communicating values and establishing a shared culture.

Within the UK, political reforms have pushed the public sector into a more commercial and managerial style meaning some managers need to make marketing decisions. A considerable amount of market research has in any case carried out on behalf of public sector bodies such as the national or local government. Social problems concerning (say) the elderly or disabled may call for information about their opinions and circumstances to help inform policy decisions.

Test your understanding 3

First run in 1994, Cancer Research UK's Race for Life, is the largest women-only fundraising event. Women are invited (for a fee) to walk, jog or run 5k at a choice of hundreds of Race for Life events taking place each year. The event will help to raise millions of pounds to fund the charity's life saving work into all forms of cancer.

Required:

Explain, using examples, how Cancer Research UK (a not-for-profit organisation) has been able to use the traditional marketing mix to increase the success of its running series.

5 Chapter summary

Further aspects of marketing

Differences between B2B and B2C
- Definition of B2B and B2C marketing
- Features of B2B marketing

Internal marketing
- Definition
- Implications

Social marketing and corporate social responsibility
- Advantages of adopting a socially responsible approach

Marketing in a not-for-profit context
- Problem 1: Multiple objectives
- Problem 2: Absence of markets

6 Practice questions

Question 1

Which of the following is not a feature of business to business (B2B) marketing?

A   Industrial buyers have a lower purchasing power than consumers.

B   A close relationship between buyers and sellers than compared to business to consumer (B2C) marketing.

C   Fewer buyers than B2C marketing.

D   Demand for the product is derived from consumer demand.

(2 marks)

Question 2

Which of the following statements is false with regards to the not-for-profit sector?

A   Marketing is difficult because there is no marketplace within which customers can choose competing goods and services.

B   A desire to meet customer's needs is constrained by the requirements to meet wider social goals.

C   The not-for-profit sector will have a number of financial objectives and non-financial social objectives.

D   The not-for-profit sector is unable to successfully adopt marketing principles.

(2 marks)

Question 3

Internal marketing is about:

A   fulfilling the needs of employees and managers.

B   ensuring employees are able to support the organisation's marketing activities.

C   promoting the company's products to employees in order to increase sales.

D   reducing expenditure on advertising.

(2 marks)

Question 4

Explain why a fast food restaurant may decide to adopt a socially responsible approach.

(4 marks)

Question 5

Sam is the Chief Executive Officer (CEO) of T Inc, a tobacco company. He has traditional views about the purpose of business in general and his own organisation in particular. Though he is frequently pressured by a variety of groups and organisations that think he should run his organisation differently, he sticks firmly to the view that the overriding purpose of business is to make money for the shareholders. His son, Frank, who is being coached to take over the CEO role, takes a very different perspective. In his view, T Inc has a responsibility to a wide range of stakeholders.

Required:

(a) Explain how:
   (i)   Sam would justify his view that the overriding purpose of the business is to make money for the shareholders.
   (ii) Frank would justify his view that T Inc has a responsibility to a wide range of stakeholders.

(12 marks)

(b) Describe the stages Frank should go through in determining the priority of the goals of T Inc when he becomes CEO.

(8 marks)

(Total: 20 marks)

Test your understanding answers

Test your understanding 1

A mixture of

- Economic/task factors (price, delivery, location, quality, reliability, customer care, after care, etc.)
- Non-task factors (personal risk or gain, previous decisions, politics, those influencing the purchaser, perception, etc.)

As a result, significant B2B marketing mix features include quality assurance, reliability, delivery, price and after sales service.

Test your understanding 2

- **Environmental impact** – the product may deplete natural resources or emit harmful gases. In 2008 the DIY store B&Q decided to end the sale of patio heaters due to their environmental impact.
- **Harmful product** – products such as addictive drugs, alcohol and fast food may fulfil a customer's short term needs but could result in long term damage.
- **Vulnerable consumers** – marketers have a responsibility towards vulnerable groups such as children who are unable to fully evaluate decisions. For example, in the UK in 2007, TV advertisements for unhealthy food were banned during kids TV programs.
- **Deceptive practices** – for example, a customer may perceive that a certain mobile phone deal fulfils their needs. However, not reading or understanding the small print may mean that they don't know what they are committing themselves to.
- **Labour practices** – for example, a customer may buy a product because it fulfils their need for good value. However, they may be unaware that the labour used to produce the product are paid a poor wage and are subject to substandard working conditions. E.g. in 2008 Primark, the UK clothing company, were found to be using Indian suppliers who sub-contracted the work to smaller suppliers who, in turn, relied on child labour.

Test your understanding 3

Product

- Brand image is bright and consistent.
- The product fulfils many women's need to keep fit whilst also fulfilling a need to raise money for charity.
- The distance, 5k, is challenging but manageable for most.

Price

- The fee is affordable for most women.
- The fee is higher than an average race entry but most women will be willing to pay more since the money is donated to a good cause.
- Women will also be encouraged to raise sponsorship money.

Promotion

- The product is promoted using adverts on TV, in women's magazines and in gyms.
- The website is easy to navigate, branding is consistent, on-line entry is available and the site contains helpful advice with regards to training and sponsorship.
- Celebrity endorsement has been used. Many popular women celebrities have completed the race.

Place

- A wide choice of accessible locations.
- Scenic locations making the event enjoyable.

Question 1

A

Question 2

D

Question 3

B

Question 4

- **Unique selling point** - the market for fast food is highly competitive. The support of socially valuable causes can act as a unique selling point for the business and attract more customers to the business.

- **Increased sales** - customers may be willing to pay more for a product bought from a responsible company. For example, the fast food restaurant may have a policy of supporting British farmers. This may be important to consumers and they may be willing to pay more for these products.

- **Can reduce company costs** - social responsibility can actually reduce costs, e.g. due to less wastage.

- **Change before new legislation is introduced** - the business will gain positive publicity if they put practices in place before new legislation is introduced.

Question 5

(a)

    (i)   Stakeholders are any people or groups that have an interest in a particular organisation. Although there are a large number of stakeholder groups that might have an interest in a company, the most important group is usually seen as the shareholders.

           Sam would argue that there are a number of reasons for this:

           The reason why a company exists is to make money for its owners, i.e. for its shareholders. The company belongs to them and so they should always be given the highest priority.

           Although there are other stakeholders such as employees, suppliers, etc. they are given their rewards through items such as high wages, bills being paid on time, etc. It is only possible to do these if the company is profitable, i.e. this is the same goal as keeping the shareholders happy.

    (ii)   Frank would argue that the responsibility of the company stretches to more than just the shareholders. For example:

           T Inc could increase profitability at the expense of its employees (by paying them lower wages) or suppliers (by taking extended credit). Although these are both of benefit in the short term to the profits of the company and therefore to the shareholders, it is unlikely that they will bring long-term benefits.

           The company is operating in the tobacco industry and as such is high profile. If the company is seen to be acting irresponsibly it might be forced by government to adopt certain procedures, which will lead to increased costs. It is therefore more sensible to consider the environment and local community since it is more cost effective in the long term.

           Frank would argue that any modern organisation must see itself as being in co-operation with a large number of other people: suppliers, customers, employees, etc. If it views itself as purely catering to shareholders and the pursuit of profit it will be unlikely to be successful in the modern business environment.

(b)   The process that Frank needs to go through in determining the priorities of stakeholders is sometimes known as stakeholder mapping.

      Firstly, Frank will need to draw up a list of all stakeholders from both inside and outside the organisation.

Secondly, Frank should identify what each group wants from T Inc. For example:

- Shareholders want increased profits and dividends.

- Employees want increased wages and working conditions.

- Government wants taxes and some contribution towards healthcare costs from both T Inc and from their customers.

- Action groups might want T Inc to stop targeting young people for advertising campaigns.

- Political groups might want to ban/limit the use of T Inc's products through smoking bans (as was introduced in 2008 in the UK).

It can be seen from the above list that it is not possible to meet the expectations of each group since some are in direct opposition to others.

Thirdly, Frank should look at how much influence and power each group has. For example, shareholders (particularly institutional ones) can sell their shares and depress the share price if they are unhappy with the decisions being made by T Inc. As such they are powerful. On the other hand, low-grade employees may not have many other job opportunities so they have much less power to influence decisions.

Finally, Frank will have to set goals and objectives that meet the expectations of those groups with the most power whilst meeting the minimum requirements of each group with some power.

HR Theories and Practices related to Motivation

Chapter learning objectives

Lead	Component
E1. Explain the relationship of human resources (HR) to the organisation's operations	(a) Explain how HR theories and activities can contribute to the success of the organisation.
E2. Discuss the activities associated with the management of human capital	(b) Discuss the HR activities associated with the motivation of employees.
	(c) Describe the HR activities associated with improving the opportunities for employees to contribute to the firm.

1 Theories of Human Resource Management

1.1 Introduction

There are a number of theories of human resource management (HRM) relating to ability, motivation and opportunity.

Theorist	Year	Theory
Taylor	1911	Scientific management – workers motivated by money
Maslow	1954	Hierarchy of needs
Vroom	1964	Expectancy theory
Herzberg	1968	Two factor theory
Handy	1976	Psychological contracts
McGregor	1981	Theory X and theory Y
Lawrence and Lorsche	1984	One type of contingency theory
Schein	1990	Four categories of worker

(**Note:** the years are for illustration purposes and will not be required in the exam).

Before reviewing these theories it is useful to consider what motivates employees and why this is important to the employer.

Test your understanding 1

(a) What motivates you to go to work?

(b) Would you still work if you won £20 million in the lottery?

(c) Why do organisations care about their employees being motivated?

Illustration 1

There are a number of well documented cases about lottery winners who have returned to work after scooping the jackpot.

- Carl Prance and his family won £6.9 million in October 07. However, ten months after he became an instant millionaire, the railway worker is back to normal – getting up at 5 o'clock in the morning for a shift.

- Millionaire lottery winner Maria Murray could earn £75,000 per year interest on her winnings but she continues to serve fried breakfasts and cups of tea to factory workers every morning for the minimum wage per hour.

1.2 Content and process theories of motivation

There are two broad classes of motivation theory:

Content theories	Process theories
• Ask the question **'What'** are the things that motivate people? They are also referred to as **"need theories"** and assume that human beings have a set of needs or desired outcomes which can be satisfied through work.	• Ask the question **'how'** are people motivated. They attempt to explain how individuals start, sustain and direct behaviour and assume that individuals are able to select their own goals and means of achieving those goals through a process of calculation.
• Content theories assume that everyone responds to motivating factors in the same way and that there is one best way to motivate everybody.	• Process theories change the emphasis from needs to the **goals** and **processes** by which workers are motivated.
• For example, Maslow's theory, Herzberg's theory.	• For example, Vroom's theory.

1.3 Taylor's scientific management

- Taylor concluded that workers are motivated by obtaining the highest possible remuneration (money).

- He believed that by analysing work in a scientific manner, the **'One Best Way'** to perform a task could be found.

- By organising work in the most efficient way, the organisation's productivity will be increased and this will enable the organisation to reward its employees with the remuneration they desire.

Steps in scientific management

Taylor's scientific management consisted of four principles, each of which has relevance to the topic of operations as well as HR management:

- Work methods should be based on the scientific study of the task, i.e. they should be planned in a way to maximise productivity.

- Select, train and develop the most suitable person for each job, i.e. scientific management of staff.

- Managers must provide detailed instructions to workers to ensure work is carried out in a scientific way.

- Divide work between managers and workers - managers apply scientific principles to planning and supervising the work and workers carry out the task.

Illustration 2 - Pig iron study

Taylor suggested that if workers were moving 12.5 tonnes of pig iron per day, and they could be incentivised (by money) to try to move 47.5 tonnes per day, left to their own devices they would probably become exhausted and fail to reach their goal.

However, by first conducting experiments to determine the amount of resting that was necessary, the worker's manager could determine the optimal time of lifting and resting so that workers could lift 47.5 tonnes per day without tiring.

Interestingly, only 1/8 of pig iron workers were capable of doing this. They were not extraordinary people but their physical capabilities were suited to moving pig iron. This led Taylor to suggest that workers should be selected according to how well they are suited to a job.

1.4 Maslow's hierarchy of needs

Maslow's theory suggests that within each employee there is a hierarchy of needs and the individual must satisfy each level before they move onto the next. The employee will seek to satisfy the five hierarchical needs from bottom to top:

Maslow's heirarchy of needs

Related aspects at work

- Challenging job
- Creative task demands
- Advancement opportunities
- Achievement in work

- Merit pay increase
- High status job title

- Compatible work group
- Friendships at work

- Job security
- Fringe benefits

- Basic salary
- Safe working conditions

(Pyramid levels, top to bottom: SELF-FULFILMENT, EGO, SOCIAL, SAFETY/SECURITY, BASIC/PHYSIOLOGICAL)

Maslow's hierarchy explained

Maslow's theory may be summarised and simplified by saying that everyone wants certain things throughout life, and these can be placed in five ascending categories, namely:

- **Basic or physiological needs** - The things needed to stay alive: food, shelter and clothing. Such needs can be satisfied by money.

- **Safety or security needs** - People want protection against unemployment, the consequences of sickness and retirement as well as being safeguarded against unfair treatment. These needs can be satisfied by the rules of employment, i.e. pension scheme, sick fund, employment legislation, etc

- **Social needs** - The vast majority of people want to be part of a group and it is only through group activity that this need can be satisfied. Thus the way that work is organised, enabling people to feel part of a group, is fundamental to satisfaction of this need.

- **Ego needs** - These needs may be expressed as wanting the esteem of other people and thinking well of oneself. While status and promotion can offer short-term satisfaction, building up the job itself and giving people a greater say in how their work is organised gives satisfaction of a more permanent nature. An example might be being asked to lead groups on a course.

- **Self-fulfilment needs** - This is quite simply the need to achieve something worthwhile in life. It is a need that is satisfied only by continuing success, for example opening and running a new office.

Test your understanding 2

Violet is the managing director of a successful design company. Assess her motivation using Maslow's hierarchy.

Implications for managers

In order to motivate their employees, managers must understand the current level of needs at which the employee finds themselves and take steps to ensure that these current needs and the subsequent higher needs are satisfied.

Test your understanding 3

(a) Explain the criticisms/ limitations of Maslow's theory.

(b) Why might a graduate starting a new job who had already satisfied the basic needs on Maslow's hierarchy then seek to satisfy needs in a different order?

The Vroom expectancy model

Vroom believes that people will be motivated to do things to reach a goal if they believe in the worth of that goal and if they can see that what they do will help them in achieving it.

Vroom's theory may be stated as:

Force	= **valence × expectancy**
where	
Force	= the strength of a person's motivation
valence	= the strength of an individual's preference for an outcome, e.g. a promotion
expectancy	= the probability of success, e.g. the opportunities that exist for promotion

1.5 Herzberg's two factor theory

Herzberg's needs based theory identified two sets of factors on the basis that they "motivate" in different ways.

Hygiene factors must be addressed to avoid dissatisfaction and include:

- Policies and procedures for staff treatment
- Suitable level and quality of supervision
- Pleasant physical and working conditions
- Appropriate level of basic salary and status for the job
- Team working.

However, in themselves hygiene factors are not sufficient to result in positive motivation.

Motivators will not cause dissatisfaction by not being present but can increase motivation if present. They include:

- Bonus
- Sense of achievement
- Recognition of good work
- Increasing levels of responsibility
- Career advancement
- Attraction of the job itself.

Most are non-financial in nature.

Implications for managers

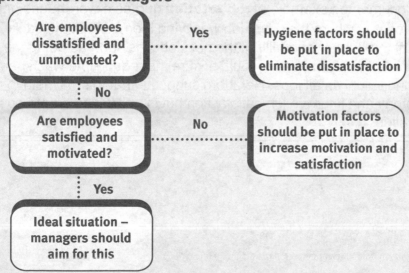

Herzberg went on to define three ways that management can attempt to improve staff satisfaction and motivation

- **Job enrichment** (sometimes called 'vertical job enlargement') - a deliberate, planned process to improve the responsibility, challenge and creativity of a job.

Illustration 3

Typical examples of **job enrichment** include delegation or problem-solving.

For instance, suppose an accountant's responsibilities for producing quarterly management reports end at the stage of producing the figures. Job enrichment could involve extending the responsibilities so that they included the preparation of figures and submitting them to senior management. This alteration in responsibilities could not only enrich the job but also increase the workload, leading to delegation of certain responsibilities to clerks within the department, the cascading effect enriching other jobs as well.

- **Job enlargement** (sometimes called 'horizontal job enlargement') - widening the range of jobs, and so developing a job away from narrow specialisation. There is no element of enrichment.

- **Job rotation** - the planned rotating of staff between jobs to alleviate monotony and provide a fresh job challenge.

Illustration 4

The documented example of **job rotation** quotes a warehouse gang of four workers, where the worst job was tying the necks of the sacks at the base of the hopper after filling; the best job was seen as being the fork-lift truck driver. Job rotation would ensure that equal time was spent by each individual on all jobs. Herzberg suggests that this will help to relieve monotony and improve job satisfaction but is unlikely to create positive motivation.

Improving the opportunities for employees contribution

This section considers practices aimed at creating opportunities for employees to contribute to the organisation whether through job design, communications, involvement procedures or engaging in formal negotiating and bargaining.

A relatively recent concept of organisational citizenship behaviour (OCB) has grown up to describe the efforts of those who voluntarily undertake innovative, spontaneous tasks that go beyond their normal job role. Organ (1988) describes such behaviour as

...discretionary, not directly or explicitly recognized by the formal rewards system and that in aggregate promote effective functioning of an organization.

Clearly such behaviour is most apparent in organisations that have positive inclusive cultures that value team work and adopt supportive management approaches. The approach adopted by a particular manager can in many situations have a significant effect on efficiency, effectiveness and motivation. The potential impact of work groups on individual motivation has long been recognised and was famously illustrated by the Hawthorne Studies. Elton Mayo's research over a 5-year period at the Hawthorne Works of the Western Electric Company in Chicago indicated that work satisfaction depends to a large extent upon the social relationships. These are both informal between workers in a group and between workers and their bosses. The effects of the group proved more powerful than altered working conditions, new payment systems, rest breaks, varying the length of the working day, and offering food and refreshments.

This thinking naturally goes to the heart of job design and the methods by which team working is encouraged. Traditionally, jobs have been designed on the basis of the scientific management approach with a high degree of specialisation and strict controls. This is highly effective for bringing about conformity in many situations, but is hardly conducive to commitment. A number of other approaches to job design attempt to build more interest, variety, challenge and collaborative working into jobs.

Self-directed work teams have emerged from group technology developed by motor manufacturer Volvo. The initiative arose as a result of recruitment and retention problems for production line jobs which involved repetitive working procedures.

Under cellular manufacturing methods, teams form a cell that jointly make a substantial proportion of the finished product rather than singly assemble one component of it. Cellular production often forms part of programmes of quality improvement. Indeed 'Total Quality Management', which seeks to move the emphasis away from detecting faults to preventing them, stresses employee involvement and team working as important ways of achieving this.

Job redesign can therefore be used to help develop individuals and groups within the workplace.

The job characteristics model sets out the links between characteristics of jobs, the individual's experience of those characteristics, and the resultant outcomes in terms of motivation, satisfaction and performance. The model also takes into account individual differences in the desire for personal growth and development (what Maslow called 'self-actualisation'). The heart of the model is the proposition that jobs can be analysed in terms of five core dimensions as follows:

- Skill variety: the extent to which a job makes use of different skills and abilities.

- Task identity: the extent to which a job involves a 'whole' and meaningful piece of work.

- Task significance: the extent to which a job affects the work of other organisation members or others in society.

- Autonomy: the extent to which a job gives the individual freedom, independence and discretion in carrying it out.

- Feedback: the extent to which information about the level of performance attained is related back to the individual.

These five core dimensions induce the three psychological states critical to high work motivation, job satisfaction and performance. These three states are defined as follows:

- Experienced meaningfulness: the extent to which the individual considers the work to be meaningful, valuable and worthwhile.

- Experienced responsibility: the extent to which the individual feels accountable for the work output.

- Knowledge of results: the extent to which individuals know and understand how well they are performing.

Jobs that have high scores are more likely to lead their incumbents to the experience of these critical psychological states than jobs that have low scores.

1.6 Handy's psychological contracts

- Psychological contracts exist between the employee and the employer.

- Unlike the employment contract the psychological contract is highly subjective, not written down and not legally binding

- Handy suggested that they cover the following:

	Employee	Employer
What do they want?	Want their needs to be satisfied	Want employee to work hard. Will have a set of expectations for each employee
What are they willing to give?	Will offer their energies and talents	Payment, benefits and other outcomes, e.g. a promotion

Implications for managers

- A psychological contract can exert a strong influence on behaviour because it captures what employees really believe they will get in return for what they give.

- If employees feel that the employer has broken promises, or violated the contract, employee reactions range from mild irritation or reduction in effort to handing in their notice.

- In order for managers to motivate and retain employees they must understand the importance of the psychological contract.

Illustration 5

Kate has worked as a trainee accountant with the same company for the past two years. She is ambitious and enjoys her work. Her manager asks her to produce a report that is outside of her normal role.

The report turns out to be difficult and time consuming and she has to put in long hours to complete the report on time as well as carrying out her normal work.

She meets the deadline and sends the report to her manager. However, she receives no acknowledgement. The next day she finds out that her manager has successfully presented the findings of the report to his boss and has taken the credit for the report.

Kate is angry and has decided that she will never do any extra work for her boss again and has even started looking for another job due to the breach of her psychological contract.

> ### Types of psychological contract
>
> There are three types of psychological contract:
>
> - **Coercive contracts** – which are not freely entered into and where a small group exercise control by rule and punishment. Although the usual form is found in prisons and other custodial institutions, coercive contracts also exist in schools and factories.
>
> - **Calculative contracts** – where control is retained by management and is expressed in terms of their ability to give to the individual 'desired things' such as money, promotion and social opportunities. Most employees of industrial organisations 'enter into' such a contract.
>
> - **Co-operative contracts** – where the individual tends to identify with the goals of the organisation and strive for their attainment. In return the individual receives just rewards, a voice in the selection of goals and a choice of the means to achieve such goals. Most enlightened organisations are moving towards such contracts but it must be emphasised that if they are to be effective, then the workers must also want them – if such a contract is imposed on the workforce, it becomes a coercive contract.
>
> In all cases the employees must know the results of their increased efforts and the management must understand the individual's needs.

1.7 McGregor's Theory X and Y

McGregor presented **two opposite sets of assumptions** made by managers about their staff.

Theory X assumptions:

- people dislike work and responsibility
- people must be coerced to get them to make an effort
- subordinates prefer to be directed, wish to avoid responsibility, have relatively little ambition, and want security above all.

Theory Y assumptions:

- physical and mental effort in work is as natural as play or rest
- the average human being does not inherently dislike work, because it can be a source of satisfaction

- people can exercise self-direction and self-control to achieve objectives to which they are committed.

- people can learn to enjoy and seek responsibility

Test your understanding 4

Explain how management style should differ depending on whether individuals are theory X or theory Y type employees.

Lawrence & Lorsche and Schein

Lawrence and Lorsche

Contingency theory is based on the idea that there is no one best way to manage. One form of contingency theory was developed by Lawrence and Lorsche:

Type of environment	Management methods
Stable	<ul><li>Detailed procedures</li><li>Centralised decision making</li></ul>
Unstable	<ul><li>Decentralisation</li><li>Employee participation</li><li>Less detailed procedures and fewer rules</li></ul>

Schein

Schein usefully categorises individuals in terms of their primary motivation, partially drawing off Taylor's assumptions regarding an individual's preoccupation with financial reward.

Categories of worker:

Rational economic man	Self-interest and maximisation of gain are prime motivators.
Social man	Socialisation and acceptance at work are critical motivators.
Self actualising man	Challenge, responsibility and pride are key issues.
Complex man	A blend of workers' expectations and whether the firm meets these is the motivator.

2 Practices relating to Motivation

2.1 Reward systems

A reward system can help in keeping staff highly motivated in order to deliver high performance.

The aims of a reward system

- **Motivation** - the reward scheme should encourage desirable behaviour and should recognise that different employees will be motivated by different factors.

- **Quality of staff** - the reward scheme should help to attract and retain the best staff.

- **Consistency and fairness** - the reward scheme should provide a fair and consistent basis for motivating and rewarding employees.

- **Reward performance** - the scheme should reward performance, e g by promotion through developed pathways.

- **Recognise factors other than job performance** - the reward scheme should recognise other factors such as the level of responsibility or additional tasks taken on.

- **To control costs** - it is important that the reward scheme assists in controlling salary costs.

- **To achieve organisational goals** - the reward scheme should assist the organisation in achieving its goals.

- **To comply with legislation/ regulation**

Incentive schemes

- An incentive scheme links pay to performance.

- It can be tied to the performance of an individual or a team of employees.

- The scheme should link performance to organisational goals.

There are three main types of incentive scheme:

- **Performance related pay** (PRP)
    - Piecework: the faster the employee works, the higher the output and the greater the reward.

    - Management by objectives (MBO): key results are identified for which rewards will be paid on top of salary.

    - Points system: this is an extension to a MBO reward system where a range of rewards is available based on a points system derived from the scale of improvements made, such as the amount of cost reduction achieved.

    - Commission: typically paid to staff in sales functions, where the commission earned is a proportion of sales.

- **Bonus schemes** – similar to PRP in that rewards will be paid on achievement of defined goals. However, it is usually a one-off scheme whereas PRP is generally a continual policy.

- **Profit sharing**
  - Usually available to a wide group of employees (often company wide) where payments are made in the light of the overall profitability of the company.
  - Share issues may be part of the scheme.

Note: make sure you distinguish between individual rewards (e.g. piecework) and team/group rewards (e.g. profit share).

> ### Test your understanding 5
>
> Explain the difficulties associated with incentive schemes

> ### Total reward package
>
> A total reward package (TRP) would draw together all of the financial and non-financial benefits available to employees.
> Employees are motivated by factors other than pay. For example, Maslow's needs from bottom to top are:
>
> - Physiological needs such as a competitive basic salary.
> - Safety needs such as a good pension scheme.
> - Social needs such as work nights out.
> - Ego needs such as an opportunity for a merit pay increase.
> - Self-fulfilment needs such as a challenging job and achievement in work.

2.2 Flexible working arrangements

Flexible working arrangements can be used to increase employee motivation. Flexibility in work patterns can be achieved in many ways:

Flexitime	The need to work a standard set of hours but less restriction on when these hours are worked;
Shift system	Working outside of normal working day patterns;
Compressed week	Standard hours within fewer days in a shift rotation;
Job sharing	Two employees share a standard hour week;

Part-time	Fewer hours than the standard weekly number;
Teleworking	Technology has enabled employees to work away from the office, usually at home.

Test your understanding 6

Explain the advantages and disadvantages for the **employer** of flexible working arrangements.

It is also important to consider the flexible working arrangements from the **employee's** point of view:

Advantages for the employee	Disadvantages for the employee
• Cost and time savings, e.g. because the employee works at home or does not travel to work at peak times.	• Increased costs, e.g. employees have to pay for additional utilities when working from home.
• Flexibility to fit work around family life and other commitments.	• Loss of social interaction, e.g. due to the flexible hours or working from home.
• Increased enjoyment of work since feel employer is listening to their needs.	• Lack of support, again due to the flexible hours or working from home.

2.3 Workforce flexibility

Flexible working arrangements encompass one type of flexibility within organisations. 'Workforce flexibility' is the term used to describe a much broader range of flexible working options:

• **Functional flexibility** – employees have the ability to move between tasks as and when is required. This will allow an organisation to react to changes in production requirements and levels of demand.

Achieving functional flexibility

Functional flexibility can be achieved by:

• Training staff in a wide variety of skills.

• Recruiting staff with a wider variety of skills.

• Introducing a programme of job rotation.

- **Numerical flexibility** – the use of non-core workers allows the organisation to adjust the level of labour to meet fluctuations in demand. For example:
  - Temporary workers
  - Part time workers
  - Overtime

Handy's Shamrock organisation

Handy suggested the idea of a 'Shamrock' organisation. People linked to an organisation are said to fall into three groups. Each group will have different expectations and it is important that they are managed and rewarded in an appropriate way. The groups are:

- **The professional core** – includes managers and technicians. They should be rewarded through a high salary and benefits since they are essential to the continuity of the organisation.

- **The contractual fringe** – contracted specialists, rewarded with a fee.

- **Flexible labour force** – part time and temporary workers provide flexibility

---

- **Financial flexibility** – this is achieved through variable systems of rewards, e.g. bonus schemes, profit sharing. By linking rewards to performance a number of improvements in performance should be realised.

- **Flexible working arrangements** – as discussed in section 2.2. Arrangements that result in a variability of labour work time, e.g. flexible hours or a compressed working week, are sometimes referred to as 'temporal flexibility'.

2.4 Arrangements for knowledge workers

Knowledge workers are people who create knowledge and produce new products and services for the organisation to sell. For example:

- Research staff
- Chemists
- Architects

As we move from a traditional manufacturing economy to a service economy, it is recognised that knowledge is a primary source of competitive advantage.

Implications for human resource management

- **Selection criteria** – employees should be selected for their skills, i.e. knowledge, as opposed to their ability to do a particular job.

- **Sharing of knowledge** – encouraged by:
    - Team working
    - Job rotations

- **Retention of knowledge** – this can be achieved by:
    - Filling vacancies internally.
    - Ensuring there is a well defined career path to increase motivation and hence retention.

- **Performance appraisal** – the appraisal must:
    - Prioritise the development of knowledge skills if the employees are to believe that the organisation takes those seriously.
    - Encourage employee input into their own development, skills and careers.

Commitment of knowledge workers

Key contributing factors to employee commitment are:

- The degree of flexibility and autonomy within the workforce.

- An emphasis on performance-related pay. Performance could be measured by, for example, the amount of quality information about a product published professionally on a web site that will help sell more of that product. The more motivated the knowledge worker is, the more quality information he or she will create.

- Appraisal systems that monitor and reward knowledge contributions and application e.g. knowledge turned into information, into documents, into content.

- Profit-sharing or equity-based forms of reward. Quality information about a product published professionally on a web site will help sell more of that product. The more motivated the knowledge worker is, the more quality information he or she will create.

- Career progression – make it clear that those who contribute quality information on a consistent basis will move up through the organisation.

2.5 Employee involvement

Employees should be given the opportunity to contribute to the organisation. **High performance work arrangements** rely on all employees for their ideas, intelligence and commitment to make the organisation successful. Increased motivation and positive financial benefits can be gained from:

- Greater employee participation in job design – job enrichment, enlargement and rotation can all result in increased motivation.

- Open and honest communication.

- Empowered, involved and listened to employees.

- A willingness for the employer to compromise and bargain with employees.

3 Chapter summary

HR theories and practices related to motivation

Theories of human resource management

- Content and process theories
- Taylor's scientific management
- Maslow's hierarchy of needs
- The Vroom expectancy model
- Herzberg's two factor theory
- Handy's psychological contracts
- McGregor's theory X and Y
- Lawrence and Lorsche
- Schein

Practices relating to motivation

- Reward systems
- Flexible working arrangements
- Workforce flexibility
- Arrangements for knowledge workers
- Employee involvement

4 Practice questions

Question 1

In Frederick Herzberg's theory of motivation, basic pay is regarded as:

A   A motivator

B   A satisfier

C   A hygiene factor

D   A resource

(2 marks)

Question 2

When a performance appraisal scheme is ineffective, this may be due to:

A   a lack of objective criteria for the appraisal of personality.

B   under-performing employees.

C   excluding discussions about pay.

D   a lack of objective criteria for the appraisal of performance.

(2 marks)

Question 3

One example of a flexible work arrangement is a compressed work week. A compressed work week involves:

A   working for longer-than-usual hours on some days in exchange for a day off work.

B   working for some days at home instead of in the office.

C   allowing employees to choose their hours of attendance each day, provided that they work a full day.

D   allowing employees to work less than the standard number of hours each week.

(2 marks)

Question 4

Content theories of motivation tend to focus mainly on:

A   the needs of the group.

B   feelings of complacency or dissatisfaction.

C   the needs of individuals.

D   the use of 'carrots' and 'sticks' as devices.

(2 marks)

Question 5

A company pension scheme is an example of which need in Maslow's hierarchy?

A   Basic needs.

B   Self-fulfilment needs.

C   Safety needs.

D   Retirement needs.

(2 marks)

Question 6

Discuss the strengths and weaknesses of Herzberg's theory of motivation.

(4 marks)

Question 7

Explain the nature of a psychological contract between an individual and an organisation, and describe the three types of psychological contract identified by Handy.

(4 marks)

Question 8

Explain what is meant by hygiene factors and motivators and explain what action should be taken by managers if they identify that both sets of factors are absent in the organisation.

(4 marks)

Question 9

List the hierarchy of needs and examples of hygiene/ motivators. What parallels can you draw between the two approaches?

(4 marks)

Question 10

Harriet has just been appointed to take charge of part of an accounting department concerned with processing information from the operating division of a large company.

Based on her previous experience she has determined that the running costs of the department are too high, due to absenteeism, lateness, low productivity and time spent in correcting errors.

Investigation of the design of the jobs in the department reveals that each employee is trained in a task which is made as simple as possible. The equipment used is maintained by a service department. Strict discipline ensures that clerks do not carry on conversations during working hours, and tasks are performed in exactly the order and method laid down.

Harriet has decided that performance can be improved by changing the job design.

Assume that Harriet's superiors approve the changes, that correct training is provided and that resistance by the clerks to change is properly overcome.

Required:

(a) Discuss the likely consequences for organisations and employees of designing jobs which are repetitive, routine and lacking in significant skill requirements.

(10 marks)

(b) Distinguish between job enrichment and job enlargement and give examples of these techniques in action.

(10 marks)

(c) Describe five changes that might achieve improved job satisfaction.

(10 marks)

(Total: 30 marks)

Question 11

CP is a small but successful company which specialises in selling car and home insurance to individuals. All sales are made over the telephone, and there are no personal callers to the company's offices. The company employs 25 staff, 22 in the telephone sales department and the remaining 3 running all the accounts and administration functions. As a consequence of its recent success in the market, CP is planning to expand its operations.

The company has been evaluating its cost structure and has discovered that the cost of providing office space for each worker is $3,500 per annum. New workers would require office space with a cost per worker of $4,000 per annum. This amounts to a significant cost in the company's operating budget. The Management Accountant has calculated that 90% of office costs can be avoided if the telephone sales staff worked from their homes. This idea has, so far, been discussed only at board level.

At present, employees appear to enjoy working in the office, where they spend most of their time using the telephone and computer system to sell insurance. Coffee and lunch breaks are normally spent in the rest area where staff also compare some notes and queries concerning their jobs. All the data that they need to perform their job is otherwise available on the computer system. This data includes:

* records on each customer;

* access to a value added network (VAN) providing costs of insurance from other companies which sell insurance;

* word-processing and other systems for producing letters and insurance quotes to customers.

The proposal to work from home was put to staff last week and this has met with some initial resistance although the Management Accountant stressed that this proposal was only a possibility.

Write notes to the Managing Director explaining:

(a) from the viewpoint of the staff, the potential benefits that will be gained by home working. Explain the concerns that staff may have over home working and whether the IT infrastructure can help alleviate these concerns.

(12 marks)

(b) what can be done to encourage staff to accept the proposed change.

(8 marks)

(Total: 20 marks)

Test your understanding answers

Test your understanding 1

(a) The answer depends on the individual. Factors that may motivate you to go to work include money, enjoyment of the work, challenge, opportunity to achieve something, enjoyment of the social side of work/ friends at work.

(b) Again, the answer depends on the individual. Some people would not return to work but others would. This leads us to believe that factors, apart from money, motivate individuals to go to work.

(c) Motivated employees are important to the organisation since:

– If individuals are motivated they will work more efficiently and productivity will rise.

– They may produce a better quality of work.

– Motivation may result in employees exercising their creativity and initiative in the service of organisational goals.

– Motivation will reduce staff turnover and the associated costs.

Test your understanding 2

Statements	Satisfied	Not Satisfied	Explanation
Self-achievement needs	✓		Self-achievement needs should be satisfied by the succuss of the business.
Ego needs	✓		Ego needs should be satisfied by being MD.
Social needs	✓		Social needs are met by being part of the Board of Directors (Note: you could have argued that some MDs may feel isolated and that the Board is against them.)
Safety/ security needs	✓		Security needs will be met by a generous pension scheme and a long notice period.
Basic/ physiological needs	✓		Basic needs are satisfied by a high salary.

Test your understanding 3

(a) The following are criticisms/ limitations of Maslow's hierarchy:

   – Individuals have different needs and not necessarily in the same order.

   – Individuals may seek to satisfy several needs at the same time.

   – Not all of these needs are or can be satisfied through work.

(b) A graduate might then seek to meet social needs before worrying about job security and long term security of pension arrangements.

Test your understanding 4

Based on their assumptions, supervisors will adopt a corresponding management style:

- If you believe that you have Theory X workers, then you adopt an authoritarian, repressive style with tight control. Effectively the workforce are a problem that needs to be overcome by management.

- If you believe that you have Theory Y workers, then you adopt a participative, liberating, developmental approach. Employees will be viewed as assets who need to be encouraged and empowered.

Test your understanding 5

- Increased earnings do not act as an incentive to all employees. A total reward package, which includes a range of financial and non-financial rewards, may be needed to motivate employees.

- Employee efforts may be undermined by external factors which are outside of their control, e.g. recession.

- Employees may feel that the scheme is unfair leading to conflict.

- Sole responsibility for success is often difficult to judge.

- There may be conflicts, e.g. a goal of higher productivity, in a piecework system, may be at the expense of quality.

Test your understanding 6

Advantages

Flexible working arrangements may fulfil the needs of the individual resulting in:

- Increased employee motivation and productivity;
- Increased commitment to the organisation;
- Attracting talented individuals because of the availability of such conditions;
- Reduced absenteeism and staff turnover.

In addition, the company may reduce costs, e.g. due to a reduction in office space if employees work at home or a reduction in the number of full time workers in favour of part time workers.

Disadvantages

Flexible working arrangements such as working from home or working non-standard hours may result in:

- Difficulties in co-ordinating staff;
- Loss of control of staff;
- Dilution of organisational culture;
- Less commitment to the organisation;

In addition, some costs may actually increase, e.g. due to the extra cost of providing equipment for employees to work from home.

Question 1

C

Question 2

D

Question 3

A

Question 4

C

Question 5

C

Question 6

The strengths of Herzberg's theory

The motivation-hygiene theory has clear implications for management. If this theory is correct then management, in seeking higher levels of performance, should give more attention to the job-content factors, such as opportunity for achievement, recognition and advancement: these are the motivating factors. The theory also points out that money may not be the most potent motivating force; and neither are the other content or hygiene factors such as fringe benefits and supervision. For managers, Herzberg's theory offers some clear ideas that may be translated into specific work-design policy.

The weaknesses of Herzberg's theory

In Herzberg's study, about 80% of the participants were motivated by the motivating factors he defined, and fewer than 70% were affected by the failure to maintain the hygiene factors. This shows that his ideas have a limited application to certain types of worker. In addition, his theory does not allow for:

- the differences in the type of employee;
- the workers who are principally motivated by financial reward;
- the skill levels required by the work;
- the challenges associated with the work.

Question 7

A psychological contract between an individual and an organisation is a 'contract' in the mind of the individual. In return for the organisation satisfying some of the individual's needs, the individual will give some of his/her energy and talent to the organisation.

Handy's three types of psychological contract are:

- **A coercive contract**: the individual is forced to work in the organisation without his consent. Examples are a prisoner in prison and, in some cases, a student at school.

- **A calculative contract**: control of the rewards that satisfy the individual's needs (pay, promotion, and so on) is in the hands of the organisation's management. The individual decides how much effort it is worth putting into the job to get the rewards.

- **A co-operative contract**: the individual identifies with the objectives of the organisation and works hard to attain them – in return for fair rewards, and a voice in the selection of targets or objectives and in the means of achieving them.

Question 8

- A hygiene factor is something that does not motivate employees but it will result in unmotivated employees, if they are not present.

- A motivator is something that, if present, will motivate staff but the absence of motivators will not result in unmotivated staff.

- Managers should begin by ensuring that hygiene factors, such as supervision and acceptable working conditions, are in place.

- Only once these hygiene factors are present, should the managers take action to ensure that motivators, such as a bonus scheme or opportunity for career advancement, are in place.

Question 9

Hierarchy of needs	Motivators	Hygiene factors
Self-fulfilment needs	Opportunity for advancement	Sports/ social facilities
Esteem needs	Acknowledgement	Working conditions
Social needs	Increased responsibility	Pension
Safety/ security needs	Work challenges	Pay
Basic/ physiological needs		

There is a clear relationship between Herzberg's 'hygiene factors' and the lower level of Maslow's 'Hierarchy of Needs.' Likewise there is a close relationship between the motivators and Maslow's higher needs.

Question 10

(a) **Consequences of routine, repetitive jobs**

McGregor concluded that there are two types of worker; theory X and theory Y. Theory X type staff dislike work, will prefer to be directed, avoid responsibility and have very little ambition. These types of staff would actually prefer a routine, repetitive and low skilled job.

However, theory Y type staff will enjoy and seek responsibility and want to be able to exercise self-direction and self-control. It is likely that the staff within the accounts department are theory Y type staff. For these types of worker, routine work results in subjective feelings of monotony and boredom and this in turn leads to less than optimum performance by the workforce.

Studies of workers in car assembly factories in various parts of the world have confirmed that a large proportion of the workforce dislikes the repetitive nature of assembly line work, and that it is strongly associated with above average levels of absenteeism, labour turnover and industrial action. These problems are most apparent in times of full employment, but their lack of visibility in times of high unemployment and job insecurity does not mean they disappear but that workers are less ready to risk their jobs by taking any form of industrial action.

All the problems which characterise low discretion, routine work, as highlighted by Harriet, inflict costs in terms of poor quality work, lower levels of production, costs of cover for absent employees, loss of output and damage to trust and cooperation between management and employees.

The kind of behaviour exhibited by employees required to carry out tedious work operations is often explained as arising from a lack of need fulfilment. Theorists such as Maslow and Herzberg, for instance, argue that routine, repetitive work does not meet the higher level social and self-actualising needs of people. Employees frustrated by the lack of self fulfilment in their work seek to avoid it by frequent absence from the organisation on the grounds of sickness or by seeking more interesting and challenging work elsewhere. Their readiness to take industrial action is explained in terms of yet another means of venting their frustration by striking for some socially acceptable reasons such as higher pay and/or better working conditions.

(b) Job enrichment and job enlargement

Job design is a method of redesigning jobs by taking into account the needs of individual workers as well as the objectives of the organisation. For the individual this can lead to greater job satisfaction and greater control over his/her work environment. It may also be a vehicle for increasing the participation of employees in the immediate work area.

In an effort to improve the variety of work for employees, additional tasks are often added to those contained in the current job description.

Job enrichment (sometimes called vertical increase) – provides the employee with extra tasks that demand use of authority, skills, behaviour and decision-making at a higher level than that required in his or her normal job.

This gives the manager:

– more time to concentrate on higher level tasks.

– an opportunity to assess the potential of the employee.

– an opportunity to develop communication.

Employees have motivation factors provided, e.g. recognition, achievement, growth. They also have a chance to prove their potential and gain rewards and an opportunity to work with less supervision.

Examples include:

– a senior could be taken 'on site' by a manager/partner to gain experience and eventually be given an area of client visits that he/she alone would organise.

– a clerk could be given training on computer terminals and word processors so that he/she could carry out secretarial and machine room operations as well as the normal tasks.

Disadvantages of job enrichment include:

– the new jobs have to come from somewhere or someone, so there may be organisational problems. There can also be friction between colleagues when one of them is 'specially chosen'. Less capable employees may be worried about the additional skills required.

– there is the risk in certain areas that control by segregation of duties might be lost. For example, the cashier who opens the mail and writes up the books might be vulnerable to corruption if inadequately supervised.

Job enlargement (sometimes called horizontal increase) occurs when additional tasks are given to the employee essentially at a similar or lower level than his or her present job, giving the job a longer cycle time. This reduces the amount of repetition and may require the exercise of a wider range of skills.

Unfortunately, it is unlikely to be a positive motivator, but it does provide recognition and job variety.

This technique gives the manager the benefits of a busier workforce capable of carrying out a variety of tasks with the ability to assess potential or training needs.

The employee has job variety and can develop new skills and can show potential and develop positive attitudes.

Examples of job enlargement include the following:

- A salesperson, even if only a booking clerk or building society cashier could advise customers on more services/bargains available.
- Retail salespeople could become more involved in inventory control, and ultimately ordering/buying.

(c) **Changes that might achieve improved job satisfaction**

A range of measures is available to Harriet to try to reduce the level of dissatisfaction felt by the staff and to motivate them to work harder.

Several of these involve some form of job redesign. Much of the routine work that the clerks do is reminiscent of the scientific management approach to work design, which amongst other things, involves job simplification by breaking a job down into a number of very simple tasks which are easy to perform. It has been widely adopted because of its assumed efficiency. Workers become adept at completing the tasks quickly because of their constant repetition. Unfortunately, as already indicated, this kind of work leads to frustration and stress and workers behave in ways that detract from both their own performance and that of the organisation.

Job satisfaction might be improved if Harriet were to adopt the following five changes:

Job enlargement – aims to give employees greater variety in their work by adding extra tasks of the same level as before. This 'horizontal extension of the job', though criticised for not giving any real increase in responsibility, often works in practice to bring about improved morale and/or productivity.

Job enrichment – is usually applied to the 'vertical extension of job responsibilities'. It implies giving an employee more responsibility through the introduction of both senior (higher) and junior (lower) level tasks into their workload. This, in turn, acts to add interest and challenge to a job by giving people tasks through which they can gain a sense of achievement.

Job rotation – allows an element of variety to be introduced into a job by switching an employee from one undemanding job to another undemanding job. This is obviously not much of an improvement but it does involve a little more variety.

Work groups – involve employees working together in a self-organised, autonomous group, which is collectively responsible for reaching its own production targets. Tasks within each group are allocated by the members and each group is responsible for the rate and quality of its output. Reportedly first established in the British coal mining industry under the 'composite longwall method', subsequent developments have shown that autonomous work groups can help to improve job satisfaction and hence employee morale.

Quality circles – are small, voluntary groups of about eight to ten shop-floor employees who meet regularly to identify problems of quality, productivity, safety, etc., to set targets to improve the situation caused by problems and to implement any required changes. The latter point is significant because unlike other forms of employee participation, quality circles permit the employees themselves to implement changes agreed by the management, thus implying a degree of grass-roots decision-making, which is new to most shop-floor situations.

(**Note:** marks would be awarded for other relevant points).

Question 11

(a) Potential benefits to staff

- Less time wasted commuting and therefore there is more time to pursue personal interests.

- Less stress and expense incurred in travelling.

- A more relaxed dress code. Suits, collars and ties will be needed rarely.

- More flexible work patterns that can be fitted around family life and other commitments and interests.

- Fewer interruptions and less time wasted by the trivial matters that typically arise in most offices. The more peaceful and relaxed environment should mean that tasks are completed more efficiently and effectively.

- Assuming there are suitable communication links, staff will have more freedom about where they live and even how long they can be away during the holiday season as their business could be conducted from almost anywhere.

The concerns of staff

- Staff realise that the proposed change will have dramatic effects and are right to be concerned. The level of an individual's concern will vary, depending on how much they enjoy office life, their home circumstances and how comfortable they feel with advanced computer systems.

- Work plays a very important role in most people's lives. In addition to providing income, work can also help meet social, ego and self-fulfilment needs. Home working will greatly reduce social opportunities for staff and they will meet colleagues only occasionally; they may fear isolation. Ego needs (the need to be looked up to and respected) will be harder to fulfil in the relatively solitary world of the home worker.

- Staff may feel cut off from important information that they need.

- Learning and problem solving opportunities will be reduced. In addition to formal training, most employees learn a tremendous amount informally by watching and by discussing problems with colleagues. Often, employees will learn by listening in on discussions being carried on between two other parties.

- Working from home may have negative effects on home life. The equipment will have to be sited somewhere in the employee's house; work time may encroach on private time as there is no longer the formal cut-off of going home from work.

Question 11

- Some employees may have more interruptions at home than they would have in the office.

- Home working may make career structures more limiting. More people are working on their own and there might be less management to carry out. Furthermore, promotion will be on fewer success criteria as the only results seen by head office will be sales; managerial and human qualities will be more difficult to display.

Use of the IT infrastructure

The infra-structure can help as follows:

- Email will provide easy communication (albeit written) between staff.

- Voice and video attachments will make it possible for staff to talk to and see each other. This will reduce their feeling of isolation.

- Communications equipment and software will allow access to data about customers and the value added network.

- Standard letters and forms can be used by the word processor to produce quotations and other commonly required documents.

- The provision of on-line help and electronic performance support systems will help staff learn on demand (just-in-time learning).

(b) **How staff could be encouraged to accept the proposed change**

- Participation in the decision making process and in the establishment of new work norms.

- It is unlikely that all work can be carried on from home without the need of meetings or visits to the office. Pointing this out should help to reduce fears about isolation.

- Emphasise the benefits that there should be (see above).

- Consider offering help to staff for the establishment of suitable work areas at home. At the very least office furniture will have to be supplied. If a separate area is not available, the furniture will have to be carefully chosen so as to fit in with domestic furniture.

- Emphasise that CP will pay for the installation of an ISDN line which is equivalent to two additional phone lines. One line will be used for IT; the other as a conventional business line. Help towards additional heating costs may be appropriate as staff will now occupy their own houses most of the day.

–   Additional efforts should be made to arrange out of hours social events to reduce feelings of isolation and loss of social contact.

–   Instead of enforcing immediate changeover of all staff, many of whom may be reluctant to cooperate, it might be possible to ask first for volunteers. These people could be seen as a pilot operation from which, no doubt, both staff and the company will learn. Every effort should be made to maximise the success of this operation so that other staff members will also be encouraged to change.

–   Staff will be aware that the company will save money and may expect some financial inducements to change their work practices.

Conclusion

Home working offers great potential benefits to this organisation but it represents a fundamental change in the culture and work practices of staff, who have legitimate worries. However, by addressing these worries and attempting to win their cooperation, staff concerns should be outweighed by the very considerable benefits which should be obtained by them.

Managing Human Capital

Chapter learning objectives

Lead	Component
E1. Explain the relationship of human resources (HR) to the organisation's operations	(b) Explain the importance of ethical behaviour in business generally and for the line manager and their activities.
E2. Discuss the activities associated with the management of human capital	(a) Explain the HR activities associated with developing the ability of employees.
	(d) Discuss the importance of the line manager in the implementation of HR practices.
	(e) Prepare an HR plan appropriate to a team.

1 Introduction

Human resource management (HRM) can be viewed as a strategic approach to acquiring, developing, managing and motivating an organisation's key resource. This should help the organisation achieve its stated objectives through the best use of its employees.

Note that HRM is not simply a renaming of old "personnel" departments but a radical change in emphasis:

The role of personnel versus the role of HRM

Personnel	HRM
• The **traditional** approach to managing human resources.	• The **modern** approach to managing human resources.
• Concerned with **operational** matters, e.g. recruitment to fill a current vacancy.	• Concerned with **operational and strategic** matters, e.g. training to fulfil the current and future needs of the organisation.
• Employees seen as **costs**.	• Employees seen as **assets**.
• Employees motivated by **payment and coercion.**	• Employees motivated by **consent and involvement**.
• Line manager's role is more **transactional** with an emphasis on **negotiation**. Key managers are seen to be personnel and industrial relations specialists.	• Line manager's role is now one of **transformational leadership** with an emphasis on **facilitation**. Line managers are seen as key within an HR emphasis.

The last point is a critical one - line managers are now seen as the key players in HR issues. As you read through the different aspects of this chapter, consider to what extent you would expect your boss to be involved and when would "experts" be included.

2 Human Resource Planning (HRP)

The organisation's **HR plan** is a strategy developed within the context of the organisation's corporate strategic plans.

- Its aim is to define and close the gap between the demand for labour and the supply of labour within the organisation.

- A typical HR plan looks forward 3-5 years and is a cyclical process.

Reasons for creating a HR plan
(1) To rationally plan recruitment;
(2) To rationally forecast future costs to assist in budgeting and control;
(3) To smooth change management in redeployment, redundancy etc.;
(4) To assist in planning the education, development and training needs of staff;
(5) To adapt more quickly to ever changing circumstances.

The stages of HRP are as follows:

> **Stage 1: Strategic analysis**
> - The organisation's strategic objectives will have implications regarding the number of employees and the skills required over the planning period (e.g. development of a new product or expansion into a new market)
> - The broader strategic environment should also be considered (e.g. trends in population growth, pensions, education and employment rights of women

> **Stage 2: Internal analysis**
> - An 'audit' of existing staff should be carried out to establish the current numbers and skills
> - Also consider:
>   - Turnover of staff and absenteeism
>   - Overtime worked and periods of inactivity
>   - Staff potential

> **Stage 3: Identify the gap between supply and demand**
> - Shortages or excesses in labour numbers and skills deficiencies should be identified

> **Stage 4: Put plans into place to close the gap**
>
> *Adjustments for shortfall*
> - Internal: Transfers, promotions, training, job enlargement, overtime, reduce labour turnover
> - External: Fill remaining needs externally. Consider suitability and availability of external resource
>
> *Adjustments for a surplus*
> Consider use of natural wastage, recruitment freeze, retirement, part time working and redundancy

> **Stage 5: Review**
> Measure the effective use of the human resource and their contribution towards the achievement of the organisation's objectives

Stage 4 of the HR plan.

In stage four of HRP a number of plans will be created and used:

Recruitment plan	Numbers and types of people, when required, recruitment programme
Training plan	Number of trainees required and training programme
Redevelopment plan	Programme for transferring staff
Productivity plan	Setting targets and developing incentive schemes
Redundancy plan	Location, selection process, package details
Retention plan	Career development programmes

Test your understanding 1

Describe **four** problems in implementing the HR plan

Effective HRP can anticipate future difficulties while there is still a choice of action. Coupled with good communication, consultation and participation with the staff involved, planning should help alleviate harmful effects to individual members of staff or to the organisation.

HR in different organisational forms

Organisational HR practices inevitably vary dependent upon the individual size and culture of the organisation and availability of specialist HR or personnel managers to support management in carrying out their duties.

The need to respond to a fast moving environment has led to organisations moving from traditional hierarchies to adopting more flexible organisational structures including fluid matrix or project-based firms. Alongside these virtual or networked firms have grown up. Inevitably these non-traditional structures have presented new HR challenges and required managers to adapt traditional approaches to these local contexts.

Clearly HR thinking and practice needs to evolve in responses to these challenges of flexibility and environmental uncertainty, specifically in the areas of:

* planning horizons
* staff appraisal where there may be no formal supervisor/subordinate reporting relations
* remuneration strategies where outputs are not easily attributable to individuals alone
* the structure of the workforce and the use of consultants and contractors
* development, promotion and succession planning.

New forms of organisation have resulted in changing HR needs. For example:

Project based teams

Employees are organised into work teams, e.g. for a particular project or customer group. HR implications:

- Multi-skilled employees are required.
- Intensive training will be needed.
- A movement away from traditional hierarchies to flatter structures.

Virtual organisations

Technology has resulted in the development of virtual organisations. Virtual teams work together using the World Wide Web, networked computers and teleconferencing.

This can bring huge benefits for the employer in terms of the flexibility to recruit the most talented individual for a particular role. However, it can also bring additional challenges with regards to HR since geographical spread will make all elements of HR (i.e. recruitment, selection, inductions, appraisals and training and development) more difficult.

3 The HR Cycle

Each of these activities will be reviewed in turn.

4 Recruitment

4.1 Introduction

Recruitment involves attracting a field of suitable candidates for the job.

The best recruitment campaign will attract a small number of highly suitable applicants, be cost effective, be speedy and show courtesy to all candidates.

The recruitment plan includes:

Assessing the need to recruit

When considering recruitment, there are two questions that managers must address. The first is whether there is really a job, and the second is whether there is someone suitable who is already employed by the organisation. There are many alternatives to recruitment, e.g.

- promotion of existing staff (upwards or laterally)

- secondment (temporary transfers to another department, office, plant or country) of existing staff, which may or may not become permanent

- closing the job down, by sharing out duties and responsibilities among existing staff

- rotating jobs among staff, so that the vacant job is covered by different staff, on a systematic basis over several months

- putting the job out to tender, using external contractors.

4.2 Job analysis

Job analysis is 'the process of collecting, analysing and setting out information about the content of jobs in order to provide the basis for a job description and data for recruitment, training, job evaluation and performance management. Job analysis concentrates on what job holders are expected to do.' **Armstrong**

Such an exercise is frequently necessary since all too few organisations have a precise picture of the work that people do to achieve organisational objectives.

Test your understanding 2

Explain the importance of job analysis for a large supermarket chain, such as Tesco.

Methods of analysing and defining roles would include:

- Interview with existing post holder or supervisor

- Direct observation

- Questionnaires

- Manager trying the job

While HR specialists may be able to assist this process, though the use of standardised questionnaires for example, job analysis usually falls to the line manager as he or she will have the best idea of what the new role will entail and why recruitment is needed.

4.3 Job descriptions

After a full job analysis has been carried out, a job description can be drawn up identifying the precise nature of the job in question.

Test your understanding 3

Prepare a job description for a London based role as a Finance Director in an internet media company which is about to become a public company.

Job descriptions

Most job descriptions include all of the following points.

- The title of the job and the name of the department in which it is situated.

- The purpose of the job, identifying its objectives in relationship to overall objectives.

- The position of the job in the organisation, indicating the relationships with other jobs and the chains of responsibility. For this purpose, many firms refer to existing organisation charts.

- Wage/salary range.

- Principal duties to be performed, with emphasis on key tasks, and limits to the jobholder's authority. Usually under this heading is included an indication of how the job differs from others in the organisation.

- A further breakdown of principal duties is made identifying specific tasks in terms of what precisely is done and in what manner, and with some explanation, both in terms of quantity and quality.

- Aspects of the 'job environment' should be considered. Descriptions should be made of how the organisation supports the job, in terms of management and the provision of key services. The working conditions should be considered in terms of both the physical environment and the social environment (is the job part of a group task?). The opportunities offered by the job should be identified; these are especially important in a recruitment exercise.

- No job description is complete without a full identification of the key difficulties likely to be encountered by the jobholder.

Most of the content of a job description will be generated by the line manager. However, an HR department can help through the use of standardised templates, discussions over grading and salary and the position of the role in the wider organisation.

4.4 Person specifications

The **person specification** defines the personal characteristics, qualifications and experience required by the job holder in order to do the job well. It therefore becomes a specification for the attributes sought in a successful candidate for the job, a blueprint for the perfect person to fill the role.

Rodgers recommended that the following categories should be covered in a person specification:

Category	Example
B - Background/circumstances	Details of previous work experience and circumstances, e.g. family background, criminal record.
A - Attainments	Details of qualifications and any relevant experience.
D - Disposition	The individual's goals and motivations, e.g. where do they see themselves in 5 years time?
P - Physical make-up	Appearance, speech, health and fitness may be important.
I - Interests	General interests and hobbies will be important, e.g. being a member of a football team demonstrates teamwork skills.
G - General intelligence	Not necessarily academic qualifications but may refer to practical intelligence, e.g. problem solving ability.
S - Special attributes	Skills such as the ability to speak another language or IT skills.

As with job analysis and job description, the prospective line manager is usually in the best position to construct a person specification but many managers will appreciate assistance here from HR specialists who may have more experience.

Fraser's 5-point plan

A similar blueprint was devised by **Fraser**. He referred to it as the Five Point Plan, to include the following considerations:

- **F**lexibility and adjustment – emotional stability, ability to get on with others and capacity for stress.
- **I**mpact on other people – appearance, speech and manner.
- **R**equired qualifications – education, training, and experience.
- **M**otivation – determination and achievement.
- **I**nnate abilities – 'brains', comprehension and aptitude for learning.

Illustration 1

Care must be taken not to transgress one of the laws relating to discrimination, as in the case of a job advertisement seeking 'a female Scottish cook and housekeeper', which was barred both on the grounds of race and sex discrimination.

Test your understanding 4

Are there any circumstances when discrimination on the basis of physical make-up is acceptable?

4.5 Source candidates

It is important to know where suitable candidates may be found, how to make contact with them and to secure their application. The following sources are available:

Source	Comment
Job centre	Free but may not find a suitable candidate.
Recruitment consultant	Reduces burden on employer and may be a source of expertise but expensive and may not understand the organisation's needs.
Job fair	Can meet people face to face but may not attract enough suitable candidates.
National press	Good coverage for national jobs but advertisements are expensive and short-lived.
Local newspaper	Useful for local staff and cheaper than national but may not attract sufficiently qualified people.
Internet	Good as long as target people are frequent internet users.
Radio and TV	Expensive but sometimes can produce a large number of suitable candidates.
Specialist journals	Already degree of selection but may contain many similar advertisements.

Sourcing candidates usually involves the HR department unless the firm is particularly small. Partly this is to ensure that any advertisements comply with any legal requirements on diversity and discimination, but also because the HR department will have more experience of recruitment consultants and the different advertising media.

5 Selection

5.1 Introduction

Selection is aimed at choosing the best person for the job from the field of candidates sourced using recruitment.

Any selection process needs to ensure:

Reliability	to give consistent results;
Validity	as a predictor of future performance;
Fairness	selection in a non-discriminatory way;
Cost effectiveness	in terms of managers' time and other options available

5.2 Application forms

Application forms are used to obtain relevant information about the applicant and allow for comparison with the person specification of the job. They should also give the applicants some ability to express themselves beyond the limited factual remit of the form. Their usefulness includes:

- eliminating unsatisfactory candidates

- saving interview time by selecting only the most suitable candidates for interview

- forming an initial personal record for an employee.

Application forms are likely to be standardised to some extent and hence will be produced by HR professionals with input from the line managers.

5.3 Selection interviews

Interviews are by far the most widely used selection technique. Their purpose is to:

- find the best person for the job
- ensure the candidate understands what the job is and what the career prospects are
- make the candidate feel that they have been given fair treatment in the interview.

Line managers would normally expect to be part of the interviewing panel for new employees for their departments.

Face-to-face
by one person

Group interview
with other candidates

Succession of interviews
obtain better view of candidate

INTERVIEW OPTIONS

Problem solving
candidate asked to solve a hypothetical problem

Panel interview
interview by group of people

Stress
candidate deliberately placed under stress by aggressive interviewer

Interview options

An interview process can be:

A face-to-face interview – carried out once by a single representative, usually of the employing organisation. It is considered the best situation for establishing rapport and is certainly cost effective in terms of people employed. While it does have the advantage of placing candidates at ease, enabling the interviewer to gain a true picture of the applicant, the selection decision relies heavily on the judgement of one individual.

A problem-solving interview – this is a face-to-face interview where the candidate is set a hypothetical problem. For example, a problem may be put to a prospective industrial relations trainee concerning the action they would take following a fight between a foreman and a shop steward where both participants told a different version of the incident and a work stoppage had ensued. The drawback with such interviews is that the quality of the answers is very difficult to assess and compare to those given by other candidates.

A stress interview – this is another face-to-face interview, where the candidate is put under deliberate stress usually by an aggressive interviewer, who attempts to disparage the candidate's answers at every opportunity. This method of interviewing proved successful during the war for selecting undercover agents and was in vogue a few years ago for selecting managers, based on the theory that their ability to handle stressful situations was the best test of their ability. Research evidence concerning stress interviews suggests they are of dubious value and can actually cause harm by alienating favourable candidates.

Succession of interviews – by different interviewers (e.g. operating manager and personnel officer). Common practice in leading companies is to conduct several face-to-face interviews, rather than a single panel interview. Obviously this type of exercise is more costly and can be more wearing on the candidate, but it may enable a more balanced judgement to be made.

Group interview – where candidates are brought together and observed by assessors, who give the group a problem to discuss or a situation to sort out. It is a sort of committee exercise. This method can identify personal reactions such as tact, dominance and persuasiveness.

Panel interview – candidates are interviewed before a panel of two or more people, in some cases as many as six or seven. For some senior posts in some local authorities in Britain, panels of 20 or more can be found. The usual panel size is between two and six interviewers, depending upon the nature of the job and the customs of the employing organisation. Panel interviews have the advantage of sharing judgements and most panels have the authority to reach immediate decisions. Their main drawback is the question of control: with so many people, irrelevancies can be introduced and a particular line of questioning can soon be destroyed. The success of a panel interview often depends upon careful planning and effective chairmanship. While they can be impressive in terms of ritual, panel interviews can be particularly unnerving for some candidates.

Advantages of selection interviews

* Places candidates at ease

* Highly interactive, allowing flexible question and answers

* Opportunities to use non-verbal communication

* Opportunities to assess appearance, interpersonal and communication skills

* Opportunities to evaluate rapport between the candidate and the potential colleagues/ bosses

Test your understanding 5

The validity of a face-to-face interview as a means of gauging a person's ability, character and ambition is regularly challenged. Briefly explain the main shortcomings of the interview technique.

5.4 Selection testing

Intelligence tests – measuring general intellectual ability e.g. an IQ test

Aptitude tests – testing specific abilities e.g. clerical and numerical ability

Medical examinations – test to eliminate candidates with health problems

Selection tests

Proficiency tests – measuring the ability to do the work involved in the job e.g. job simulation

Psychometric tests – contain features of all other types of test. Candidates are scored based on their answers to a list of questions

Personality tests – Reveal what a person is really like e.g. likes, dislikes, what they would do in certain situations

Many of the above techniques would lie outside the expertise of the line manager and so specialists would be called in to carry out the testing and feed back.

5.5 Assessment centres

- The idea of the assessment centre grew out of the obvious shortcomings of the selection interview and other selection techniques.

- Assessment centres, usually provided by external consultants unless the firm is particularly large, allow the assessment of individuals working in a group or alone by a team of assessors, who use a variety of assessment techniques.

GROUP DISCUSSIONS — PRESENTATIONS — QUESTIONNAIRES — SIMULATIONS

WRITTEN TESTS — ASSESSMENT CENTRE — GAMES

ROLE PLAY EXERCISES — SELF-APPRAISAL — PEER RATING — SPEECHES

- Groups of around 6-10 candidates are brought together for one to three days of intensive assessment.

- The assessment centre can be designed so as to test the applicant's competencies against the criteria set out in the person specification.

Different approaches to selection tests

The main types of test that can be used as part of a selection process as follows:

Cognitive tests which relate to thinking processes and include tests of intelligence, ability, aptitude, communication, numerical skills, etc. Usually intelligence tests are described to candidates as 'aptitude' or 'skills' tests and comprise mathematical or number skills, communication or verbal skills and a general logic or problem-solving testing. Originally they were work-related, such as typing tests, but gradually more abstract forms were developed for aptitudes seen to be important for some jobs. Manual dexterity, mechanical, numerical ability and spatial testing are included in this category.

Personality tests which involve assessing non-cognitive and non-intellectual characteristics of an individual, usually the emotional make-up, reflected in the style of behaviour. Beaumont (1993) noted that 'there is probably no subject more controversial in occupational psychology than the merits and demerits of personality assessment'. Results from personality tests have to be interpreted carefully alongside the applicant's other known attributes. Many categories of personality tests exist, including questionnaires, which have doubtful validity if candidates attempt to predict likely required answers. Such techniques tend to have low reliability and less predictive validity. The most-well known personality test is the Cattell 16 PF (Personality Factors) which provides 16 basic dimensions, such as extrovert/introvert, tough-minded/tender-minded, along which individuals score from 0 to 10. These standard-ten or 'sten' scores can be aggregated to produce higher-level factors such as leadership or toughness. This test has norms against which candidates can be compared, and also has a 'motivational distortion' score, which can be used to assess how far the candidate has tried to manipulate their responses. There are several books interpreting the scores of such tests and computer software that can produce written narratives explaining the results.

Psychometric testing is sometimes also undertaken in this context. The term 'psychometric' derives from 'psyche' meaning the mind and 'metric' meaning measuring so psychometric applies to both personality and cognitive testing. The quality of tests used ranges from good to of dubious quality. Others are expensive to administer and score, often requiring the involvement of the commercial consultants. Organisations intending to use such tests should first seek guidance from the British Psychological Society, the American Psychological Society or other reputable agencies in other countries. In psychological testing, ethical considerations should be applied to critical aspects of the science. Since administration, scoring and interpretation of tests is a skilled operation only qualified people are entitled to use them. Credible Psychological Societies require proper training of test administrators and interpreters and there is a strong recommendation to give the candidates feedback on their results.

Psychometric testing

In the following extracts from an article by Bryan Appleyard the growth and usefulness of psychometric testing is reviewed:

Welcome to the weird world of psychometrics. If you want to work for a big company there's at least a 70% chance that before being given a job you will be subjected to a personality test by one of the big four – MBTI (Myers-Briggs Type Indicator), 16PF (16 personality factors), OPQ (occupational personality questionnaire) or Hogan – and an ability exam measuring verbal reasoning and numeracy.

These are basically IQ tests by another name...according to the Association of Graduate Recruiters, it's because nobody trusts university degrees any more. It has just issued a report saying degree standards are inconsistent and, as a result, companies are turning to psychometrics. But Ceri Roderick at occupation psychologists Pearn Kandola adds two other reasons. 'Companies want to know things like the motivational characteristics of recruits and the technology is now available to do these things.' There's also a fourth reason: the need to compete for quality recruits. 'There's a war for talent,' says Professor David Bartram of the British Psychological Society (BPS), 'companies are fighting to get the best people.' All of which means there is now a rapid proliferation of psychometrics consultancies, most of them offering candidates the chance to do all the tests online. . . .

Sceptics think the whole enterprise is misguided. In America a book – The Cult of Personality by Annie Murphy Paul – has cast doubt on the intellectual credibility of psychometrics…

In support of Paul's book the author Malcolm Gladwell questions the very idea of measuring personality: 'We have a personality in the sense that we have a consistent pattern of behaviour. But that pattern is complex and that personality is contingent: it represents an interaction between our internal disposition and tendencies and the situations that we find ourselves in.'. . .

But are Gladwell and Paul right to question the whole theory on which they are based? The history of psychometrics marches hand in hand with the history of IQ testing. Alfred Binet, the French psychologist, produced the first modern IQ test in 1905 and Walter Dill Scott subjected 15 engineering graduates to the first psychometric test in 1915. Both ideas were inspired by the conviction that there could be no reason why the human mind should be impervious to scientific investigation. . . .

Psychometrics works, but only if the tests are properly applied, rigorously interpreted and accompanied by traditional interviews. This means that they do not necessarily speed up the recruitment process. They might, however, help weed out unsuitables in advance, a huge benefit at a time when all companies are swamped with applicants for attractive jobs.

Source: Appleyard, B. (2007) Want a job? Let's play mind games. Sunday Times, 22 July.

Test your understanding 6

Explain why assessment centres are part of a competency-based selection process used by many major employers when recruiting staff for their graduate training scheme?

Drawbacks of assessment centres

- The assessment centre must be rigorous or else there is a temptation to select the person who just seems the most sociable or likeable.

- The cost of setting them up, administering them, staffing them and producing results can be extremely high.

5.6 References

The purpose of references is to confirm facts about the employee and increase the degree of confidence felt about information given during the other selection techniques.

References should contain two types of information:

- Straightforward factual information. This confirms the nature of the applicant's previous job(s), period of employment, pay, and circumstances of leaving.

- Opinions about the applicant's personality and other attributes.

> ### Content of references
>
> A standard form to be completed by the referee might pose a set of simple questions about:
>
> - job title
> - main duties and responsibilities
> - period of employment
> - pay/salary
> - attendance record.

Problems with references

Opinions should obviously be treated with some caution. Allowances should be made for:

- prejudice - favourable or unfavourable
- charity - withholding detrimental remarks
- fear of being actionable for libel

5.7 Employment offer and negotiation

- **Offer of employment** – once an eligible candidate has been found, an offer can be made, in writing or by telephone, subject to satisfactory references.

- **Negotiation** – it may be necessary to reach a mutually agreeable compromise over some aspects of the employment contract, e.g. pay, hours of work or holiday allowance.

> ### Offer of employment
>
> An effective offer of employment must not contain anything that cannot be delivered and should contain the following elements:
>
> - Must be a written document – a written statement is a legally binding document, which should help to seal the offer. A telephone call to break the good news to the successful candidate is fine, but should not go into too much detail about the offer in conversation.
>
> - Must contain sufficient detail – must contain the job title and location with details of pay, benefits, hours of work, holiday as well as the terms and conditions of employment, including notice period, sickness payment schemes, pension scheme details, disciplinary and grievance procedures and an outline of the probationary period where one is in force.
>
> - Should offer an opportunity to make further contact before a final commitment is made – a clear but informal opportunity for further discussion, which may lead to negotiation on terms and conditions of employment.

6 Induction

The purpose of an induction is to ensure the most effective integration of staff into the organisation, for the benefit of both parties.

The benefits of a good induction programme include:

- Quick and effective assimilation into organisational life

- A well planned programme will reassure employees. This will aid motivation and improve performance

- Increased commitment since it can provide a positive reflection of the organisation while the employee is still comparatively receptive and has not been subject to negative views

- Reduces staff turnover and associated costs

Induction programmes may focus on company wide issues, in which case they will usually be designed and run by the HR department, and/or focus on departmental practices and procedures, in which case they may be set up by the line manager.

Illustration 2

In 2008 the average UK employee turnover rate was 17.3% and the average cost of employee turnover was £5,800 for each employee. A major reason why employees leave within the first six months to a year is a poorly planned induction process. Therefore, there are significant savings to be made from implementing an effective induction process.

A good induction programme would typically include:

Pre-employment	• joining instructions • conditions of employment • company literature
Health and safety	• emergency exits • first aid facilities • protective clothing • specific hazards
Organisation	• site map - canteen, first aid post etc • telephone and computer system • organisation chart • security pass and procedures
Terms and conditions	• absence/ sickness procedure • working time including hours, breaks and flexi-time • holidays • probation period • discipline and grievance procedure • internet and email policy
Financial	• payment date and methods • benefits and pension • expense procedures

Training	• discuss training opportunities and agree training plan • career management
Culture and values	• organisation background • mission and objectives

7 Training and Development

7.1 Introduction

```
          Distinction between
          training and
          development
```

Training – Formal learning to achieve the level of skills, knowledge and competence to carry out the *current* role

Development – The realisation of a person's potential through formal and informal learning to enable them to carry out their *current and future* role. It is more individually orientated than training

Benefits of training

Some of the benefits of training for the individual and for the organisation include:

Individual	Organisation
• Improved skills • Potential qualifications • Increased confidence • Increased job satisfaction	• Motivated and hence productive employees • Increased competence and confidence • Lower staff turnover • Improved health and safety • A more flexible workforce

Illustration 3

There are various indicators of organisational health, which may well suggest that training is necessary. Such indicators might include labour turnover, absenteeism or the level of grievances. For example, several studies have shown that inadequate training often leads to workers failing to achieve production targets, which affects their chances of gaining financial incentives. Many such employees experience frustration, which manifests itself in grievances and labour turnover.

7.2 The stages in the training and development process

Stage 1: Identify training and development needs

Stage 2: Set training objectives

Stage 3: Plan the training

Stage 4: Deliver the training

Stage 5: Evaluate the training

Stages in training and development

- **Identifying training needs** – this could include an investigation into the organisation's current performance as well as mapping the corporate skills base. It should drill down to the level of the individual to target specific needs.

- **Setting training objectives** – as with all objectives these should have clear, specific, measurable targets in relation to the behaviour and standard of behaviour required in order to achieve a given level of performance.

- **Planning the training** – this covers who provides the training, where the training takes place and divisions of responsibilities between trainers, line managers or team leaders and the individual personally.

- **Delivering/implementing the training** – a combination of formal and on-the-job training programmes will be used.

- **Evaluating training** – assessment of cost versus benefit using feedback forms, end of course tests, assessment of improved performance in the work place and impact on corporate goals.

7.3 Methods of training and development

Training and development methods for individuals	Training and development methods for groups
• External and in-house courses	• Lectures
• Computer-based training	• Discussions and role plays
• Coaching/ mentoring	• Business games
• Job rotation	• Outdoor pursuits
• Project work	

7.4 Kolb's experiential learning cycle

Kolb suggests that learning is a series of steps based on **learning from experience**. He suggested that classroom learning is false and that learning should be an active process if it is to be effective.

7.5 Honey and Mumford's learning styles

Honey and Mumford suggest there are four different learning styles:

Learning style	Explanation
Activists	Involve themselves fully and without bias in new experiences. They are open-minded, enthusiastic, constantly searching for new challenges but are bored with implementation and long-term consolidation.
Reflectors	Prefer to step back to ponder and observe others before taking action. They are in general cautious, may be perceived as indecisive and tend to adopt a low profile.
Theorists	Adapt and integrate information in a step-by-step logical way. They prefer to maximise certainty and feel uncomfortable with subjective judgements, lateral thinking and anything flippant.
Pragmatists	Are keen to try out new ideas, theories and techniques to see if they work in practice. They are essentially practical, down-to-earth people, like making practical decisions, act quickly on ideas that attract them and tend to be impatient with open-ended discussions.

Test your understanding 7

State the most effective learning methods for each of Honey and Mumford's learning styles

Illustration 4

It is generally agreed that a combination of different types of learners will make an effective team in an organisation. In discussing an issue, the most likely question the Reflector will pursue is 'Why it is important'; the Theorist, in contrast, will be interested in 'What it is all about'; the Pragmatist will be concerned with 'How it can be applied in the real world'; and the Activist will be keen to know 'What if we were to apply it here and now'.

8 Appraisals

Appraisal is the systematic review and assessment of an employee's performance, potential and training needs.

8.1 Benefits of appraisal

Benefits for the employer	Benefits for the employee
• **Feedback and objective setting** - the appraisal is an opportunity for the employer to give feedback and to set the employee's objectives for the following period.	• **Feedback and objective setting** - the appraisal is an opportunity for the employee to receive feedback and to set the objectives for the following period.
• **Promotion** - it provides a formal system for assessing the performance and potential of employees, with a view to identifying candidates for promotion. This will assist with HRP.	• **Future prospects** - a formal appraisal system offers employees an opportunity to discuss further prospects and ambitions.
• **Training** - it provides a system for identifying training needs, in order to raise the level of efficiency and effectiveness.	• **Training** - appraisals can be used to identify and agree further training, to improve employee competence.
• **Improved communication** - if well managed, communication and hence working relations can be improved between managers and staff.	• **Pay and rewards** - the appraisal can be used as a basis for considering pay and rewards.
• **Career planning** - discussions concerning longer term development and career planning can be had and appropriate action taken.	• **Voice concerns** - appraisals can provide a platform for staff views and to voice concerns.

8.2 The stages of performance appraisal

Stage 1: Identify the criteria for assessment, e.g. a number of objectives may be set based on job analysis

Stage 2: Manager prepares an appraisal report. Note: sometimes the appraisee prepares a report and they are compared

Stage 3: Appraisal interview is carried out between the job holder and the manager

Stage 4: Agreement of future objectives and solutions to problems, e.g. training needs are agreed and action points implemented

Stage 5: The manager's own supervisor reviews the assessment for fairness

Stage 6: Follow up – progress and success is monitored

The appraisal interview

The appraisal interview is the point at which the employee and manager meet formally to discuss performance and agree targets for the forthcoming period. It is a vitally important stage in the process and must be planned well. Prior to the interview the supervisor or manager who is appraising needs to be prepared. The following are documents that may be available, and should have been read and copied for the interview:

- the job description (or a clear idea of the appraisee's job)

- a statement of performance such as the rating sheet or the appraisal form

- a diary or record book which highlights the good and bad points of the employee's performance over the review period

- peer assessment

- comments from clients, customers or other outside agencies

- the employee's self-assessment form

- the employee's file with background notes on attendance, timekeeping, personality, temperament and family.

From this information the manager can draw up a list of points to be discussed during the interview. Other documentation includes the appraisal form for both parties to complete at interview, including an assessment of past performance from the last appraisal, a set of objectives for the forthcoming review period, a development and action plan and a section for signatures and comments.

Once you have done your homework and have the information you need to hand, there are a few points to bear in mind about appraisal interviews:

The environment and atmosphere are important. Planning too many interviews in one day is not a good idea, nor is holding them at an inconvenient time. The interviewee should not be intimidated by the physical setting of the interview; sitting on a huge chair behind a large desk may be appropriate for a disciplinary interview but is not appropriate for an appraisal interview. Constant interruptions during the interview should be avoided because it is discourteous, disruptive and shows a lack of professionalism.

Your approach should be sketched out, with the main points you wish to make, prior to the interview. It also helps if the interviewee has an understanding of what is going to happen. A highly-structured interview plan with a rigid order of items goes against the spirit of the more freewheeling joint appraisal/problem-solving interview. Note taking during the interview should only happen if the appraisee has agreed.

Conducting the interview

The first steps are to put the employee at ease, explain the purpose of the interview and then discuss the employee's progress. During the discussion there are many social communicating skills at play. The following list of skills is a guide of 'must do's' while conducting the interview:

- Ask open questions requiring more than a yes or no answer.
- Ask closed questions only when clarification is needed.
- Allow time for the appraisee to ask questions.
- Refrain from asking multiple or confusing questions.
- Encourage conversation with body language and appropriate cues.
- Periodically summarise, reflect and check your understanding.
- Build upon answers.
- Refrain from talking too much.
- Handle difficult or sensitive areas carefully.
- Be tolerant of pauses and silences.

- Listen carefully, making sure that the interviewee knows you are listening.
- Keep the conversation from wandering off into irrelevant areas.

The present approach in staff appraisals is to encourage the manager to act as a counsellor rather than a judge or a critic. The emphasis is on helping the subordinate to overcome any shortcomings and become more effective in the future. This requires open appraisals which are frequently held, often in an informal atmosphere, at pre-set dates. Much of the success or failure of such schemes is determined by the face-to-face attitude generated by the manager at the counselling sessions.

At the end of the interview, the manager should sum up the whole discussion, and restate any decisions, commitments, agreements or recommendations that have been made. This ensures that there is a full understanding about the future actions or plans of both parties. Agree on alternative courses of action in case the first is not possible. Note that the action plan should include:

- training and development needs
- recommended action along with the key dates by which the action is to take place
- the resources needed for support.

After the interview the manager or supervisor should inform the appraisee of the results of the appraisal and write up on the following:

- agreed action plans on training, promotion, etc.
- the shortcomings and weaknesses that were discussed and the results
- any help or assistance the employee needs and what was promised at the interview.

The follow-up procedures will include taking the steps to help the employee attain the agreed objectives by:

- providing feedback
- training
- rescheduling work
- altering work methods
- upgrading equipment.

8.3 The barriers to effective appraisal

Lockett suggests that appraisal barriers can be identified as follows:

Confrontation	• Differing views regarding performance. • Feedback is badly delivered.
Judgement	• Appraisal is seen as a one-sided process – the manager is judge, jury and counsel for the prosecution.
Chat	• An unproductive conversation. • No outcomes set.
Bureaucracy	• Purely a 'form filling' exercise. • No purpose or worth.
Annual event	• A traditional ceremony, carried out once or twice a year.
Unfinished business	• No follow up. • Points agreed are not actioned.

Relationship between appraisal and the reward system

In many organisations there is a link between performance and pay. There are many problems in linking pay to performance including:

• employees concentrating on goals that have a definite link to the reward system

• inducing conflict when rewarding some employees more than others

• financial constraints due to recessionary factors, or poor company results

To overcome some of the difficulties of linking pay to performance it is necessary for those carrying out the appraisal to be well trained and skilled at carrying out the process. Schemes need to be uncomplicated, free from bias and subjectivity, and perceived to be fair by those who are to be appraised.

8.4 Appraisal and career development

Appraisal has a clear link to career development. Career development sees the interaction of three concepts:

Education – a process results in a formal qualification, e.g. CIMA

Training – e.g. IT training required for the job the employee is doing now

Development – e.g. training in management skills for the job the employee may be doing in the future

Career planning and development

Career planning has traditionally been viewed as an organisation-driven activity that enables human resource managers to concentrate on jobs and building career paths so providing for logical progression of people between jobs. These career paths, particularly for people such as management accountants, have tended to be mainly within one specialised function and represent ladders on which individuals could progress within their functional specialism. Organisational career planning suffered severe setbacks from the layoffs during the recession of the late 1980s and early 1990s.

In addition these core concepts have increasingly been challenged due to a number of other developments including:

- Non-traditional organisational structures emerging. These flatter organisation structures have removed some career paths entirely and reduced opportunities in other areas. Additionally these structures imply a need for multi-skilling and teamwork at the expense of promotion 'ladders' found within traditional hierarchies. Increasingly workers are seeking to be 'multi-skilled' often developing a good understanding of more than one function rather than specialists.

- The development of general management skills and the concept of cross-functional career paths long been accepted as the norm in Japanese firms.

- Increasingly, career development has become led by the individuals themselves. An individual philosophy of building a portfolio of experience qualification and networks arose in order to develop a career outside a single organisational structure. This individual career planning focuses on individuals' goals and skills. It considers ways in which each individual might expand his or her capabilities and enhance career opportunities both within and outside a particular organisation. (Within the UK the Association of Graduate Recruiters recently warned that career paths no longer exist: only crazy paving that the individual lays himself or herself!)

Given this background, it is unsurprising that succession planning as an alternative to external recruitment may be seen as of decreasing HR significance. Problems have in any case always been associated with succession planning, including:

- Retention. Unlike other assets that have received investment, employees who are well trained especially those who are over-trained in anticipation of future developmental moves and are highly marketable.

- Individual failure. A failed assignment damages the individual, the company and the working relationships. 'Failure' may be attributable to one of a number of HR defects including poor control or managerial judgement, the over-promotion of individuals, and defective appraisal monitoring systems.

- Timing. One person failing to move because of personal circumstances can hold up the development of others unless some other kind of arrangement can be made. Slow promotion or development can lead to frustration and (for instance) graduate staff leaving shortly after becoming useful to the organisation. As the process depends on political expediency, many talented staff find that their present manager is reluctant to release them.

- Size of organisation. For a multi-national organisation, extensive relocation can be financially costly and for the family potentially distressing, demotivating and stressful. For many in small organisations a feeling of 'waiting for dead people's shoes' (as the old expression has it) may exist.

- Overseas postings. The issues of combining multi-cultural groups and three types of employee (the parent country nationals (expat), the home country national and the third country national) may prove problematic. Planning the correct combination of these staff is virtually impossible because of competing priorities and so many firms merely rely on the ability of all employees to 'mutually adjust' to each other and the new situation.

9 Termination

The E1 syllabus does not say much about termination but you should be aware of the following.

- Context - The HR cycle

    The last stage of the HR cycle is termination. Ultimately all staff cease to be employees for one reason or another. Even this stage needs to be managed effectively.

- Methods of termination

    The main ways a contract of employment is terminated are voluntary leaving (for example to move to another job), retirement, dismissal (for example, for misconduct) and redundancy (for example, where a whole business unit is closed down). Detailed legislation surrounds the last two of these and managers need to ensure that employee rights are not compromised. Legal issues are discussed in the next section.

- Context - HR planning

    When forecasting the HR resource requirements for a business, it may be that a surplus of staff is identified. While some of this surplus may be reduced through "natural wastage" (i.e. staff leaving to find new jobs or through retirement) the rest must be accomplished through any of the following:

    - Freezing recruitment of new staff

    - Retraining staff to fill vacancies elsewhere within the organisation

    - Reduced working hours (e.g. job share, part-time working arrangements)

    - Redundancy - usually a last resort.

10 Legal Issues

10.1 Introduction

Throughout this chapter we have seen how line managers are often central to HR management. However, in the context of the legal aspects of employment, they are advised to use the services of specialists, whether within the organisation or external consultants.

While **employment legislation** can vary considerably from country to country, it typically refers to the following:

Area	Typical Terms
Rights	Gives employees certain rights, such as: • a right not to be unfairly dismissed • a right to a redundancy payment if made redundant and • a right to a minimum period of notice to terminate the contract.
Contracts	Requires an employer to provide employees with a written statement of certain particulars of their employment. The statement typically includes details of: • pay • job title • place of work • length of notice and • details of disciplinary or grievance procedures.
Working hours	Limits the hours of work to an average of 48 a week, say. It also gives the right to: • four weeks paid leave a year and • one day off each week, say.
Rights of parents	Gives parents of children under five the right to request flexible working arrangements. Gives rights for maternity and paternity leave.

Legislation relating to **discrimination** typically includes the following:

Legislation	Typical terms
Pay	Must include an equality clause into all contracts of employment If workers of the opposite sex do the same job or a different job of equal value. Deals not only with pay, but other terms, e.g. holiday and sick leave.
Sex Discrimination	Discrimination in employment affairs because of marital status or sex is illegal. This applies especially to the selection process as it offers protection to both sexes against unfair treatment on appointment.
Racial discrimination	Prohibits discrimination on grounds of: • race • nationality or • colour unless there is a genuine occupational qualification, e.g. for reasons of authenticity.
Disability Discrimination	Prohibits discrimination on the grounds of disability.

10.2 Disciplinary procedures

The purpose of discipline is not punishment but is to improve the future behaviour of the employee and other members of the organisation.

> **Test your understanding 8**
>
> State **four** types of situation that may require disciplinary action by managers.

An organisation has a statutory duty to demonstrate that any dismissal is fair. Otherwise the dismissed employee will have a variety of rights open to them. The existence of written disciplinary procedures is designed to protect the employee and the employer.

Many orgãnisations adopt a progressive disciplinary procedure:

- **The informal talk** – for a minor infraction by an employee with no previous record of disciplinary action.

- **Oral warning** – for repeated violation.

- **Written warning** – becomes a permanent part of the employee's record.

- **Suspension without pay** – if previous steps were of no avail.

- **Demotion** – punishment by way of loss of pay or status.

- **Discharge** – reserved for the most serious offences.

Key requirements of any disciplinary policy will be:

Immediacy	Fast response to the misdemeanour;
Advance warning	Of the sanctions for breaches, in the staff handbook;
Consistency	For all staff in terms of actions taken;
Impersonality	Action based on the crime not the person involved;
Privacy	Confidentiality of proceedings should be maintained.

10.3 Redundancy

Redundancy should be considered as the last alternative:

Test your understanding 9
Explain what courses of action are available to a company to reduce staff costs.

- True redundancy arises when the role an employee performs is no longer required, perhaps due to restructuring.

- An employee may claim unfair dismissal if, in fact, the position was not redundant.

- Organisations that act ethically will have policies for pre-redundancy consultation and post redundancy support.

Illustration 5

When the UK entered recession at the beginning of 2009, employers rushed to reduce wage costs. Many employers ignored the costly steps that must be adhered to. As a result:

- Disputes regarding unfair dismissal were up by a quarter.

- Disputes regarding unfair redundancy were up by a third.

- Failure to inform and consult on redundancy almost doubled.

11 Ethical Issues

11.1 Introduction

Ethics is a set of moral principles to guide behaviour.

Ethical obligations

Each of us has our own set of values and beliefs that we have evolved over the course of our lives through our education, experiences and upbringing. We all have our own ideas of what is right and what is wrong and these ideas can vary between individuals and cultures.

There are five factors that affect ethical obligations.

(i)   **The law** – this defines the minimum ethical standards in a given area of practice. For example, deceptive advertising is illegal and violators of this law are liable to large fines, court action and/or loss of goodwill. Some unethical behaviour is often not considered illegal, such as head hunting employees from other companies, padding expense accounts, etc.

(ii) **Government regulations** – these are also fairly clear-cut outlining what is acceptable and what is not. These regulations set standards on issues such as unfair competition, unsafe products, etc. Failure to comply with these regulations could lead to criminal charges, or fines etc. Unfortunately, there are times when these regulations do not force ethical behaviour. In the US cyclamates (artificial sweeteners) were banned because there was evidence that they were carcinogenic. Following the ban a major food manufacturer sold 300,000 cases of cyclamate sweetened food overseas. Similarly many banned food additives and pesticides etc are being sold overseas, mainly to third world countries.

(iii) Industry, institute and company **ethical codes** – are codes that clearly state the ethical standard an employee should follow within his or her organisation. These standard practices are usually followed if they are written down and the rules enforced, however many companies have 'unwritten' codes of practice or if written down, have no method of enforcing these rules. Generally, written codes clarify the ethical issues but leave the resolution to the individual's conscience. The CIMA ethical guidelines would come undert his category.

(iv) **Social pressures**

(v) **Tension between personal standards and the goals of the organisation** – we can refer back to the example involving the sale of banned substances overseas. It is not illegal, but it may be against your personal values to sell these products to unsuspecting overseas clients. What would you do if this action were a direct order from a superior? Does this take away your responsibility? As with many ethical problems there are no easy answers.

Test your understanding 10

Explain why ethical behaviour is important in business, generally, and for the manager and their activities.

Illustration 6 - Ethical dilemmas

The following ethical dilemmas may arise:

- A rival company creates the legally permitted maximum of toxic waste. Your company has a range of expensive systems that keep waste to much lower levels. Not using these would reduce costs, and there is increasing pressure from industry analysts to increase the return on investment.

- A young, talented and ambitious team leader wants you to dismiss a member of his team, who is much older than the rest and does not really fit in. However, the worker in question has worked at the company a long time with a good record of service.

- You are forced to make redundancies in a department. The Human Resources manager has said, off the record, that it must not seem that gender or ethnicity is an issue, so you must make it look fair. However, this would require you to keep some weaker individuals, and lose some good ones.

11.2 Types of ethics within organisations

Paine suggests there are two approaches to the management of ethics in tho organisation.

Compliance-based ethics

The compliance-based approach is designed to ensure the company primarily operates within the letter of the law by defining the standards required and then enforcing standards through procedures such as compliance audits.

Integrity-based ethics

This is based on the organisations defined ethical code or business values, and seeks to promote the development and maintenance of an ethically-based environment, instilling a sense of shared accountability and purpose among staff.

A combination of the two approaches is really required for successful management of ethics within an organisation.

11.3 CIMA ethical guidelines

- These guidelines state that members have a duty to observe the highest standard of conduct and integrity.

- In order to achieve the objectives of the accounting profession, professional accountants have to observe six fundamental principles:

Fundamental Principle	Interpretation
Integrity	Should be honest and straightforward in all work.
Objectivity	Should not allow prejudice, bias or influence of others to affect behaviour.
Competence	Should be professionally competent and take due care.
Confidentiality	Should not disclose information unless there is a legal/ professional right or duty to do so.
Professional behaviour	Refrain from behaviour which might bring discredit to the institute.
Technical standards	Work should be carried out in accordance with technical standards.

11.4 Dealing with ethical dilemmas

If you are faced with an ethical dilemma at work, then you should follow the following process:

(1) Obtain further information - do you have firm evidence to support concerns?

(2) Follow established internal procedures (e.g. whistle blowing help-lines)

(3) Consult with direct line management

(4) Escalate issue to higher levels of management

(5) Escalate to audit committee

(6) Seek advice from professional institute (e.g. CIMA ethics department)

(7) Finally, consider withdrawing from the engagement / situation.

Test your understanding 11

You are a recently qualified management accountant and have just accepted a new post as management accountant in Black Pearl Co, a company specialising in the provision of credit and loans to wealthy individuals. You report to Mr. Sparrow, the senior management accountant and your duties involve performing credit checks on new customers through to the preparation of monthly management accounts and cash and profit forecasts for the company.

An initial review of the receivables ledger shows one debt from Miss Swan is quite old; there have been no loan repayments for the last six months, and the outstanding balance has risen to nearly $150,000 with accrued interest. When queried, Mr. Sparrow suggests not making a provision for this amount because to make a provision would decrease profit and cash flow by an unacceptable amount.

After leaving work for the day, you go for a drink at the Parlez wine bar with the junior management accountant, Will. After a few drinks, Will informs you that Mr Sparrow is a personal friend of Miss Swan, which may be a reason Mr Sparrow does not want to make a provision at this time.

Required:

Identify which, if any, of the fundamental principles within the CIMA ethical guidelines Mr. Sparrow has broken and describe possible actions that you should take in response.

12 Chapter summary

Personnel vs HRM

Human resource planning (HRP)
- Strategic analysis
- Internal analysis
- Identify gap between supply and demand
- Put plans in place to close the gap
- Review

The HR cycle
- Recruitment
- Selection
- Induction
- Appraisal, training and development
- Termination
- Legal and ethical issues

Recruitment
- Definition
- Job analysis
- Job description
- Person specification
- Source candidates

Selection
- Definition
- Aims
- Application form
- Selection Interview
- Selection Testing
- Assessment centre
- References
- Employment offer and negotiation

Human Resource Management

Induction
- Purpose
- Contents

Training and development
- Stages
- Methods
- Kolb's experiential learning cycle
- Honey and Mumford's learning styles

Appraisals
- Benefits
- Stages
- Barriers
- Appraisal and career development

Legal issues
- Employment legislation
- Legislation relating to discrimination
- Disciplinary procedures
- Redundancy

Ethical issues
- Definition
- Types of ethics within organisations
- CIMA ethical guidelines

13 Practice questions

Question 1

Aptitude testing is most frequently used:

A   As part of a selection process

B   As part of an appraisal process

C   As part of a process of training and development

D   As part of an exit interview process

Question 2

HR selection tests that accurately predict future performance are said to be:

A   Valid

B   Equitable

C   Reliable

D   Stable

Question 3

Development can be defined as:

A   The creation and maintenance of an individual

B   The progressive alteration to the individual

C   Growth and change in the individual

D   The growth or realisation of a person's ability and potential

Question 4

A test used in the selection of individuals for jobs might ask questions about their likes and dislikes, attitudes, and what they would do in certain non-work situations. This type of selection test is:

A   an intelligence test

B   an aptitude test

C   a personality test

D   a situational test

(2 marks)

Question 5

An employer has decided to offer a job to a candidate following a selection process, but still has some doubts about whether the individual will be well-suited to the job. Which of the following options would be the most effective way of dealing with these concerns about the individual's aptitude for the job?

A   Making the employee redundant if he/she fails to perform well.

B   Offering the job initially for a probationary period.

C   Offering the candidate a low rate of pay until he/she has demonstrated the ability to do the job well.

D   Dismissing the individual for incompetence if he/she does the job badly.

(2 marks)

Question 6

The use of standard questions in job interviews helps ensure:

A   fairness.

B   validity.

C   reliability.

D   completeness.

(2 marks)

Question 7

The purpose of a person specification is to provide details of:

A   organisational size and diversity of activity.

B   the types of responsibilities and duties to be undertaken by the post holder.

C   personal characteristics, experience and qualifications expected of a candidate.

D   individual terms of engagement and period of contract.

(2 marks)

Question 8

Which one of the following is a part of the recruitment rather than the selection process?

A   Job analysis

B   Interviewing

C   Testing

D   Assessment centres

(2 marks)

Question 9

Briefly describe Kolb's experiential learning cycle.

(4 marks)

Question 10

Identify FOUR ways in which a training system would benefit the accounting function.

(4 marks)

Question 11

Discuss any FOUR factors that should be taken into account when deciding upon whether to use recruitment consultants.

(4 marks)

Question 12

Identify the objectives of performance appraisal from the viewpoint of:

(a) the individual

(4 marks)

(b) the employer

(4 marks)

Question 13

(a) Explain what is meant by the selection interview and explain the purpose of the selection interview.

(3 marks)

(b) Discuss the problems associated with using the interview as a selection technique.

(6 marks)

(c) Explain how inexperienced interviewers damage the effectiveness of selection interviews?

(5 marks)

(d) Explain FOUR key skills needed to carry out the selection interview successfully.

(4 marks)

(Total: 18 marks)

Question 14

(a) Explain why it is necessary for chartered management accountants to adhere to a professional code of conduct.

(10 marks)

(b) Describe the steps that both professional accountancy bodies and organisations more generally can take to ensure that their members take seriously the ethical principles included in their organisations' codes of conduct.

(10 marks)

(Total: 20 marks)

Test your understanding answers

Test your understanding 1

- People resources are costly and should therefore be carefully planned.

- Knowledge, expertise and skill requirements are constantly changing and it can be difficult to keep up with these changes.

- Rapid social and technical changes also make planning difficult.

- All types of forecasting will be open to uncertainty.

Test your understanding 2

- Effective recruitment depends on accurate job analysis, e.g. if the exact nature of the job is known, then it facilitates precisely worded adverts, which will assist in attracting a suitable field of candidates.

- It may eliminate the need for recruitment, e.g. the job may no longer be necessary or could be shared elsewhere in the organisation.

- To assist in determining the most appropriate method of selection.

- To help identify the need for training and the most appropriate training method.

- To establish differences between jobs so that wage and salary differentials may be determined.

Test your understanding 3

- Finance Director required **(Title of the job)**
- At least five years post qualified experience **(special requirements)**
- Experience of a dynamic industry **(special requirements)**
- Understanding of investor relations and pre-floatation requirements **(special requirements)**
- Ability to manage change and form own department **(special requirements)**
- Role includes **(brief description of role):**
  - Business and financial strategy and planning, monitoring, management and reporting
  - Reporting and accounting as per the legal requirements
  - Management of strategy for and liaison with stock market business press and the business analyst community
- Excellent package including competitive salary and share options **(remuneration)**
- Responsible for a growing team of 18 people **(number of staff directly supervised)**
- Report directly to the Managing Director **(responsible to)**
- Located in London with approximately 20% travel to other European locations **(location and special attributes, e.g. shift systems, willingness to travel)**

Test your understanding 4

Discrimination may be acceptable in certain circumstances, e.g:

- Army soldiers must be fit, healthy and be able to carry heavy kit.
- Firemen must be a certain height so that they can reach the equipment.
- An Italian restaurant can choose to recruit only Italian waiters and waitresses.

Test your understanding 5

Shortcomings of selection interviews include:

- too brief to 'get to know' candidates
- interview is an artificial situation
- 'halo' effect from initial impression
- contrast problem - an average candidate following an awful one will look very good
- qualitative factors such as motivation, honesty or integrity are difficult to assess
- prejudice – stereotyping groups of people
- lack of interviewer preparation, poor questioning, poor retention of information
- environmental factors, e.g. an unsuitable location, noise, lack of time

Test your understanding 6

- An assessment centre uses a wide range of assessment methods and it is therefore argued that the approach is more thorough and therefore more successful than the more traditional approaches. If nothing else, the process takes longer and allows the potential employer to see the candidates over a longer period of time. The opportunity to get to know a potential employee could prove to be invaluable. This contrasts well with the very time-constrained, artificial interview situation.

- It has been shown that they are much better at predicting a successful match between the selected candidate and the employer. The wider the range of techniques used, the more successful the result in terms of reliability and validity.

- Avoidance of single–assessor bias.

- The development of skills in the assessors, which may be useful in their own managerial responsibilities.

Test your understanding 7

Activists - they enjoy learning through games, competitive teamwork, tasks, role-plays and on-the-job training.

Reflectors - the reflector prefers learning activities that are observational such as carrying out an investigation or work shadowing.

Theorists - the theorist prefers learning to be structured, allow time for analysis and provided by other theorists, e.g. classroom based courses.

Pragmatists - the pragmatist prefers learning activities that are as close as possible to direct work experience. They will only engage in formal training, such as lectures or computer based training, if it reflects their actual job.

Test your understanding 8

- Excessive absenteeism
- Inadequate work performance
- Breaking safety rules or other rules
- Improper personal appearance

Test your understanding 9

- **Improved HR planning in future** - should eliminate or minimise any staff surpluses.

- **Reduced overtime** - a removal of or big reduction in overtime payments could lead to huge cost savings and most staff should accept that such a step is required during more challenging times.

- **Recruitment freeze** - the organisation could take immediate steps to put a freeze on recruitment. This combined with natural wastage of staff could make a significant contribution to reducing staff costs. Not only will there be a smaller number of staff to pay but recruitment costs will also be saved. This step should cause little disruption to the business and staff should be accepting of the move as long as it does not result in an increased workload.

- **Retirement** - forced retirement, for those over the retirement age, is a possibility. Voluntary early retirement, for those close to retirement age, could also assist in reducing staff costs. Staff may actually view this as a good opportunity to give up work and enjoy their retirement, especially if they have a good pension in place. As long as the business can continue to operate effectively without these members of staff, there should be minimal disruption to the organisation.

- **Shorter hours** - in addition to cuts in overtime payments, the organisation may consider it necessary to reduce normal hours of working. This may be achieved through a shorter working day or week. As long as there is sufficient human resource, the move should cause minimal disruption. However, the significant reduction to an individual's salary may make this unpopular amongst employees and the organisation should proceed with caution.

- **Job sharing** - this would involve two employees working shorter hours by agreeing to share a role. This would have a similar impact to that discussed above and as a result should be approached with caution. A voluntary scheme could be put in place before any compulsory moves are made.

- **Redundancy** - this should be considered as the last alternative. This is due to the high level of disruption that may be caused as well as upset to staff. Redundancy is an unpleasant experience, even if a generous redundancy payment is made. Managers must follow the laws governing redundancy and must ensure that any remaining employees remain motivated. Voluntary redundancy should be offered before any attempt is made to terminate employment compulsorily. The organisation will prefer to use voluntary severance as it avoids problems over selection, hardship and resentment. However, it is worth remembering that the organisation must maintain a balanced workforce and that oversubscription is a possibility. As a result it should reserve the right to refuse a volunteer.

Test your understanding 10

Ethical behaviour is important since:

- Ethical principles **may** be enforced by the law. For example, an ethical manager would select employees on the basis of who can best perform the job. This is enforced by legislation and regulation covering the areas of recruitment and selection.

- Ethical principles are not always enforced by the law. However, a business with high ethical standards may gain competitive advantage since individuals and other businesses will often prefer to purchase from this type of business.

Test your understanding 11

Identifying the ethical dilemma

Mr Sparrow appears to be basing business decisions on his friendship with other people. In this sense the following ethical principles may have been breached:

- Firstly, *Integrity* – members should be honest and straight-forward in all personal and business relationships.

- Secondly, *Objectivity* – members do not allow bias or conflict of interests in business judgements.

It certainly appears that Mr Sparrow has been less than objective. Without the friendship with Miss Swan, it appears that the customer would have been sued by now to recover the outstanding money. The action also appears to lower the integrity of Mr Sparrow because the level of trust you have in his actions will now be lower – you can no longer be sure of his motivations.

Action

You now have a possible reason for Mr Sparrow not pursuing Miss Swan for the outstanding debt; although to be clear this is only hearsay and may yet be determined to be incorrect. To progress matters, you could ask Mr Sparrow if there are any other reasons he can think of as to why the debt from Miss Swan remains unpaid – this gives him the chance to explain that Miss Swan is a personal friend.

If Mr Sparrow denies knowledge of friendship, then there is simply his word against Will's – it will be difficult to report the case to CIMA's ethics committee for lack of objectivity because there is no breach of principles that can be proven.

However, there is still the issue of the outstanding amount from Miss Swan. You can suggest that a provision is made, although again Mr Sparrow may reject this assertion.

Other options available to you therefore include:

- Reporting directly to the board on the issue,
- Taking advice from CIMA's ethics department.

It appears no further action can be taken due to lack of any firm evidence.

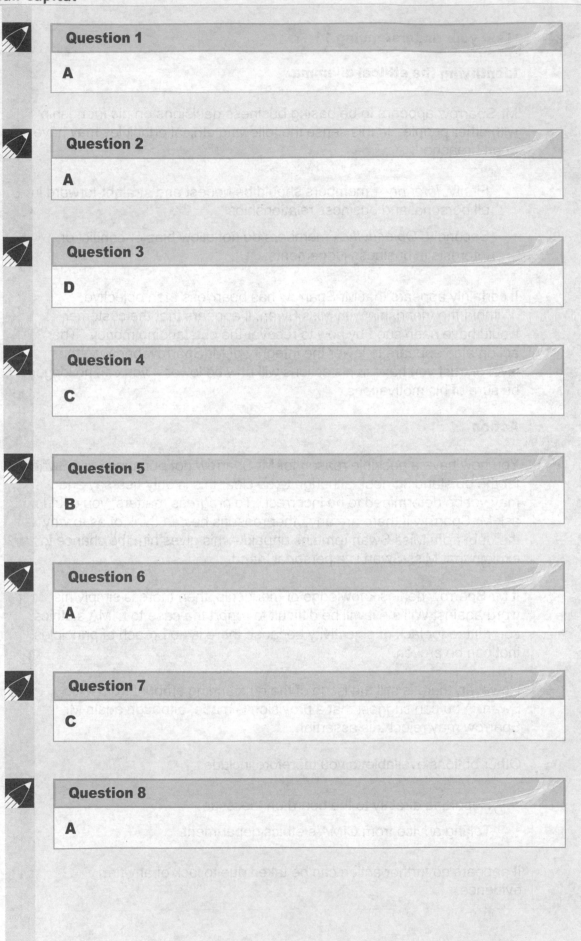

Question 1

A

Question 2

A

Question 3

D

Question 4

C

Question 5

B

Question 6

A

Question 7

C

Question 8

A

Question 9

Kolb suggests that learning is a series of steps based on learning from experience. He believes that classroom learning is false and that actual learning comes from real life experiences. Experiential learning comes from 'doing', thus ensuring that learners actually solve problems. Kolb's experiential learning cycle (shown below) identifies the four steps:

- The first step is where the person is learning something new,
- then the experience is reviewed,
- then the experience is accepted or rejected, and
- the fourth step is when the person calculates how and when to apply what has been learned.

Question 10

The most likely benefits of a training system for the accounting function of an organisation are:

- more efficient use of staff resources as staff understand their duties more clearly, so that, for example, difficult accounting entries will be dealt with more intelligently.

- greater flexibility of operation as more staff acquire more skills, allowing for replacement of those concerned with maintaining one set of records by those working on others if workload or absences demand it.

- greater ease in introducing new techniques as a training system will exist to help with the changeover, particularly useful if the accounting records are being computerised.

- improved staff morale and greater capability for dealing with staff turnover as the training programme automatically provides for career succession.

Question 11

Any organisation which is considering the use of external recruitment consultants would make its decision upon the following:

- The availability, level and appropriateness of expertise available within the organisation and its likely effectiveness.

- The cost of using consultants against the cost involved in using the organisation's own staff, recognising the level of the vacancy or vacancies against the consultant's fee.

- The particular expertise of the consultants and the appropriate experience with any particular specialised aspect of the recruitment process.

- The level of expertise required of potential employees and therefore the appropriate knowledge required of the consultants.

Question 12

(a) **The objectives of appraisals from the viewpoint of the individual**

- It compares the individual's performance against a set and established standard.

- It identifies work of particular merit done during the review period.

- It provides a basis for remuneration.

- It establishes what the individual has to do, regarding the objectives of the organisation.

- It determines the future employment of the individual e.g. to remain in the same job, be transferred, promoted or retire early.

- It determines whether the individual is in a job where proper use is being made of his or her skills and talents.

- It establishes key results which the individual needs to achieve in work within a set period of time.

- It identifies training and development needs.

(b) **The objectives of appraisals from the viewpoint of the organisation**

- It monitors human resource selection processes against results.

- It identifies candidates for promotion, early retirement etc.

- It helps to identify and provide a record of any special difficulties/hazards surrounding the job, perhaps not previously realised.

- It identifies areas for improvement.

- It provides a basis for human resource planning.

- It helps formulate the training plan.

- It improves communication between managers and the managed where the organisation adopts the joint problem-solving approach in their appraisal system.

Question 13

(a) The selection interview is a formal discussion where an employer assesses an applicant for a job, and where an applicant decides whether he or she wants to take it.

The purposes of the interview are:

(i) to find the best person for the job;

(ii) to make sure the candidate understands what the job itself entails, and the career prospects associated with it;

(iii) to make the candidate feel that they have been given fair treatment during the interview.

The main limitations of the selection interview are that they fail to provide accurate predictions of how a person will perform in the job, partly because of the nature of interviews, partly because of the errors of judgement by interviewers.

(b) The following problems are often associated with poor selection decisions:

(i) **Scope**

An interview is too brief to 'get to know' candidates in the kind of depth required to make an accurate prediction of work performance.

(ii) **The 'halo' effect**

A tendency for people to make an initial general judgement about a person based on a single attribute, such as being neatly dressed or well spoken. This single attribute will colour later perceptions, and might make an interviewer mark the person up or down on every other factor in their assessments.

(iii) **Contagious bias**

The interviewer changes the behaviour of the applicant by suggestion. The applicant might be led by the wording of a question or non-verbal cues from the interviewer, and changes what he or she is doing or saying in response.

(iv) **Stereotyping**

Stereotyping groups people together who are assumed to share certain characteristics, for example, women or vegetarians, then attributes certain traits to the group as a whole. It then assumes that each individual member of the supposed group will possess that trait.

(v) **Incorrect assessment**

Qualitative factors such as motivation, honesty or integrity are very difficult to assess in an interview.

(c) Inexperienced interviewers are one of the main reasons why the selection interview is often ineffective. Inexperienced interviewers might:

(i) be unable to evaluate the information they obtain from a candidate;

(ii) fail to compare a candidate against the requirements for a job or a personal specification;

(iii) prepare to plan for the interview inadequately;

(iv) avoid taking control of the direction and length of the interview;

(v) have a tendency either to act as an inquisitor and make candidates feel uneasy or to let candidates take over the interview;

(vi) show a reluctance to probe into fact and challenge statements where necessary.

(d) The skills of interviewing involve those of:

(i) planning and preparing for the selection interview. Information gathering and research are the primary activities involved in selection interviewing and form the basis of an effective selection interview;

(ii) analysing the application form and other information about the candidate to decide on the main areas of questioning. An interviewer should have a very clear idea of the applicant in terms of their knowledge, skills, and experience, and be aware of the personal situation of the applicant;

(iii) questioning the candidate in an appropriate way. Focused and relevant questioning is vital for the interviewer to obtain the necessary information on which to base the selection decision;

(iv) evaluating the candidate by objectively analysing and evaluating the information which has been obtained from the interview.

Question 14

(a) CIMA have a professional code of conduct which, amongst other areas, includes:

- keeping client matters confidential;

- a requirement to serve the public interest (which overrides the point noted above);

- to behave with objectivity and integrity;

- to maintain technical competence.

The main reason for this code is that the role of the management accountant (MA) within the organisation is that of a provider of information. If the MA were to provide false or misleading information (through technical incompetence or not being objective) this might lead to senior managers making incorrect decisions. This would then have an impact on stakeholders of the company such as shareholders and creditors.

At the present time accountancy in most countries is self-regulating. This means that the conduct of accountants is left to the professional bodies rather than being legislated. Because of this CIMA (and the other professional bodies within the UK) must be seen not only to have a code of conduct but also to enforce it.

The accountants within any organisation are in a crucial position in that they have access to confidential information. Employers must be confident that this information will be kept confidential to the organisation. Although an employee being a member of a professional body does not guarantee this it should provide some assurance.

Finally, it is important for MAs to comply with a code of conduct since if they did not it would damage the entire profession.

(b) The reason why a code of conduct is required is because instances will arise in which an MA will face conflicts between what is good for the organisation and what is good for them personally.

From the point of view of the professional body, the code of ethics must be enforced rigorously. This means investigating suspected cases where the code has not been followed. If the allegations are proved then the offender will be punished either financially or, in extreme cases, struck off the register of members.

As far as individual organisations are concerned there are a number of steps that can be taken to try and ensure that employees act in an ethical manner.

The simplest and most effective method would be to employ the right kind of staff in the first place. Recruiting staff who have high personal ethical standards should mean there will be no ethical problems in the future. The obvious drawback to this approach is in identifying these qualities in applicants.

Many organisations will formalise ethical behaviour through procedures and rules that must be followed (and that carry disciplinary action if they are not). The drawback with this approach is that it is almost impossible to draw up guidelines on every single circumstance and so some measure of personal responsibility will always remain.

An increasing number of organisations have instituted ethics committees which oversee the working practices and procedures in an organisation. If these are to be successful they need to be high-profile and set up at a high enough level within the organisation. The drawback with this approach is that it can give general but not specific guidelines.

From the above, it can be seen that there is no single approach which will ensure that all employees behave ethically all of the time.

Pillar E

E1 – Enterprise Operations

Specimen Examination Paper

Instructions to candidates

You are allowed three hours to answer this question paper.
You are allowed 20 minutes reading time **before the examination begins** during which you should read the question paper and, if you wish, highlight and/or make notes on the question paper. However, you will **not** be allowed, **under any circumstances**, to open the answer book and start writing or use your calculator during the reading time.
You are strongly advised to carefully read ALL the question requirements before attempting the question concerned (that is all parts and/or sub-questions). The requirements for questions 3 and 4 are contained in a dotted box.
ALL answers must be written in the answer book. Answers or notes written on the question paper will **not** be submitted for marking.
Answer the ONE compulsory question in Section A. This has ten sub-questions on pages 2 to 4.
Answer the SIX compulsory sub-questions in Section B on page 5.
Answer the TWO compulsory questions in Section C on pages 6 to 8.
The list of verbs as published in the syllabus is given for reference on page 9.
Write your candidate number, the paper number and examination subject title in the spaces provided on the front of the answer book. Also write your contact ID and name in the space provided in the right hand margin and seal to close.
Tick the appropriate boxes on the front of the answer book to indicate the questions you have answered.

TURN OVER

© The Chartered Institute of Management Accountants 2009

E1 – Enterprise Operations

SECTION A – 20 MARKS

[the indicative time for answering this section is 36 minutes]

ANSWER *ALL* TEN SUB-QUESTIONS

Instructions for answering Section A

The answers to the ten sub-questions in Section A should ALL be written in your answer book.

Your answers should be clearly numbered with the sub-question number and ruled off so the markers know which sub-question you are answering. **For multiple choice questions you need only write the sub-question number and the answer option you have chosen**. You do not need to start a new page for each sub-question.

Each of the sub-questions numbered from **1.1** to **1.10** inclusive, given below, has only ONE correct answer. Each is worth two marks.

Question One

1.1 A deliberate addition of new, stimulating requirements to a person's job normally carried out by someone more senior is called

A   job enrichment.

B   job enlargement.

C   responsibility 'creep'.

D   multi-skilling.

(2 marks)

1.2 Employers wishing to attract and retain talented employees by bringing together pay and non pay elements and emphasising a positive organisational culture are said to operate a

A   benefit scoping strategy.

B   total reward package.

C   talent strategy package.

D   a consolidated remuneration package.

(2 marks)

1.3 Which of the following does NOT represent a 'spoke' in Cousins' strategic supply wheel?

A   Performance measures

B   Organisational structure

C   Organisational culture

D   Cost/benefit analysis

(2 marks)

1.4 Customers' direct participation in the delivery process is a feature of

A cellular production.

B the value chain.

C the service industry.

D lean product manufacture.

(2 marks)

1.5 An operations management programme involving a series of long term continuous development practices is referred to as

A queuing theory.

B a sustainability program.

C optimised production technologies improvement.

D stakeholder engagement strategy.

(2 marks)

1.6 The acronym/phrase/term 'BRIC' is normally associated with

A a Japanese quality development technique.

B a stock control method.

C supplier development through buying, relating, investing and collaborating.

D the emerging combined economies of Brazil, Russia, India and China.

(2 marks)

1.7 Organisations engaged in off-shoring

A have some operations carried out in a different country.

B diversify their operations.

C brand themselves as 'global'.

D maximise competitive advantage by being based in a particular country.

(2 marks)

1.8 Which of an organisation's competences should NOT be outsourced?

A Allied competences

B Core competences

C Complementary competences

D Residual competences

(2 marks)

Section A continues over the page

TURN OVER

1.9 A formal definition of a level of service to be provided is usually found in

A documented quality assurance arrangements.

B a marketing plan.

C a corporate strategy.

D a service level agreement.

(2 marks)

1.10 A country's earnings from investment abroad is included in its

A Gross Domestic Product.

B Gross National Product.

C Relative Trade Balance Index.

D Quality of Life Index.

(2 marks)

Reminder

All answers to Section A must be written in your answer book.

Answers or notes to Section A written on the question paper will **not** be submitted for marking.

End of Section A

Section B starts on the opposite page

SECTION B – 30 MARKS

[the indicative time for answering this section is 54 minutes]

ANSWER *ALL* SIX SUB-QUESTIONS IN THIS SECTION - 5 MARKS EACH.

Question Two

(a)   Explain the benefits a collaborative process of Human Resource planning might bring to an organisation.

(5 marks)

(b)   Explain what types of costs are associated with internal failure costs and the significance of these for an organisation with a reputation for quality.

(5 marks)

(c)   Describe the features and benefits of SERVQUAL to organisations where it might be relevant.

(5 marks)

(d)   Identify the key issues for a manufacturing organisation considering adopting Six Sigma philosophy.

(5 marks)

(e)   Explain why a business with shareholders might take into account the interests of a wider group of stakeholders when considering a policy decision.

(5 marks)

(f)   Identify the nature and effects of risks for an organisation considering doing business in a country that has a government and political system that it is unfamiliar with.

(5 marks)

(Total for Section B = 30 marks)

End of Section B

Section C starts on the next page

TURN OVER

SECTION C – 50 MARKS

[Indicative time for answering this section is 90 minutes]

ANSWER *BOTH* QUESTIONS IN THIS SECTION – 25 MARKS EACH

Question Three

CW is an established charity based in the capital city of the developed country of Statesland. It raises funds locally to finance clean water and sustainable agricultural projects in some of the poorest areas of the world. CW relies heavily on the work of unpaid volunteers and prides itself on low operating overheads and directing a large proportion of its income to 'on the ground' projects. CW's sources of income involve donations from the public and the operation of charity shops in the north of the country selling unwanted clothes and household items. Recently however, a downturn in the economy, 'charity fatigue' and competition from other causes has made fund-raising more difficult. It is clear that CW needs to either reduce the level of projects it currently funds or increase income.

The Chief Executive of the charity has convinced her Board of Trustees that the charity needs to professionalise its operations, be more 'outward facing' and employ modern marketing practices. Consequently, an independent consultancy firm with expertise in this area has been engaged to advise the charity. Trustees are supportive of the Chief Executive but are worried that certain marketing practices, particularly promotional activities, might be seen as unethical and damage the good reputation of the charity.

In the first meeting between a partner of the consultancy firm and the Board of Trustees, a number of areas were covered including
- a discussion of the application of the marketing mix to the charity, and
- market research options for CW.

A second meeting has been arranged. You work for the consultancy firm and have been asked to produce some briefing notes for the partner to help him with this second meeting.

Required:

Prepare briefing notes for the partner that addresses the following questions:

(a) Explain what aspects of marketing could be helpful to CW. (Do not include matters covered in the first meeting or segmentation and targeting.)

(10 marks)

(b) Explain the processes and implications of market segmentation and targeting to CW.

(10 marks)

(c) Identify two types of promotional activity and for each explain the ethical concerns that might arise for CW using them.

(5 marks)

(Total for question three = 25 marks

Section C continues on the opposite page

Question Four

The S1K group has grown from a single optician's shop in a provincial town into (what it describes as) a 'lifestyle retail group'. S1K's policy is to buy existing shops in fashionable city centre shopping malls which it believes are 'underperforming'. In addition to traditional services offered by opticians, S1K offers eye correction (laser) treatment, designer sunglasses, cosmetic tinted contact lenses and, for certain spectacle frames, a range of complementary jewellery. S1K also plans to sell own-brand 'augmented' products and treatments such as eye creams and drops, make-up, etc. at premium prices from its premises. S1K is due to expand from thirty to thirty five geographically diverse shops in the south of the country within the next year.

The Board of S1K recognises the challenges ahead and has recently appointed a new Chief Executive who has a background in both retail operations and information solutions. He has just completed an initial review of systems and technology within S1K. His main findings are highlighted below:

- The opportunities for the use of information technology (IT) need to be grasped, particularly in the implementation and running of the information system network in support of management operations both in shops and in the main functional areas of S1K's headquarters.

- Systems are generally weak and the benefits of modern software applications lacking. The accuracy and completeness of information received by headquarters from shops needs to improve and there needs to be better coordination of activities. Through its acquisition policy S1K has 'inherited' a series of shops operating independent systems of varying sophistication and effectiveness. Several different systems are used and some are very inefficient. (For example, the equivalent of over 40% of a full time workers time is spent manually analysing and searching for information in shops.)

- Internet possibilities are being missed and there is no virtual network.

- Common computerised stock records will also be required when new products and treatments are sold.

- Some shops still use manual systems, others use basic stand-alone computers, but none take full advantage of software capabilities and most only use basic software functions. The financial system is the only shared system.

- The existing financial system is struggling to cope with the rapid growth of the group. Replacement software is due to go ahead within the next six months. Although the software does not fit existing business processes exactly, it has the clear advantage of giving S1K access to an industry best practice system and is identical to that used by all its main competitors. As such, it is a good choice. The least problematic implementation approach is a phased approach, and a programme of events for implementing was drawn up by the previous project manager who has now left S1K. A replacement project manager from within S1K needs to be appointed to oversee the introduction of the project as a matter of priority.

The requirement for this question is on the next page

Required:

(a)   Identify the ways in which information technology and information systems might improve S1K's operations.

(10 marks)

(b)   Discuss the Chief Executive's analysis of ways of overcoming potential problems in the implementation of the new financial system.

(10 marks)

(c)   Identify the main individuals and groups S1K's Human Resources Department should target first for training and whether training provision should be made in-house or not.

(5 marks)

(Total for Question Four – 25 marks)

Total marks for Section C = 50 marks)

End of Question Paper

The Examiner's Answers – Specimen Paper
E1 - Enterprise Operations

SECTION A

Answer to Question One

1.1	A
1.2	B
1.3	C
1.4	C
1.5	B
1.6	D
1.7	A
1.8	B
1.9	D
1.10	B

SECTION B

Note: The answers that follow in Sections B and C are fuller and more comprehensive than would have been expected from a well-prepared candidate. They have been written in this way to aid teaching, study and revision for tutors and candidates alike.

Answer to Question Two

Requirement (a)

Human Resource planning is an organisational activity that will culminate in the production of an HR strategy to support corporate activity and aspirations. Critically, it will involve wide consultation within the organisation.

A means of gaining a realistic, strategic perspective. The process of Human Resource planning will provide a framework for clearly and rationally agreeing upon organisational challenges and obstacles that will arise in the future. Participants in the process will, as a consequence, be better able to face such challenges when they occur.

Agreement on priorities. The collaboration and discussions involved in the process should act as a focus for discussion, agreement and an establishment of common ground. In so doing, a shared focus on organisational priorities should emerge. This should in turn help define operating and functional priorities.

Commitment and ownership of the plan. A sense of ownership of the ultimate plan and a commitment to its accomplishment should be achieved through collaboration and communication.

Underline the value of people to the organisation. The intense focus on people issues should confirm the importance of people in delivering corporate aspirations. Hopefully, it will also assist defining necessary specific staff development activities essential for organisational success.

Overcome departmentalism. The collaborative nature of the process should help overcome departmentalism and provide a basis for stronger future working relationships. It should also help in strengthening or positively shaping an organisational culture.

Motivation and personal development. The inclusion of individuals within the process may prove to be a source of motivation by offering participants a better understanding of corporate issues and an opportunity to participate in a strategic process.

Suggest a plan of action. The actions arising from the process should be clearly understood by those involved and allow a smooth transition for the organisation rather than hurried responses to environmental and other factors.

Help match future organisational activity with its human resources. The process will ultimately allow for an identification of potential solutions to a particular need:

- Increasing supply of human resources to meet increased organisational demand. (Through for example, retraining / re-skilling; increased use of IT; outsourcing; recruitment & selection; etc.)
- Reducing supply of human resources to meet reduced organisational demand. (Through, for example, early retirements, redundancy, short-time working, sabbaticals, job-sharing, more flexible working patterns, etc.).

Requirement (b)

Internal failure costs are costs associated with finding and correcting sub-quality products before they reach the customer.

Types of costs:
- time to rework inspection rejects,
- materials to replace/rework inspection rejects,
- time to repair faulty machines,
- scrap / lost materials,
- excessive inspections/checking,
- lost income from the sale of cheaper goods marked as 'seconds'.

Significance:
If the organisation wishes to protect its reputation for quality these costs are preferable to external failure costs as they occur before they reach the customer. The organisation should see these costs as necessary but may wish to reduce their incidence through processes aimed at creating quality rather than detecting quality failures.

Requirement (c)

Contribution of SERVQUAL

SERVQUAL represents a structured means of assessing quality where the service is intangible by nature and rubrics used in manufacturing (such as rejects, returned goods, scrap, etc.) are not available. SERVQUAL is a quality measurement technique used by some service and retail businesses.

Organisations benefitting:
- Potentially any non-manufacturing organisation
- The concept is widely applied in areas such as healthcare, banking, finance and education

Features of SERVQUAL

Organisationally driven. SERVQUAL is instigated by the organisation itself because it has a commitment to quality and staying close to the customer.

Customer focused. SERVQUAL is based on a scale which takes account of customer attitudes in order to obtain measurements.

An established methodology and framework. SERVQUAL offers an established methodology and a comprehensive framework. The framework indicates differences between a customer's expectations for a service and their feelings of how the service was received. It involves customers answering questions about (both) their initial expectations and their perceptions of the actual service delivered.

Conceptually straightforward and seen as relevant. SERVQUAL is a straightforward concept, and is easily explained and understood by key stakeholders such as the workforce.

Identifies areas for future attention. SERVQUAL can be used to produce a checklist for future attention in order to improve service quality. Gaps will emerge between customer expectation and perception of the quality they receive. These will suggest service gaps that need to be remedied. Such gaps will arise where:

- the organisation does not understand what the customer wants, or
- the organisation is unwilling to meet customer demands, or
- the organisation fails to meet these demands despite its best attempts, or
- the customer may have gained an unrealistic perception of the organisation's service (possibly through false or misleading promises).

Inherent limitations in methodology. Virtually all approaches to quality contain limitations and SERVQUAL is no different in this respect. SERVQUAL can be complex to administer and maintain. In addition, the methodology is only pseudo-scientific by nature and results can be subjective, statistically unreliable and require interpretation.

Requirement (d)

Like TQM, Six Sigma is more than a quality enhancement programme; it represents instead more a business philosophy. The aim of Six Sigma is that processes are carried out to near perfect levels, through the elimination of defects and a tackling of production variations.

The costs and the benefits involved
The Six Sigma philosophy is only one of many approaches to quality management an individual organisation might choose to adopt. The organisation concerned should therefore review the alternative approaches in order to determine whether Six Sigma is the most appropriate for them. Six Sigma requires a high level of commitment and potentially a great deal of organisational upheaval, so it is important that the organisation is aware of this before choosing it as an option.

Cultural fit
The organisational culture needs to be receptive to the philosophy. Six Sigma can be considered to be a combination of measure, target and philosophy and these should be central to the way in which the organisation operates. If the culture is unreceptive, significant change may be necessary as Six Sigma strives for near perfection in order to 'delight' the customer. Six Sigma is very task oriented and demands high volumes for statistical methods to achieve significant results; as such, it may prove culturally unsuitable.

Top management commitment
Successful implementation of Six Sigma will require the full commitment from the top management of the organisation. Arguably, the culture of the organisation is created and managed by this group and the case has already been made that a sympathetic culture needs to be created and maintained.

The tools necessary
Improvements 'tools', including process mapping and problem-solving techniques, need to be adopted. As such, they need to be taught to the workforce and embedded within normal working practices.

Training
Much dedicated training is necessary to introduce Six Sigma. This might begin with convincing the workforce of the benefits of the approach, explaining the implications and then undertaking training in the tools and necessary metrics.

Monitoring and control metrics
Six Sigma aims for six standard deviations between the mean and the nearest specification limit in any process. To achieve Six Sigma, a process must not exceed 3.4 defects per million opportunities. Clearly, measurement and monitoring systems need to be established to allow organisations to do this.

Requirement (e)

Corporate social responsibility
The concept underpinning this thinking is known as 'corporate social responsibility' (CSR) or 'corporate responsibility'. CSR encourages businesses to balance financial profits, economic value addition and social good. This represents an ongoing commitment by a business to behave ethically, contribute to economic development and, at the same time, improve the quality of life of others (e.g. its work force and their families, the local community, society in general, etc.) CSR has been defined as having four dimensions: economic, legal, ethical and philanthropic. The thinking is as follows:

Validity of other stakeholder groups' claims on a business
Shareholders with their economic goals form one important group within a wider group of stakeholders. However, other individuals or groups also have a legitimate stake in the business and have goals, and these deserve to be taken into account when considering a policy decision. Business practices should be built around stakeholder analysis and engagement and reflect the needs and aspirations of society as a whole.

A need for a stable operating environment
If business trading is not to be disrupted, organisations need a stable social environment within which to operate. This stability helps provide a predictable climate. It follows that individual businesses understanding and responding to society's expectation is vital to maintaining such stability. (A programme of sustaining the environment for future generations might be seen as an investment in the future of the business).

Interdependence of business and society
Business cannot exist without society and society exists best with business. It follows that business must take full account of the societal expectations e.g. social and environmental concerns when making policy decisions. (A company's ultimate customer is after all a member of society).

CSR makes good business sense
Certain policies that take account of wider stakeholder groups can make good 'business sense'. Examples of where this may apply might include (for instance) the promotion of an appropriate work/life balance amongst the workforce which can reduce absences through ill health and increase productivity.

Better balanced decisions
Policy decisions that take a longer-term view combining social, environmental and economic considerations are more likely to be fully considered, balanced and soundly based.

Source of competitive advantage / relationship building
Policies based on principles of operating with integrity, being respectful of human rights and the environment, etc. might provide certain businesses with a form of advantage over competitors that are less sensitive to these issues. (Such considerations are also key in the management of relationships with governments and regulatory agencies, NGOs, etc.)

Requirement (f)

An organisation considering doing business in a country that has a government and political system that it is unfamiliar with should investigate the associated risks in terms of nature and potential impact.

Unstable trading conditions

The political system may be unstable or could easily become so, leading to social and economic upheaval in that country. This might lead to social unrest which could disrupt business. At the extremes, this unrest might involve armed conflict, riots, terrorism or the operation of anarchist groups (possibly targeting foreign businesses). Possible effects include:

- threat to organisational property
- endangering organisational personnel
- general disruption to business activity
- delays in moving goods through customs

Unfavourable Government policies

If the organisation is unfamiliar with the political system there is a clear risk. The existing or likely future government of that country may:

- give preference to local firms, or alternatively,
- more general government policies (whilst not directed specifically at foreign businesses) might create unfavourable trading conditions.

Possible effects include:

- increased taxation and other financial penalties, etc. so reducing profitability,
- making getting new business difficult due to preference given to local firms,
- reduced freedom to trade freely,
- revision of contracts gained,
- more stringent product and process requirements, restricting operating freedom,
- exchange rate fluctuations,
- technical product adaption to meet government requirements,
- difficulty in recruiting locally if the organisation is viewed unfavourably by government.

Totalitarian Government policies

From the prospect of government policies being unfavourable, policies may instead become discriminatory and harmful if a ruling group is likely to act in a totalitarian fashion. Possible effects include:

- expropriation of assets (with or without compensation),
- loss of ability to repatriate profits,
- cancellation of existing contracts,
- a use of indigenisation policies to make the organisation fit the local culture (contemporary examples might include the Zimbabwe regime which requires foreign-owned firms to transfer majority shareholding to local individuals or groups).

Lobbying and vested interests

The organisation would do well to understand the strength of political lobbying and the influence of such lobby and pressure groups within the target country. The vested interests of other stakeholders (e.g. local business people) also needs to be considered. Possible effects include:

- retaining existing business difficult,
- getting new business made more difficult.

SECTION C

Answer to Question Three

Requirement (a)

The proliferation of charitable causes and the competition between them combined with a downturn in the economy, and "charity fatigue" has made fund-raising more difficult. It is likely that those charities employing the most appropriate marketing practices will succeed in levering the greatest contribution of peoples' time and money for their particular cause.

Marketing concepts can be adapted and certain techniques and approaches used by the charity in order to maximise the generosity of supporters. (This support includes both the time of volunteers and the monetary donations of others). It is apparent from the scenario that the charity's operations are not very professional and that modern marketing practices are not currently being employed.

Become customer focused
The marketing concept is based on identifying and satisfying customer needs and being customer focused generally. CW's own customers are a different grouping from those enabling the service to be provided. A basic principle of marketing is that an organisation should satisfy customer needs but in this case CW should seek to get close to both groups. Charities, including CW, have to improve their focus on the needs and wants of all different customer (stakeholder) groups through marketing, including:
- contributors (of money and unwanted items for resale in the charity shops),
- customers of charity shops,
- beneficiaries (in this case those benefitting from the clean water and sustainable agricultural projects in some of the poorest areas of the world), and
- volunteer workers and other supporters.

Conduct a strategic review
CW would do well to conduct a basic strategic review of its current position including a simple SWOT analysis and a scan of its external environment. In this way CW will become more 'outward facing'. This process should reveal:
- positive internal strengths to build upon and opportunities that might be seized through marketing practices, and
- internal weaknesses that need to be remedied and external threats that need to be avoided or minimised through marketing practices.

In terms of potential income levels and streams, at the moment income only comes from two sources (donations and charity shops) so there is an opportunity to develop new income streams based on the strengths CW already possess. The operation of these shops and the process of obtaining donations could also be reviewed in order to improve income levels.

A concentration on external factors might usefully lead to a consideration of the activities and initiatives of competitors (other charities). How CW might respond to these initiatives and what might be learned from their operation are valuable areas of consideration.

The possibilities thrown up by this review process will need careful debate and research and should ultimately benefit the charity.

Branding
With so many charities, competition for voluntary giving is intense. Branding is particularly important in communicating a particular charity's core values, and distinguishing it from others. A belief in the worthiness of CW as evidenced by the work of unpaid volunteers and the core values that will be articulated from analysis, organisational strengths (as part of the SWOT) need to be agreed upon and a strong brand image promoted based on this thinking. In the case of CW, this is likely to emphasise the value of its clean water and sustainable agricultural projects to those who are far less fortunate than those who happen to live in Statesland. Although costs will be involved in brand development and promotional activities, the value of the CW brand if correctly communicated, should help in a number of ways:
- By overcoming suspicions that CW's charitable income will be wasted,

- By giving a reason why a donor or volunteer worker may choose CW over other charities,
- By providing a 'shorthand' image of the charity when communicating with stakeholder groups.

Relationship marketing

Relationship marketing involves an organisation seeking to develop a long term relationship with key customers in order to retain their loyalty and increase sales. This concept could be easily adapted to the charity's requirements. CW should look to identify its main donors, capture this information (possibly on a database) and keep in touch in some way. This might be achieved through newsletters and updates (either through traditional mail or emailed). One-off appeals, thanks for past support and explanations of some of the worthy projects financed by the charity should strengthen the donor/charity relationship and produce greater income flows. (It is acknowledged that an investment in IT and systems might be a necessary precursor to this). The charity also needs to recognise that it relies heavily on the work of unpaid volunteers and that an investment in strengthening these relationships is needed if continuing support is to continue.

Cause marketing

At the moment charitable donations from CW are received solely from individuals and CW might want to consider how they might obtain support from businesses and other organisations. This may prove difficult in times of economic downturn but it is an option worthy of consideration. Cause marketing involves the cooperative efforts of a business and a charity for mutual benefit. Relationships are established with a specific business (possibly local to CW's base) and would go much further than the organisation merely making a charitable donation. The organisation would 'adopt' the charity. It may make the relationship known in the media and might (for instance) collaborate and allow workers to participate in the running of events, promotions and certain aspects of the charity. The business would receive good public relations and CW would gain obvious benefits.

Requirement (b)

Implications for CW

The reality is that every market (whether industrial, domestic or charitable) consists of potential buyers/customers/donors with different needs, and with differing decision making and behaviour. Market segmentation is a technique based on recognition of this fact. The different variables within the market such as attitudes may be grouped into distinct **segments** or parts of an entire market. This then gives the possibility of a different marketing approach being taken for each market segment. The organisation itself may, however, consider that it is either undesirable or impractical to **target** every segment in this way and may make decisions accordingly.

For CW, the implications of market segmentation and targeting is that it needs to analyse its market and make rational decisions as to how it addresses itself to its customers and potential customers.

Quite apart from the outcomes of the analysis, one valuable result of the process is that CW will, for the first time, build a mental picture of who the customer currently is and who it might be in the future.

In common with all organisations, CW is offering its market a mix of product, promotion, price and place. (CW is possibly doing this at the moment without much thought). This mix is, however, powerful as it represents a set of available tools or ingredients from which effective marketing strategies can be developed and customer needs satisfied. The implication for CW is that by undertaking segmentation and targeting it can, for the first time, adopt a more sophisticated marketing approach and the appropriateness of its existing mix reviewed in order to better meet the needs of the target segment(s).

Process of segmentation

Market segmentation involves subdividing a total market into distinct subgroups of customers, where any subgroup can be selected as a target market to be met with a distinct marketing mix of product, promotion, price and place. For CW this will involve subdividing the total potential market for charitable support in Statesland.

The value of market segmentation to CW is that, although within the total market, widely different groups may exist. Each group consists of people (or organisations) with common needs and preferences, which perhaps react to a certain marketing mix in a similar way.

Segmentation can take place on virtually any basis but CW might identify the following variables as relevant:

- *Geographical area:* It seems that the current target is the region around the north and capital of Statesland but other areas (and indeed neighbouring countries) may also have potential.
- *Age:* The age profile of potential donors.
- *Gender:* The choices to be made in terms of gender are to focus marketing on males, females or both.
- *Income:* The income profile of potential customers.
- *Business/Individual:* Currently income comes solely from individuals but the potential for corporate 'customers' should not be excluded.

Other segmentation variables might be identified as relevant including occupation, social class, lifestyle, etc.

Process of targeting

Once the process of segmentation has been completed, targeting follows on naturally. At this stage the choice is made over which of the identified market segments the charity should target with its marketing efforts. This will involve weighing up the potential of one segment against another and realistically considering the ability of CW to serve such segments.

A narrowing down of *potential* segments should take place in order to establish a viable, *practical* focus on potential customers. Marketing wisdom suggests that since the purpose of these processes is to identify target markets, segments must be:

- *Measurable.* (Meaning that abstract segmentation by 'personality' for example might be elusive and difficult to measure. A segment identified as 'those with a belief in charitable giving' might present less difficulties in measurement.)
- *Accessible.* (The segment must be 'reached' by the charity without any undue difficulty through (for instance) promotion.)
- *Substantial.* (The likely revenue streams from the segment must outweigh the effort in reaching the segment or segments.)

It is highly likely that national statistics exist that indicate levels of charitable giving and may indicate sources (either geographical or corporate versus individual) and the potential of a segment might be gauged. This is, of course, only relevant so long as CW can access the segment concerned.

Any market segment can become a target market, requiring a unique marketing mix in order for the organisation to exploit it successfully. Recognition of market segments will enable any organisation to adopt a more refined marketing approach to a given group of potential customers. These same principles apply to CW, and like any organisation they have potentially three main targeting strategies available to them:

- *Undifferentiated:* Targeting the whole market with one marketing mix (something arguably they may be doing already by default).
- *Differentiated:* Targeting several segments with distinctive mixes unique to each segment (which can be expensive and complicated if many segments are targeted).
- *Concentrated:* Targeting a single segment with a single mix.

Once this process is completed and target segments identified, precise marketing mixes will need to be determined in order to position the charity to its potential customers.

Requirement (c)

Trustees are supportive but worried that certain practices particularly promotional activities might damage the good reputation of the charity. Having targeted a particular segment, CW needs to consider and avoid promotional practices that might be considered unethical.

Promotion of charities involves engaging in persuasion, more specifically engaging in ways of convincingly communicating the benefits of the charity to supporters and potential supporters. There are potentially many individual promotional tools available, but the following represent those most likely to be considered by CW:

Advertising

Advertising is a non-personal promotion of ideas and is targeted at a specific market through some media channel such as TV, radio, newspapers, posters, billboards, fliers, on-line advertising, etc.

Ethically questionable practices:

TV and radio advertising are expensive media and these may be seen as inappropriate for a charity that prides itself on low overheads and directing a large proportion of its income to "on the ground" projects. The big ethical dangers are, however, potentially overstating claims in promoting the charity or not applying money raised in the way 'promised' in the advertising material.

Sales promotion

Sales promotion is impersonal and short term by nature and involves offering incentives to encourage sale of products by stimulating consumer purchasing. Sales promotion might therefore be used in CW's charity shops.

Ethically questionable practices:

The difficulty of this is that if promotions such as special offers, discounts, BOGOFs (buy one get one free) are used donors may feel 'let down considering that donated products could have been sold for much more. An additional downside is that stocks could be depleted as a result of the activity.

Personal selling

Personal selling is an option that involves a direct, often one to one contact with potential customers. The salesperson verbally presents the benefits of the charity in the hope of gaining a donation. This may take the form of telesales or 'cold' calling by salespeople knocking on doors, or stopping members of the public in the street.

Ethically questionable practices:

This approach could be expensive as the costs of employing salespeople needs to be 'covered'. It would also go against what CW prides itself on, namely low overheads and directing income to 'on the ground' projects. In addition, tactics that pressure vulnerable members of the public or the application of undue pressure to get a donation are dangers (particularly where bonuses to sales people are based on income attracted).

Direct mailing

Direct mailing involves widespread distribution of promotional literature and brochures, through traditional mail systems or emails.

Ethically questionable practices:

The danger of this is that the literature and messages are seen as junk mail or SPAM and the efforts could be counter productive if recipients are irritated by the approach. If the approach is seen as invasive or bullying then it is clearly ethically inappropriate.

Answer to Question Four

Requirement (a)

It is clear from the scenario that S1K's operations might be improved considerably through both information technology and information systems.

Use of information technology

The new Chief Executive believes that the opportunities for the use of information technology (IT) needs to grasped, particularly in the implementation and running of the information system network and in support of management operations. The opportunities that IT offers are evident in a number of ways including the following:

- *Strengthening current operating and managing systems.* S1K's systems are generally weak and clearly these need to be improved upon and developed. In theory, it would be possible to have effective information systems without using information technology (IT). The size and complexity of the group means that IT is the only practical delivery option for meeting S1K's expanding information needs arising from an expanding product range and (soon) 35 geographically diverse shops.

- *Standardising operations.* IT would allow S1K to operate a number of different types of systems each designed to assist management, group coordination and decision making. This will involve a move from the current stand alone applications to common integrated technology and systems.

- Offering a platform for greater accuracy and completeness of information through the introduction of IS.

- *Increasing operating efficiencies.* Currently the equivalent of over 40% of a full time workers time can be spent manually analysing and searching for information. IT can offer the platform to perform these functions in a less time hungry fashion. The time released should enable more value adding activities to be undertaken and potentially allow for a speedier answering of telephone and customer queries.

- *Simplifying procedures.* S1K's shops operate independent systems of varying sophistication and effectiveness, some based on manual systems rather than information technology. IT and the associated IS applications offer the potential to simplify and ensure consistency of operations.

- *Offering a platform for further system enhancement.* With appropriate information technology in place, the opportunity is then open in the future to introduce further information system networks and systems to support management operations and ensure greater group cohesion.

Use of information systems

- *Internet access.* The installation of internet access in all shops would enable email systems which offer speed and versatility, allowing easy communication, and the facility to send electronic attachments, so making returns to S1K's head office more efficient.

- *Maximising the benefits of a website.* Many organisations now use the potential offered by websites. By investing in a well designed web site, S1K could:
    - use it as a means of advertising and staying in touch with customers,
    - develop an online booking system for optical and other appointments.

- *Operating a network*, where a number of computers and devices are linked. As S1K operates throughout the south of the country the most appropriate computer systems configuration would be through a wide area network (WAN). Operations can be improved through the use of such a network in the following ways:
    - Speeding up communication between S1K's central management and headquarters functions and individual shops.
    - Improving inter-shop collaboration. A WAN would provide e-mail access and easier inter-shop communication and cooperation. This would allow resource and information sharing between S1K's growing number of shops.

- *New financial system software.*
  - The new financial systems software will be able to cope with the size and complexity of the group in a way that the existing software cannot.
  - This software has the clear advantage of giving S1K access to an industry best practice system and is identical to that used by all its main competitors.

Requirement (b)

The existing financial system is struggling to cope with the rapid growth of the group and replacement software is due to go ahead within the next six months. Based on his past experience, the Chief Executive has analysed potential implementation problems and solutions.

The potential problems appear to be as follows:
- Mismatch of software and business processes
- The implementation approach to adopt
- The current absence of a project manager

Mismatch of software and business processes
The new software does not fit existing business processes exactly. Despite this, the Chief Executive believes the software is 'a good choice'. This is based on two reasons identified in the scenario:
- It would give S1K access to an industry best practice system
- It would mean that S1K has the same opportunities as all its main competitors who use identical software

Realistically, given the timescale, an additional point is that S1K has already committed itself to take the software, will already have incurred some costs and will probably be contractually obligated to take the software.

The software is an 'off the shelf' package designed to perform specific financial functions of the business. As such, it is less expensive than a bespoke option. A bespoke solution would require some expertise to carry out software development and it is probable that S1K may need to employ outside sources for the purpose. Thus, such a process might be lengthy and costly.

Changing the business processes to correspond with software requirements represents a change initiative that staff may respond to negatively. Negative responses should be challenged. Competitors are using the software already and it is reasonable to assume that it will encapsulate industry best practice. The indications are, that because of its rapid growth and acquisition policy, S1K may operate in an inconsistent and possibly inefficient fashion, so a change in practices might be a positive thing.

The implementation approach to adopt
There are several potential implementation approaches S1K could adopt. Again the Chief Executive has backed previous decisions made by S1K, in this case those made by the previous project manager who has drawn up a staged programme of events for implementation.

The Chief Executive believes this approach to be the 'least problematic' for S1K. This staged approach allows for a degree of pilot testing to be carried out prior to full implementation across the organisation. The phased approach is often used in large system projects or in organisations that are geographically dispersed (like S1K). This might involve implementing a complete system in one geographical location at a time. If the system operates as expected then a further transfer can be made with existing systems retired in an orderly, staged way. Currently staff are likely to be experiencing 'change fatigue' from the instability caused by takeovers and a change of Chief Executive and this staged approach looks eminently sensible.

The phased approach is less risky given that the project manager would be new to the role and risk will be reduced as issues found in small-scale use of the new system can be remedied in time for wider software roll-out.

Alternatives S1K may have considered include:

- *Direct approach.* Under this approach, at a predetermined point in time all old systems cease and the new financial system becomes operational. This approach has the highest risk, as there is no opportunity to validate the new system's output with the old.
- *Parallel approach.* This approach involves both old and new systems processing the same current data together for an agreed time (e.g. for a month). The outputs of the new system would be compared with those from existing systems to determine whether the new system is operating as expected. The downside of this approach is that implementation of the new system is delayed. This might indicate to S1K's workforce that management does not have complete confidence in the new system. Furthermore, additional time and effort would be taken in operating both old and new systems together.
- *Retrospective pilot.* This approach involves operating the new system with 'old' data (e.g. last month's financial data). The results produced by the new system can then be crosschecked with the results already processed by the existing systems. If there are no difficulties the old systems can then be withdrawn in favour of the new system. Like the parallel approach, additional time and effort would be taken in operating both old and new systems together to obtain duplicate output.

The absence of a project manager

The project manager who was overseeing project implementation has now left S1K. Clearly the introduction of such an important project as this needs to be properly managed and must not be left to chance. The Chief Executive's judgment that a replacement project manager should be appointed as a matter of priority seems well founded. However, he feels that the appointment should come from within S1K. The advantage of this is that the individual would have a good local knowledge. On the downside, there is no indication as to whether anyone within the group possesses the necessary expertise. Indeed, the system deficiencies within S1K suggest that little IS project management experience exists. This may be an error of judgment and a better option might be to buy in the services externally from a specialist IS project manager on a short term contract.

Requirement (c)

Main individuals and groups to be targeted

New project manager: Project management skills

Effective project management is crucial to the successful implementation of this important system. For the S1K employee who is appointed to oversee the introduction of the financial system it is likely that training in the technical skills of project management will be needed. If the appointee is inexperienced, or unfamiliar with what is required of a project manager, then this training is a priority. It is best provided by placing the individual on an externally facilitated training event.

Senior S1K managers: behavioural considerations

Support from the top is crucial for any significant change. In this case, senior management must be seen to support the new software initiative. They should understand the Chief Executive's analysis and a general overview of the system and its benefits could help, possibly through executive training seminars. This training is best provided in-house, possibly in conjunction with the Chief Executive (if possible) and the new project manager.

Central headquarters finance staff: training in all aspects of the new system

The new software is an 'off the shelf' package designed to perform specific financial functions of S1K's business. Finance staff will need to understand all aspects of the new package. This staff group will require regular returns from shops and, if properly trained, they can act as a source of advice and guidance to users in shops. Often software suppliers offer training options either as part of the contract or for an additional fee. Alternatively, as the software appears to be widely used within the industry, private training courses might already operate. The most convenient means of training staff would, however, be onsite but externally facilitated if this can be arranged.

System users in shops: general training in computer systems

Some shops still use manual systems, others use basic stand alone computers, so it is conceivable that some staff will not have sufficient confidence or experience to use any new application. Targeting further technical training might be beyond such staff without ensuring they first obtain a degree of computer literacy. S1K may have sufficient expertise in-house to provide such basic support and tuition for such individuals.

System users in shops: training in specific aspects of the new system

Detailed user instructions on how to operate the new system in shops will be needed (including procedures, commands and data-entry requirements, etc.). On-the-job training while staff are actively using the new system would be most appropriate. As shop users make returns to headquarters, appropriately trained headquarters staff could be used for the purpose. User manuals, 'help lines' and dedicated support teams might also be needed to support this process. Later, updates as users become familiar with the system may help consolidate growing knowledge and skills.

Users' managers: behavioural considerations

S1K's shop managers will be called upon to help ensure that potential disruption caused by the introduction of the system is kept to a minimum. Successful user acceptance is vital and local managers are also best placed to achieve local buy-in. Users' managers should therefore be made aware of the benefits of the system and the reasons for its introduction. In addition, an outline understanding of the elements of the system for which they are responsible should also be given. This training could be carried out by in-house staff through seminars and workshops, etc. Managers participation in such events could help get their full commitment and engender feelings of 'ownership'.

Index

Index

Index